Michigan's
Upper Peninsula

D0870032

Michigan's Upper Peninsula

A Great Destination

Amy Westervelt

The Countryman Press
Woodstock, Vermont

SECOND EDITION

Explorer's Guides Michigan's Upper Peninsula, A Great Destination
ISBN 978-1-58157-138-7

Interior photographs by the author unless otherwise specified
Maps by Erin Greb Cartography, © The Countryman Press
Book design by Joanna Bodenweber
Composition by Eugenie S. Delaney

Published by The Countryman Press, P.O. Box 748, Woodstock, VT 05091
Distributed by W. W. Norton & Company, Inc., 500 Fifth Avenue, New York, NY 10110
Printed in the United States of America

10 9 8 7 6 5 4 3 2 1

This book is dedicated to the people of the U.P.
Would that more people shared your kindness,
honesty, and community spirit!

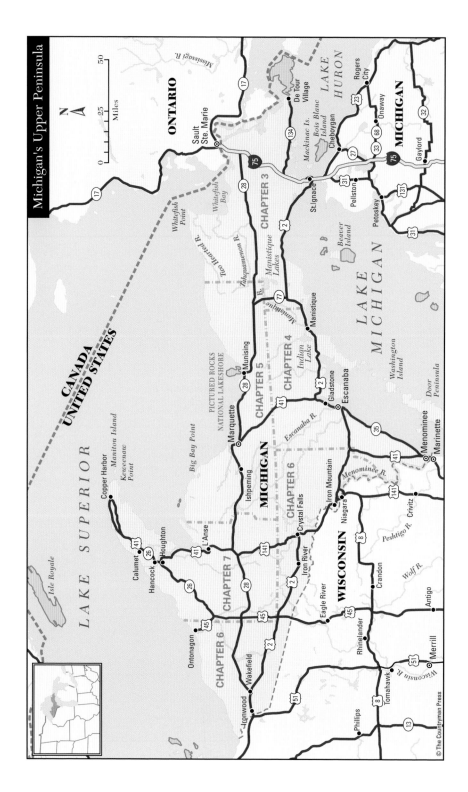

Michigan's Upper Peninsula

Contents

Acknowledgments

ALTHOUGH THE FORMAT HAS CHANGED A BIT, the first edition of this book is the foundation for this updated edition, and all the people I thanked the first time around are still deserving of gratitude: my husband, parents, brother, and, of course, all my lovely Yooper friends—the nicest, most sincere group of people I've come across, particularly Mrs. Donna Weigel. I am also indebted to Michaelanne Petrella for helping to check my facts, Kim Grant for giving me the opportunity to write this book in the first place, Lisa Sacks for dealing with all the editing and coordinating of this edition, and Kermit Hummel and Countryman Press for publishing it.

LEFT: Tucked away in a hemlock forest, Sable Falls are among the U.P.'s most picturesque.
Matt Girvan

Introduction

WHEN I ARRIVED IN MICHIGAN FROM CALIFORNIA, I expected snow and lakes and friendly midwesterners. What I did not expect was that, having traveled the world from Brazil to Italy, Morocco to Jordan, I would find one of my all-time favorite vacation destinations here: the Upper Peninsula.

As I've been telling friends and family for years, the U.P. is one of the best-kept secrets in America. In the summer, swimmers, kayaks, small pleasure boats, and yachts skim across crystal-clear lake waters; cyclists ride through mountains and woods or take it easy closer to shore, enjoying the views; hikers find indescribably beautiful waterfalls and rock formations, not to mention an incredible variety of birds and wildlife. In fall, leaves turn from green to gold to fiery orange and bright red, rivaling the famous fall foliage of New England. In the winter—OK, in the winter it is freezing cold in the U.P., but you know what? It's still beautiful. The snow is always white and soft; there's none of that dirty, salty city snow up here. Cross-country skiers have mile after mile of wide-open or woodland snow at their disposal, and even with all those skiers, there's enough room for snowmobilers to tear it up for miles without anyone telling them to keep it quiet or slow it down. And there's no need to forgo the fishing in winter. Ice fishing for walleye, whitefish, and trout is great fun, and the lakes freeze up enough by mid-December. When the ice begins to melt and leaves begin to sprout on the trees, April marks the start of trout-fishing season, and it's hard to imagine a better place to watch the magic of spring. Lilac runs riot over the islands, cherry blossoms explode with color, and birds sing cheerful tunes along the shore and in the woods. Though summer is warm and lovely, it is the only time of the year when crowds form in certain parts of the U.P. (Mackinac, Pictured Rocks). For those who prefer to avoid crowds, I recommend heading up in the spring, just after the first

LEFT: The coastline near Grand Marais is some of Lake Superior's most beautiful. Matt Girvan

11

In spring, the U.P. is awash in wildflowers.   Matt Girvan

blooms (April and May) but before the summer crowds, or in September when the crowds have left but the sun is still shining and the leaves are just starting to turn.

No matter what time of year it is, visitors are always treated to a warm, friendly Yooper welcome. (Yooper is slang for locals in the U.P. and comes from U.P.-er). People still wave hello to strangers, and although there are certain local treasures that residents are hesitant to share, most are happy to show off their home by pointing visitors in the direction of the best local sights and eats. Perhaps even more important, they have no problem steering tourists away from sights that aren't what they're cracked up to be.

My goal is that this guide be your own personal Yooper traveling companion—friendly and knowledgeable, pointing you toward secret waterfalls and charming B&Bs, romantic dinner spots, and the best piping-hot pasties, all while entertaining you with ancient legends and juicy bits of modern history.

The Way This Book Works

MICHIGAN'S UPPER PENINSULA is larger than the four states of Connecticut, Delaware, Massachusetts, and Rhode Island combined, with a continuous 1,700-mile shoreline provided by Lakes Superior, Michigan, and Huron. Within these boundaries, the 384-mile-long peninsula stretches from Drummond Island in the east to Ironwood in the west, reaching 233 miles wide from Menominee in the south to Copper Harbor at the tip of the Keweenaw Peninsula.

It's a lot of territory to cover. In the first edition of this book, we used the Great Lakes as a navigation system. This time around, because I've learned more about how people use this guide, it's divided by region and split into smaller chapters that group popular attractions together. The regional chapters move from east to west, and there are eight chapters total: History; Transportation; The East (Tahquamenon, Mackinac, and the Soo Locks); South Central (Beaches, Ghost Towns, Big Spring, Escanaba, and Manistique); North Central (Pictured Rocks and Marquette); Southwest (Iron Country and the Porkies); Northwest (Houghton, Keweenaw, and Isle Royale); and Information.

The first two chapters of this book cover the intriguing history of the U.P., from Native American tribes to French fur trappers to British and American soldiers, and transportation—getting to and getting around this large region. Then, within each regional chapter, you'll find a brief characterization of the region and what to expect when you visit, both in summer and in winter (a *very* important distinction!), along with recommendations for lodging, dining, shopping, and activities.

It is important to remember that the U.P. has many more trees than people and several more miles of isolated wilderness than developed civilization, so there will be some areas with limited lodging and dining options. Other areas, like Mackinac Island and its environs, are major

In May, before the summer season begins, Mackinac is nearly empty and absolutely lovely.

tourist destinations with plenty of restaurants and resorts to choose from. Another important fact to keep in mind: Winter is considered the off-season in the U.P., which means that a restaurant that was full of diners in June may well be boarded up in December. Some innkeepers shut their doors as well, and even those that remain open are surprised to hear from tourists outside the main season (May through September). Many establishments that stay open for the majority of the year tend to take the month of April off. All of which is to say, a spontaneous trip to the U.P. might not be the greatest idea between December and May, but with a little planning, you'll be just fine.

I have personally tested the waters throughout the U.P. in every season and included only those establishments I enjoy myself and would recommend to a good friend. I've marked those restaurants and lodging options that exceed all expectations with a star, for those looking to plan an extra-special trip.

Within each regional chapter, lodging prices are noted by dollar symbols, according to the following range:

$—Less than $100 a night
$$—$100 to $150 a night
$$$—$150 to $200 a night
$$$$—Over $200 a night

DINING PRICES

A similar dollar-sign scale, $ to $$$$, is used to indicate dining prices as well. The number of $ signs relates to an average price that refers to a dinner consisting of an entrée, appetizer or dessert, and glass of wine or beer (tax and gratuities not included). Following is a breakdown of the dollar value range of these tags:

$—$15 or less
$$—$15 to $30
$$$—$30 to $50
$$$$—$50 or more

History

TRIBES, TIMBER, MINES, AND GHOST TOWNS

THOUGH IT MAY SEEM a harsh place to live by today's standards, Michigan's Upper Peninsula has been considered an ideal home by an assortment of inhabitants, from early Native American settlers to French fur trappers, British miners, Finnish fishermen, and the all-American Henry Ford. The area was and still is rich in natural resources that lent themselves to both early rural life and modern industrialization—fresh water, lakes and streams chock-full of fish, a thriving deer population, huge forests, and large amounts of copper and iron ore. Though copper and iron mining didn't really take off until the mid-1800s, Native Americans mined for copper on Isle Royale and throughout the Keweenaw Peninsula (in the northwest of the U.P., jutting up into Lake Superior) to make tools and jewelry as early as 3000 B.C.

These very early settlers disappeared to parts unknown, replaced by the Ojibwa (also known as Chippewa) and Menominee Indian tribes, both part of the Algonquian language group, beginning in A.D. 800. The Ojibwa and Menominee lived off fish and nuts and had the peninsula to themselves until the first European explorers discovered the area in the 1620s. French fur traders soon had a thriving beaver pelt business in the U.P., establishing Sault Ste. Marie and Mackinac Island as major trading posts. The British eventually wrested the area and the fur trade away from the French, only to be supplanted by the Americans after the Revolution.

British influence returned to the U.P. several decades later in the form

LEFT: The Ojibwa people, longtime residents of the Upper Peninsula, continue to honor their traditions in celebrations like this one on Mackinac Island, which holds a special place in the Ojibwa creation myth. Courtesy Mackinac Island Tourism Bureau

17

of Cornish miners who immigrated to work in the iron and copper mines in the mid-to-late 1800s, bringing with them their Cornish pasties—meat and vegetable pies that made for a portable meal, easily eaten in the mines—which remain a Yooper staple to this day. Finnish, Scottish, Eastern European, Norwegian, and Italian miners all made their way to the U.P. during the mining boom, and their influence is still felt today in the regional music (it resembles Scandinavian folk music), cuisine, and architecture. By the 1880s, the Keweenaw Peninsula provided nearly 90 percent of the nation's copper.

Meanwhile, farther south and east, in the Menominee Range, the Gogebic Range, and the Marquette Range, highly productive iron mines were booming, making the area the nation's largest iron supplier by the end of the century. Michigan's lumber boom also crept north during this period, clearing acre after acre of U.P. forest. This burst of industry in what had long been a quiet rural area piqued the interest of Michigan's great captain of industry Henry Ford in the early 1920s. Looking to control the source of his raw materials and to illustrate his version of the American dream—a combination of old-fashioned rural life and hard work with modern industrial productivity—Ford established company mining towns, bought up forests, and erected sawmills throughout the U.P. Though his

In the early 1900s, fisherman braved the rough waters of the St. Mary's River.
Courtesy Library of Congress

U.P. empire was sold off after his death, Ford's towns, with their neatly divided management and worker housing areas, community squares, and industrial complexes, can still be toured today.

Ford wasn't the only one to establish company towns in the U.P. With lumber, copper mining, and iron mining all booming at the same time, numerous towns were built throughout the peninsula in the mid-to-late 1800s. Though there are still active lumber operations in the U.P. today, and mining is experiencing a bit of a renaissance (a fact not all locals are overly pleased about, given various environmental concerns), that initial boom eventually went bust, and only some of the towns made it through the sudden downturn. Today, the area is dotted with ghost towns that stand as life-size monuments to those times.

NATURAL HISTORY

The Upper Peninsula's rich iron and copper ores are the result of volcanic eruptions, the last of which occurred roughly 3 billion years ago, creating the Keweenaw Peninsula and raising the western half of the peninsula above the eastern half. In addition to eventually creating a mining industry in the U.P., these mineral deposits and geological rumblings, combined with erosion caused by the surrounding bodies of water and the area's harsh weather, have resulted in stunning stretches of coastline. Iron, copper, and manganese have painted the shore of Lake Superior between Munising and Grand Marais, known now as Pictured Rocks National Lakeshore, with deep greens and blues, burning reds and oranges, and coal black.

The lakes and their network of rivers and streams have long dominated both the landscape and local life in the U.P. Fish from the lakes have provided locals with food for thousands of years, and the lakes—especially Superior, infamous for its unpredictable weather and swells—have claimed their fair share of fishermen in return. Rivers jump off rocks on their way to the lakes and become beautiful waterfalls all over the U.P. You can hardly drive 10 miles through the peninsula in any direction without passing a sign directing you to a nearby waterfall. One local family—the Penroses—has documented and rated all the waterfalls in the area in a popular book that puts the waterfall count at 199.

Despite decades of overfishing, and the introduction of invasive species such as the lamprey eel—a vicious carnivore that eats up to 40 pounds of fish per week and is typically found in the waters of northern Europe—the lakes and rivers of the U.P. remain full of fish, from Lake Superior whitefish to salmon, trout, and perch.

Large bodies of water and vast areas of untouched forest make the U.P. an ideal home for numerous animals, from the ubiquitous deer to the

A spectacular sweep of a colorful sandstone cliff along Lake Superior's shoreline. Matt Girvan

elusive wolf. Wolves are notoriously development-shy, and they thrive in the U.P. forests, where they can easily hide from humans and choose from plenty of deer for dinner. Another elusive mammal—the moose—also calls the U.P. home, especially the woods northwest of Marquette and the almost entirely undeveloped Isle Royale in Lake Superior. Moose were hunted to the brink of extinction in the U.P. during the mining boom, but in the 1980s, a pack of 59 moose was introduced to the Marquette area from Canada, and their numbers grew to over 300 by the late 1990s. Now lucky visitors can spot moose grazing or slurping from ponds or marshes at dawn or dusk.

Besides being drawn by the larger wildlife, people visit the U.P. from all over the world for its unique bird population. In addition to numerous bald eagles, hawks, and herons, notoriously cagey birds like the loon flourish here, sandhill cranes visit every year, and the Seney National Wildlife Refuge is home to countless rare birds like the yellow rail and the black-backed woodpecker.

SOCIAL HISTORY

Old Copper Indians to Modern-Day Tribes

Little is known about the first settlers in the U.P., except that they lived in the area approximately 5,000 years ago and they mined for copper, with which they made arrowheads and jewelry. These so-called Old Copper Indians mysteriously disappeared, eventually replaced by the Algonquian tribes—Ojibwa (Chippewa), Potawatomi, and Menominee—in A.D. 800. The Ojibwa and Potawatomi occupied most of the eastern U.P., and the Menominee occupied the central and western U.P. and much of what is now Wisconsin. Under the catchall names of Ojibwa and Menominee are several distinct regional tribes including the Soo—the common name for the Sault Ste. Marie tribe of Ojibwa who are descendants of the Anishinabeg tribe.

By the mid-1500s, the Ojibwa were joined in the east by the Ottawa (Odawa) and Huron tribes, both of which had fled from the Iroquois. These tribes are still active in the U.P. today; their history and culture are evident in the names of lakes, regions, streets, and parks. The tribes still hold regular powwows as well, and a real effort has been made to provide museums, tours, and events that delve into tribal culture.

Numerous Native American casinos have also sprung up throughout the U.P. in recent years; in some regions the casinos are the primary development for miles around.

The French Introduce Europe to the U.P.

French explorer Étienne Brûlé is generally thought to be the first European to set foot in the Upper Peninsula. Brûlé crossed the St. Mary's River into the eastern U.P. in 1620, apparently looking for a trade route to the Far East. What he discovered instead were waterways teeming with beaver. Brûlé was soon followed in 1634 by Jean Nicolet, another explorer looking for a route to the Orient who found fur instead. By the late 1600s, French fur trappers were doing a booming business in the U.P., with trading posts at Sault Ste. Marie and St. Ignace. In the early 1700s, justifiably fearful of attack from the British, the French moved their fur-trading operations to a fortified village, Fort Michilimackinac, which has since been reconstructed just outside Mackinaw City. The fort has been maintained as a historical attraction, so those interested in this period of the U.P.'s history can stop by today for a faithful glimpse of how the early traders and their families lived, dressed, and entertained themselves.

In addition to the fur trade, the French brought with them new food, customs, and religion, which they attempted to share with the Ojibwa people they met in the U.P. One of the better known of these explorers was Father Jacques Marquette who arrived in the U.P. in the late 1660s, building a mission in Sault Ste. Marie in 1668 and at St. Ignace in 1671. Marquette was not your garden-variety missionary. He had a knack for native tongues and believed, as did other Jesuits at the time, that the native people were inherently good and already believed in God.

Distinguishing him further from other missionaries of the day was Marquette's zeal and talent for exploration. In 1673, he joined explorer Louis

Daily summer performances at Fort Michilimackinac are faithful to history, complete with cannon firing. Wikimedia Commons

Jolliet and a small French and Native American crew to "discover" the Mississippi River. The Jolliet-Marquette expedition marked the first time Europeans entered the Mississippi River—the crew traveled via canoe from St. Ignace, through Lake Michigan to Green Bay, up the Fox River, and over to the Wisconsin River, which led them to the Mississippi. The priest helped to map these waterways before heading back to St. Ignace via Chicago, but the weather and the long journey caught up with him, and he died near Ludington, Michigan, in 1675. Marquette's statue looks over St. Ignace still; his mission and life are paid tribute to in the Marquette Mission Park there, and the Museum of Ojibwa Culture occupies roughly the same spot that Marquette's mission once did. The priest was also the namesake for the U.P.'s largest city and is memorialized in various other spots throughout the peninsula.

The British Are Coming

The British did eventually turn up, defeating the French in Montreal in 1760 and taking over Fort Michilimackinac and the fur trade in 1761 after victory in the French and Indian War. (They eventually moved the bulk of the fur trade to Mackinac Island, where it was protected by Fort Mackinac from the tribes and the rebellious American colonists.)

While the French had viewed the Native American tribes as neighbors, often working with, marrying, and having children with the Ojibwa, the British viewed and treated the tribes as a conquered people. Dissatisfied with the policies of the British, the Ojibwa, Potawatomi, Ottawa, and Huron tribes revolted in 1763, led by Ottawa chief Pontiac in what was later called Pontiac's Rebellion.

The American Dream

After the Revolutionary War, all of the U.P. eventually became American soil, but otherwise it was business as usual. The fur trade continued to thrive, with Mackinac Island as its hub under the watchful eye of business-man John Jacob Astor, until the 1830s.

In 1837, after the Toledo War—really more of a squabble than a war—was ended by President Andrew Jackson, Congress admitted Michigan to statehood, giving the disputed Toledo Strip to Ohio and offering Michigan the U.P. as a consolation prize. Though at the time the U.P. was described in the federal register as desolate wilderness, industry continued to prosper in the region. The opening of the Soo Locks at Sault Ste. Marie, connecting Lake Superior to the other Great Lakes via the St. Mary's River, increased the flow of goods to and from the U.P., and though the fur trade had long since declined by that point, mining and lumber kept the locks so full that

A Revolutionary War–era cannon on the shores of Mackinac Island serves as a reminder of the tiny island's role as a major trade and military hub. Matt Girvan

Miners came to work the Keweenaw copper mines from all over the world. Wikimedia Commons

the tonnage passing through them surpassed that passing through either the Panama Canal or the Suez Canal.

Though Native Americans had been mining for copper for thousands of years, the copper industry really began to boom in the U.P. in the 1860s, with production centered on the Keweenaw Peninsula. Iron mining had begun in earnest in the 1850s after an 1842 geological report of the Marquette Range by Michigan's state geologist was published, revealing large amounts of iron ore in the range. Iron was eventually discovered in the Gogebic and Menominee Ranges as well, placing three of the six principal American iron ranges in the U.P.

Immigrants came from all over the world to work in the iron and copper mines and as lumberjacks in the emergent lumber industry, but the dominant groups were from England (mostly Cornwall), Scotland, Finland, Norway, Sweden, Italy, and Poland. The descendants of these early miners are still alive and well in the U.P. today, making for a vibrant music, food, and art scene.

Industry Gives Way to Tourism, Convicts, and Casinos

The lumber and mining industries began to decline toward the end of the 19th century, due to less expensive options elsewhere in the country and beyond. It was railroad executives who first thought to turn the U.P. into a tourist destination in the late 1800s to recover profits that were slowly dropping off as the companies transported fewer and fewer loads of timber, iron, and copper. No longer a remote wilderness, the U.P. had become a viable vacation destination.

Built in 1852, the Island House on Mackinac Island was the first hotel to cater to summer visitors. Its construction was followed by that of several other hotels including the legendary Grand Hotel in 1887, and Mackinac quickly became a favorite vacation destination for visitors from "down below" and even for out-of-staters, including a U.S. president and a handful of well-known actors (Esther Williams among them). When the Mackinac Bridge was constructed in 1957, tourism increased and began to spread beyond Mackinac Island to the rest of the U.P., just in time to employ at least some of the workers who had been laid off by mining, lumber, and railroad companies.

To keep visitors entertained and locals employed, tribe-owned casinos began springing up throughout the U.P. in the 1980s. In addition to a tourist mecca, the U.P. became home to the bulk of the state's prisons, with six prisons built between 1988 and 1993. Currently the prison system

Before the Mackinac Bridge was built in 1957, visitors to the Upper Peninsula had to take a car ferry. Matt Girvan

and the casinos are the top employers in the U.P. In the summer, tourism employs far more people, but the drop-off in winter leaves many people out of work for several months.

NEIGHBORS ALL AROUND

The Upper and Lower Peninsulas of Michigan could easily be considered separate states. Downstaters sometimes look down on Yoopers as unsophisticated roughnecks, while Yoopers refer to those from "down below" as everything from trolls to fudgies (due to the number of downstate tourists that crowd Mackinac's fudge shops in the summer). The factories to the south lured a large percentage of U.P. workers in the 1940s, contributing in some part to economic problems up north. And Detroit, in its heyday, was a very cosmopolitan city that thought itself better than the mining towns up north, despite the fact that, as Yoopers are quick to point out, the Calumet Theater in the Keweenaw Peninsula predates any of Detroit's landmarks. From its large tracts of wild land to the widespread enjoyment of and respect for nature and wildlife, the U.P. actually has more in common with the neighbor on the other side of its watery borders—Canada. Even the Yooper accent sounds more Canadian than Michigan, with its Scandinavian-influenced intonations and the frequent use of *eh* to punctuate both statements and questions.

People often wonder why the U.P. is part of Michigan as opposed to Wisconsin, which is closer to the peninsula and shares a long land border (lower Michigan is connected to the U.P. only by the Mackinac Bridge). In 1835, before Michigan was formally admitted to the Union, Ohio senators lobbied for a long slice of southern Michigan at the mouth of the Maumee River. Ohio prevailed easily, and Toledo is now located in that strip, but Michigan was given the U.P. as consolation. At the time, Wisconsin was not yet populated enough to apply for statehood.

In many ways, the history of the U.P. mirrors that of the United States as a whole, and there are few places in the country where that past—from Native American culture to the Industrial Revolution to modern-day globalization—is so easily traced. In addition to still being one of the more beautiful, large, untouched pieces of wilderness left in the country, the U.P. stands as a sort of living American history museum—ghost towns, closed mines, national parks, and remnants of ancient Native American culture interspersed with modern-day Indian gaming casinos and grand old buildings in towns that today boast no more than a few hundred year-round residents.

It's hard to imagine the U.P. becoming much different in the future. Tourism increases a bit every year, but the long winter and long journey still keep the U.P. from becoming completely overrun, and the huge tracts of national forest ensure that it will never become overdeveloped. The state may build more prisons, but surely it can only need so many, and the locals and visitors can support only so many casinos. Mining companies are once again interested in the region, but they are meeting opposition from local environmental groups and Native American tribes, both of which fear the machines and chemicals employed by the companies will soil sacred lands. Meanwhile, one of the largest ethanol production facilities in the country is also being planned for the U.P., setting up an interesting contrast between "old" energy and "new" energy. And while some look to turn the U.P.'s resources into energy, others have a different idea for the region's natural products: Microbreweries and maple syrup producers are hoping to turn the U.P. into one of the country's top producers of both sorts of liquid gold. It's an exciting time in the U.P., with more young people choosing to stay up north and the economic downturn turning naturally self-sufficient Yoopers into a new crop of entrepreneurs.

Transportation

WATERWAYS, FREEWAYS, AND THE MIGHTY MAC

GETTING AROUND THE U.P. is pretty straightforward: There are only so many main roads, the major attractions are well marked (unlike in the rest of Michigan, road signs indicating attractions here are large, obvious, and placed at logical intervals before you need to turn off the main road), and it's fairly easy to travel between regions. Getting to the U.P., on the other hand, can be somewhat of a trek, depending on where you start. Whether you plan to take a short flight or a longer drive, set aside at least a week for your trip if you want to visit multiple attractions or devote weekends to particular spots. I don't recommend trying to tackle the U.P. in one fell swoop, unless you're prepared to spend a good month or two seeing everything you need to see.

GETTING TO THE U.P.

The Mackinac Bridge is the primary route between the Lower Peninsula and the Upper Peninsula. It is so much a part of life in Michigan that state residents refer to the U.P. as "above the bridge" and the Lower Peninsula as "below the bridge."

By Car

Everyone driving to the U.P. from the south will cross the Mackinac Bridge. Even some visitors from Wisconsin will bring their cars on the ferry from

LEFT: Despite the slow speed, riding through the locks in a boat is a big rush. Matt Girvan

Manitowoc, Wisconsin, to Ludington, Michigan, and then drive up and over the bridge. From Detroit to St. Ignace (the first U.P. town across the bridge), the drive takes approximately five hours; from Ludington to St. Ignace, it takes about three hours.

By Plane

Flights operated by Mesaba Air and booked by Delta fly between Detroit and Marquette (closest to Pictured Rocks National Lakeshore), Hancock (gateway to the Keweenaw Peninsula), and Pellston (closest to Mackinac Island) daily. See www.mesaba.com.

By Bus

Indian Trails operates buses between Chicago, Milwaukee, lower Michigan, and the U.P., as well as routes between destinations within the U.P. The company offers connections to routes offered by other carriers, including Greyhound, Michigan Flyer, and Amtrak. See www.indiantrails.com for schedules, routes, and fares.

GETTING AROUND THE AREA

Getting around in the U.P. generally requires a car, with the notable exception of Mackinac Island, which is car free. It is possible to get from the east to the west of the peninsula and vice versa by bus, but you'll still need some other form of transportation upon arrival at your destination. That said, biking is terrific throughout the U.P. (bikes are allowed on Indian Trails buses

Indian Trails buses crisscross the U.P. Courtesy Indian Trails

A sign describing the history of US 41 marks the beginning of the highway. Matt Girvan

for an additional $15), with numerous rides of all lengths and difficulty levels offering terrific views and an easy way to get around town. Most of the waterfront towns also have boardwalks that are ideally suited to a sunset stroll. Ferries are abundant in the U.P. but don't operate in the winter for obvious reasons.

By Car

Traffic can get backed up on US 2 during the summer, from St. Ignace in the east moving westward, so it's best to drive during off-peak hours in the summer months (early morning, midday, nighttime). In addition to US 2, which runs along the entire southern U.P. from St. Ignace in the east to Ironwood in the west, there are a handful of other main highways in the U.P. connecting various regions. US 41 runs from Escanaba in the south central part of the peninsula north to Marquette and then northwest all the way up to Copper Harbor on the Keweenaw Peninsula. I-75 connects the Lower Peninsula to the Upper Peninsula, taking drivers across the Mackinac Bridge and farther north and east up to Sault Ste. Marie. US 45 leads from the Wisconsin-Michigan border in the south up to Ontonagon in the northwest. MI 123 takes visitors to and from popular Tahquamenon Falls and can get fairly congested in the summer months.

Ferries for Isle Royale leave from Houghton and Copper Harbor. Matt Girvan

Types of Roads

The U.P. is crisscrossed with various types of roads, ranging from interstate highways to unpaved country roads. Following is a list of the road types and abbreviations used here:

CR—County road. Generally paved roads, county roads tend to link major towns or provide a direct route to a popular attraction off a larger highway.

FR—Forest road. Generally unpaved roads through national forests.

H—H road. These roads are small and sometimes unpaved and either provide scenic routes between towns or connect small towns to larger roads or highways.

MI—Michigan state road. Slightly larger than county roads, state roads typically lead from a highway to either a large town or a popular landmark. (MI 123, for example, leads drivers off US 28 to Tahqua-menon Falls and returns to the highway in a loop.)

US—U.S. highway. These highways provide the primary links between regions.

I—Interstate highway. I-75 is the only interstate highway in the U.P.; it leads up from the lower peninsula to Sault Ste. Marie in the northeast of the U.P.

Model T in the U.P.

As with the rest of Michigan, Henry Ford and the auto industry left an indelible mark on the U.P., not only with the mines, lumberyards, and company towns he set up, but also with his vehicles. And Ford wasn't

the only one. The U.P. is full of classics, both in various museums and on the roads and in the lots they once domi-nated. Old-timers in Eagle Harbor love to tell the story of when a shipment of new Chryslers had to be rescued and hauled in over the ice when its carrier was ship-wrecked on a piece of Lake Superior ice. It's easy to imagine a new Model T hop-ping down the road through the middle of many a U.P. town, and spotting one of them in reality is always a treat.

Classic cars dot the U.P. landscape.   Matt Girvan

By Rental Car

Cars are available for rent from Avis, Budget, Alamo, and National Car Rental at the Marquette airport, from National Car Rental at the Houghton County Memorial Airport in Hancock, and from Avis and Hertz at Pellston Regional Airport. Prices start at $48 a day and go up, but you can some-times find a package deal with a flight and/or hotel that drives the cost down considerably.

By Ferry

Ferry service is available to Mackinac Island, Drummond Island, and Isle Royale on varying schedules. Ferries to Mackinac book up quickly in peak season (June through August), so it's best to purchase ferry tickets well in advance. Isle Royale is also very popular in the summer, so it's a good idea to buy ferry tickets at least a week in advance, although you can sometimes squeak by with a last-minute purchase. (see page 44 for details)

By Bus

Bus service is available on Indian Trails from St. Ignace in the east to Iron-wood in the west, with a stop at Escanaba along the way. Indian Trails also operates a bus route between Calumet, in the Keweenaw Peninsula, and Marquette. See www.indiantrails.com.

1

The East

TAHQUAMENON, MACKINAC, AND THE SOO LOCKS

LIFE IN MUCH OF THE UPPER PENINSULA revolves around water, but nowhere in the peninsula is water quite so important—and prevalent—as here. In addition to the most celebrated waterfall in a region full of falls (Tahquamenon), this area is home to some of the state's best trout streams, and its cold, deep lake waters mask the most shipwrecks in a lake known for sending ships to its floor. This is also where the U.P.'s most important river—the St. Mary's—serves as both a watery border between the United States and Canada and a migratory route for people, ships, and wildlife. Another important waterway—the Straits of Mackinac—link Lake Huron to Lake Michigan and separate Michigan's Lower Peninsula from its Upper Peninsula, with the Mackinac Bridge over the Straits acting as a gateway to the eastern U.P.

The land bordering these waterways to the north makes up the eastern-most part of the U.P. and comprises more islands than any other region in Michigan. The high concentration of islands has historically made boating, paddling, and fishing both popular and necessary in the region, and the islands themselves have long been socially important, first as meeting places for the Ojibwa and then as vacation destinations for downstaters.

There is great variety among the islands of the eastern U.P.—car-free, Victorian-inspired Mackinac Island and modern, elegant Drummond Island offer four-star lodging and dining, while the islands that make up

LEFT: Arch Rock has been a Mackinac attraction since the late 1800s; this photo dates to around 1900. Library of Congress

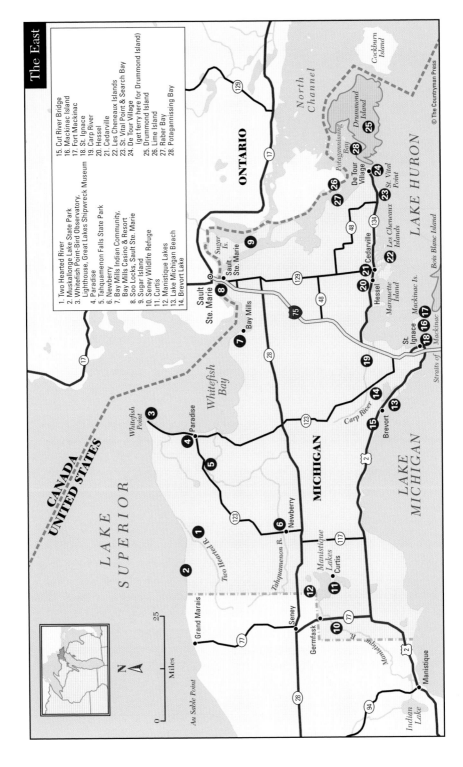

1. Two Hearted River
2. Muskallonge Lake State Park
3. Whitefish Point-Bird Observatory, Lighthouse, Great Lakes Shipwreck Museum
4. Paradise
5. Tahquamenon Falls State Park
6. Newberry
7. Bay Mills Indian Community, Bay Mills Casino & Resort
8. Soo Locks, Sault Ste. Marie
9. Sugar Island
10. Seney Wildlife Refuge
11. Curtis
12. Manistique Lakes
13. Lake Michigan Beach
14. Brevort Lake
15. Cut River Bridge
16. Mackinac Island
17. Fort Mackinac
18. St. Ignace
19. Carp River
20. Hessel
21. Cedarville
22. Les Cheneaux Islands
23. St. Vital Point & Search Bay
24. De Tour Village (get ferry here for Drummond Island)
25. Drummond Island
26. Lime Island
27. Raber Bay
28. Potagannissing Bay

© The Countryman Press

Mackinac's pleasant, car-free downtown. Aaron Bowen

Les Cheneaux (French for "The Channels" and often referred to as the Snows) are dotted with unpretentious resorts, rugged fishing camps, parks, and woodland campgrounds. Beyond the islands, the shores of Lake Huron are home to waterfront towns that range from charming (St. Ignace) to touristy (Mackinaw City).

Meanwhile, in the farthest east section of the region, Sault Ste. Marie is a city whose economic survival revolves around water, between the massive freighters moving through its Soo Locks and the groups of tourists coming to take a look at them.

Pick Your Spot

Best places to stay in eastern U.P., and nearby . . .

DRUMMOND ISLAND

At 36 miles long, Drummond ranks as the largest island in Michigan, but it remains one of its lesser known, despite efforts in the last two decades to put Drummond on the map as a travel destination.

Once home to a small logging and fishing community, Drummond has almost always had vacation cottages and lodges built to accommodate visiting hunters, boaters, and fishermen in the summer and adventurous snowmobilers in the winter. In the last 20 years or so, though, a fair amount of development has taken place on Drummond, elevating it to a sort of high-end vacation destination, at least by U.P. standards.

The island first came to some prominence in the 1980s when Domino's Pizza founder (and then owner of the Detroit Tigers) Tom Monahan bought a large portion of it with the intention of turning the island into an upscale executive retreat. Monahan built a large Frank Lloyd Wright–inspired lodge, lakefront cottages, a fine-dining restaurant, a golf course, tennis courts, and a huge 20-person sauna. In the process of building out the resort, Monahan found God in the woods of Drummond Island. The last thing he built was a beautiful and serene outdoor chapel in a peaceful glen overlooking the water: Sitting here on a clear morning it's not hard to see how Monahan might have felt touched by a higher power. After selling the resort, his baseball team, and his business and toiling for a time in Mexico as a missionary, Monahan resurfaced in Florida where he made waves with the design and development of a town and Catholic university, both named Ave Maria. Ave Maria, Florida, is run in accordance with Roman Catholic principles and has been the subject of much debate since it appeared in 2006.

Whatever the fate of Ave Maria, the Drummond Island Resort (1-800-999-6343; www .drummondisland.com; $$$) is here to stay, and since Monahan's departure, it has become a popular destination for those looking for a bit of wilderness without giving up the comforts of home (including The Rock, an award-winning golf course). The resort's sister property, Drummond Island Yacht Haven (1-800-543-4743; www.diyacht haven.com; $$) offers a more casual—-and affordable—option, with fully equipped one-, two-, or three-bedroom cabins right on the water, each with a kitchen, linens, and all the necessary cooking utensils. The cabins could use some updating, but they are clean and simple, and the lake view can't be beat. Those looking for even more solitude can rent one of dozens of Drummond Island vacation homes through Northern Properties (1-800-292-5064; www.northernprop erties.com; $$ to $$$$), which offers everything from small and affordable cabins to luxury lakefront stunners.

The newest lodging option on the island, the Drummond Island Hotel (906-493-5799; www.drum mondislandhotel.com; $) offers affordable, large rooms with one king or two queen beds and cable TV and a complimentary continental breakfast every morning. Rooms are neither charming nor rustic, just simple, clean, and comfortable. The hotel is located near Four Corners, the only thing close to a downtown on Drummond Island, and is within walking distance or close driving distance to the lakeshore, a marina, restaurants, and the island's only grocery store.

Irrespective of your home base, Drummond Island is an outdoor

You can rent this boathouse through the Drummond Island Resort for total privacy and 360-degree views.   Matt Girvan

enthusiast's paradise, with 40 inland lakes, 50 outlying islands, several protected coves, hiking and biking trails, golf, a variety of birdlife, fantastic hunting and fishing, and morel mushrooms just waiting to be scooped up and added to your next recipe.

GRAND MARAIS

Grand Marais is an idyllic stereotype of a small American seaside village, flanked by great dunes, falls, and Pictured Rocks to the west and long stretches of undeveloped Lake Superior wilderness to the east. It fills to capacity during the summer months, then returns to small-town life after the fall color season.

A small log cabin motel and several stand-alone one-, two-, and three-bedroom log cabins, known collectively as Hilltop Cabins (906-494-2331; www.hilltopcabins.net; $$), look out over Lake Superior from a small bluff above Grand Marais. Furnished with custom-made wood furniture, each cabin has a full kitchen, private bathroom, and living room, with towels and linens provided. All guests have access to a large deck with incredible views of the lake and a handful of barbecue grills. The three-bedroom cabins all have Lake Superior views, whirlpool tubs, and fireplaces. Popular both with summer tourists and with snowmobilers in the winter, these cabins book up fast, so call ahead.

Closer to the water, North Shore Lodge (906-494-2361; www.northshorelodgemi.net; $) is the only Grand Marais hotel on the beach. This cute green A-frame on Coast Guard Point isn't fancy, but it makes up for anything lacking in the luxury department with a good deal of comfort and convenience. Guests have access to a sandy private beach right out their front doors, rooms are large and clean with cable TV and in-room phones, there's an indoor pool, and the hotel operates a decent restaurant as well. Pets are allowed in all rooms, and kids stay free, making the North Shore very popular with families, who dominate both the motel and the lodge's eight housekeeping cabins. In the winter, North Shore is a favorite with snowmobilers for its proximity to the trail (it's right smack on top of it), its snowmobile rental packages, and its restaurant, which also includes a full bar. Important to note: North Shore Lodge usually closes for at least two weeks during either March or April.

LES CHENEAUX

At one time (the late 1800s, to be more precise) nearly every wealthy Midwest family had a summer home on one of the 36 small islands that make up Les Cheneaux. These people had money, but they were looking for modest family summer homes rather than elaborate retreats. So, though some of these houses (built by the likes of Eli Lilly) are large enough to qualify as mansions, and a few of the boats skimming between the islands could cost as much as you paid for your house, Les Cheneaux remains a quiet and unpretentious place to enjoy a bit of the great outdoors.

Hessel and Cedarville are two small villages on the shore of the main peninsula nearest Les Cheneaux. In addition to a handful of restaurants and lodging options, these former Native American fishing villages are home to an annual antique wooden boat show that brings boating fans from throughout the Northeast.

In Cedarville, the Cedarville Inn (1-800-222-2949; www.cedarvilleinn.net; $) is a former Comfort Inn, and it still looks a bit like a chain motel but with a number of improvements: several rooms have Jacuzzi tubs, the hotel has a 40-foot indoor heated swimming pool and a small fitness room, a handful of pet-friendly rooms cater to guests traveling with their furry friends, and a complimentary deluxe continental breakfast is served daily. The motel also rents snowmobiles and provides access to over 100 miles of snowmobile trails.

Hessel is home to the annual wood boat show, and the Hessel Bay Sunset Cabins (616-365-2035; www.hesselsunsetcabins.com; $$) provide a bird's-eye view of the action, with six simple, clean lakeview cabins set on a grassy acre of lakefront with nearly 300 feet of

The annual wooden boat show in Hessel. Courtesy Pure Michigan

sandy shoreline access, just two blocks from the Hessel Marina. Full-size kitchens with fairly new appliances also make it a great spot for families (just don't forget to bring your own towels).

In between the two towns, The Spring Lodge and Cottages (1-800-480-2282; www.springlodge .com; $) offers the sort of setting you'd expect to see in a Norman Rockwell painting. Most of the cottages have views from both decks and glassed- and screened-in living rooms. There's a large sandy swimming beach with bonfire pits, various boats are available for rent, and a number of trees provide a bit of pleasant shade on warm summer days.

MACKINAC ISLAND

Yoopers have a love-hate relationship with Mackinac Island. It's both a point of pride ("Have you been to Mackinac? It's beautiful, you should go!") and the butt of local jokes ("Stay away from Mackinac for a couple of months. The fudgies are in town!").

Mackinac is known for a few key things: It's a car-free island, so you'll see horses, carriages, bikes, and skateboards but no automobiles, which is extremely rare in Michigan; there are more fudge shops than restaurants on the island (hence the term *fudgies* for summer tourists to Mackinac); lilac blooms like crazy in the spring and summer, just in time for the annual

Lilac Festival; and all the buildings are Victorian inspired, from the celebrated Grand Hotel up on the hill (another one of Mackinac's attractions) to the few residences scattered around the island.

There are dozens of great B&Bs on Mackinac, but to avoid both high prices and crowds, many visitors opt instead to stay in St. Ignace or Mackinaw City, where ferries to the island depart several times a day.

Unlike the majority of resorts on Mackinac, the small and charming Bogan Lane Inn (906-847-3439;

Mackinac celebrates its annual Lilac Festival in early June, when the island is awash in purple blossoms. Courtesy Mackinac Island Tourism Bureau

With no cars, Mackinac's wide roads are left solely to bicycles and horses.   Matt Girvan

www.boganlaneinn.com; $$) is open year-round. It also doesn't take Internet reservations, all rooms share bathrooms, and its prices are shockingly reasonable for this part of the U.P. Innkeeper Trish Martin has lived on Mackinac all her life (she grew up in what is now the inn) and provides guests with great recommendations for exploring. Plan on booking early if you're looking to stay at Bogan Lane during the summer, as it books up quickly.

The grandest resort on the island—and the most expensive by far—is the Grand Hotel (1-800-334-7263; www.grandhotel.com; open May through October; $$$$), which sits regally atop a hill over-looking "downtown" Mackinac and has hosted presidents and Holly-wood luminaries. Esther Williams swam in the pool here, and President Harry S. Truman relaxed on the front porch, as did four other U.S. presidents and countless presidential hopefuls. Its huge white columns, manicured rose gardens, and hushed, deferential service hark back to a long-gone era of gentility and refinement. In an effort to keep that air of glamour, the hotel has a fairly strict dress code, requiring guests to wear evening wear every night (coats and ties for men, dresses or pantsuits for women). If you're going to splurge on a room here, it's worth a few extra dollars to get a slightly

Getting to Mackinac Island

Three ferry companies offer trips to Mackinac and back:

Arnold Transit Co. (906-847-3351 or 1-800-542-8528; www.arnoldline .com) This is the oldest company, but they have the fastest boats, which leave from both St. Ignace and Mackinaw City. They also offer a slower, traditional ferry.

Shepler's (1-800-828-6157; www.sheplersferry.com; 556 E. Central Ave., Mackinaw City) Shepler's leaves from both St. Ignace and Mackinaw City, but its hub is Mackinaw City. Customers can print their own tickets online. Shepler's also sells tickets to the Mackinac Historical State Park attractions on the island.

Star Line (1-800-638-9892; www.mackinawferry.com) Star Line runs hydro-jet ferries that produce a 35-foot rooster-tail spray, which is fun for kids to see. Leaves from both St. Ignace and Mackinaw City.

Keep in mind that in the early spring and later fall the companies taper their schedules back a bit and don't offer service every day. Not that it would be such a bad thing to be "stuck" on Mackinac! If you head over in April, you'll see all the folks on their way to Mackinac for "the season" with trunks of clothing and food, not unlike the way things were back in the 19th century.

The Arnold ferry makes several trips to Mackinac daily during the summer.

Courtesy Pure Michigan

Horse-drawn carriage is still a primary mode of transport on Victorian Mackinac Island.

Courtesy Mackinac Island Tourism Bureau

larger one with a view; the interior rooms can feel like you've been trapped in your grandmother's attic. A daily full breakfast, lunch, and five-course dinner are included in the hotel's rates and served in the Main Dining Room, a large and charming restaurant with cheery yellow walls, white linen table-cloths, dark green chairs, and dozens of large windows looking out over the Straits of Mackinac. In keeping with the hotel's Great Gatsby vibe, its Terrace Room offers live big band music in a swanky formal ballroom. It's worth a visit if only for the fun of pre-tending you're Esther Williams, cutting a rug to some white-hot swing music and sipping cham-pagne like it's what you were born to do.

The opulent Grand Hotel opened in 1887.

Mackinaw or Mackinac?

Both, actually. The Native American tribes in the area called it Michinni-makinong, but the name was shortened over the years by French and British settlers. In the 1600s, the French pronounced the ending as *aw* and spelled it as *ac*, which is why today Michilimackinac, Fort Mackinac, Mackinac Island, the Straits of Mackinac, and the Mackinac Bridge are all spelled with an *ac* but pronounced *aw*. Upon the arrival of the British, a village established as Mackinaw (now Mackinaw City) was pronounced as *aw* and also spelled that way.

A bit more reasonably priced than some of the other inns on the island, the Harbour View Inn (906-847-0101; www.harbourviewinn.com; open May 4 through October 31; $$$) is within walking distance to downtown but far enough away to keep summer guests from the busy tourist bustle. The inn consists of three separate buildings—the Chateau, the Carriage House, and the Guest House. The Chateau houses the lobby and several guest rooms; suites, many with private balconies, are located in the Carriage House and Guest House, which sit on opposite sides of a quiet courtyard with an outdoor spa, gazebo, and floral gardens. Not all of the rooms have air conditioning, so be sure to ask if you're booking during the summer. Although there is no restaurant on-site, a complimentary continental breakfast (pastries, fruit, yogurt, cereal, coffee, juices, tea) is served daily, and the extremely helpful, friendly staff will be happy to point you in the direction of a great restaurant.

Its great location, close to both the water and downtown but not too close to either for noise to be a problem, makes the Hotel Iroquois (906-847-3321 or, in winter, 616-247-5675; www.iroquoishotel.com; open mid-May through October 22; $$$$) popular with regular visitors and newbies alike. The grounds are beautiful, with manicured lawns butting up against jagged rocks that fall off into the ocean. Rooms in the back of the hotel have views of the water and the lighthouse, while rooms at the front have pleasant views of the Main Street boardwalk—good for people watching—so there's not really a bad room in the house. The décor is "Victorian inspired," but they've done a good job of modernizing the Victorian look with the addition of white space and some softer colors. Overall, this is a great spot for a couple's or friends' weekend away; though children are welcome here, it's much better suited to adults.

Slightly closer to downtown, Mackinac's first hotel is still one of

The Island House Hotel was the first hotel on the island to cater to families visiting in the summertime. Wikimedia Commons

its finest. Perched above Main Street near Marquette Park, the rambling crisp white, red-roofed Island House (1-800-626-6304; www.theislandhouse.com; open early May through late October; $$$$) boasts one of the island's best locations, close to downtown (two blocks) but far enough away to be peaceful and quiet even during the summer rush, with unobstructed views of the marina, the lighthouse, and the shipping lanes. Rocking chairs line the expansive front porch, and it's not uncommon for guests to spend the better part of a day here, staring out at the water. The rooms are decorated à la "Grandma's Rose Garden," with plenty of floral prints and pastel walls, but you're likely to spend more time in the large, bright lobby, one of the popular restau-

rants (1852 Dining Room, with its stellar water view, or the local favorite Ice House Bar & Grill) or on the front porch than in your room.

For more seclusion, visitors head out to the Mission Point Resort (1-800-833-7711; www .missionpoint.com; open May through October; $$$), which sits on its own quiet corner of the island. Its dozens of activities make it possible to stay at Mission Point and never leave, but because it offers a ton of options without an ounce of stuffiness—and because it allows children under 18 to stay free and children under 12 to eat free—the resort has become very popular with families.

And for those who prefer to be smack in the middle of things, fudge shops and all, the Murray

Hotel and the Inn on Mackinac (1-800-462-2546; www.4mackinac .com; open May through October; $$$) are two B&Bs in one, each with something different to offer. While the Murray Hotel is smack in the middle of Main Street and has a cool old mining-town saloon feel—you halfway expect to see women in bustles and someone in a top hat playing the piano when you walk in—the Inn on Mackinac is tucked away above Main Street and embodies everything the words *Victorian inn* bring to mind: tall, round turrets, an elaborate and colorful paint job, a large wraparound veranda. Both B&Bs feature outdoor sundecks, pools, and hot tubs.

Rooms are spacious and comfortable, with modern bathrooms and Victorian-decorated bedrooms (floral wallpaper, elaborate headboards, antique bedside tables), and home-baked bedtime cookies are offered nightly at both hotels.

MACKINAW CITY AND ST. IGNACE

Back on shore, Mackinaw City is the more newly built and thus slightly tackier cousin to St. Ignace, which comes closer to mimicking the Victorian charm of Mackinac Island. That's not to say that Mackinaw City is without its virtues: There are many affordable lodging

The Inn on Mackinac is one of several Victorian Inns on the island. Wikimedia Commons

and dining options there, and its proximity to Colonial Michilimackinac Historical State Park—the nation's longest-running archaeological digs—make it appealing to many visitors.

On the other hand, with its wooden boardwalk, waterfront restaurants, and charming old homes, St. Ignace offers the same affordable prices and proximity to Mackinac Island as Mackinaw City, but without the tacky tourist vibe.

For a bit of both worlds, try the Brigadoon Bed & Breakfast (231-436-8882; www.mackinawbrigadoon.com; open April through late October; $$$), a bright and cheery yellow Victorian home a block north of downtown Mackinaw City and walking distance to the ferry docks. Brigadoon offers eight large, elegant suites, all with fireplaces. The prices aren't the cheapest in Mackinaw City, but you'll get much more than you would for the same price on Mackinac Island. In addition to the fireplaces, all suites have sitting rooms, and bathrooms feature Gilchrist & Soames bath products, heated marble floors, and whirlpool tubs. Breakfast is a hot, full, home-cooked affair served on the veranda and paired with really good locally roasted coffee.

Equally pleasant, but with a completely different vibe, the Deer Head Inn (231-436-3337; www.deerhead.com; open year-round; $$) stays true to its name with quite a few deer heads adorning its walls. Located in the heart of downtown

Mackinaw City, steps from shopping, restaurants, theaters, and the ferry docks, the Deer Head is done up in traditional northern hunting lodge style. The inn features bear rugs, fireplaces, and lots of cozy exposed wooden walls and beams inside and a pleasant brick facade outside. All rooms have beautiful remodeled private bathrooms, fireplaces, and sitting areas.

Families visiting the area love the Northpointe Inn (231-436-9812; www.northpointeinn.com; open May 15 through October 31; $). It's a great deal with basic Best Western–style décor and a private sandy beach on the lake. A hot breakfast is included in the room rates, and the indoor pool is very kid-friendly, with several water slides and a hydro tower.

Over in St. Ignace, the Colonial House Inn Bed & Breakfast (906-643-6900; www.colonial-house-inn.com; open year-round; $$) offers a similar experience to that provided by the B&Bs on Mackinac Island for half the price. A charming restored Victorian on the waterfront, directly across from the ferry docks, the Colonial House is painted a cheerful yellow with white trim. It's easy to imagine the original owners rocking in chairs on the wraparound veranda and watching ships sail in and out of the harbor. The seven rooms manage to escape the grandma feel of so many similar establishments and pull off tasteful Victorian. Two rooms (the Verandah and the Antique) have

St. Ignace offers a handful of charming, affordable B&Bs like the Colonial House Inn, which provide easy access to Mackinac without the expense.   Matt Girvan

fireplaces, and all have private baths. A full, hot breakfast is cooked by your gracious host, Phil, and served by his lovely wife, Elizabeth, from 8 to 9:30 daily. An adjacent motel offers basic rooms with private baths; breakfast is not included but can be purchased separately in the restaurant. For summer bookings it's best to call at least two months in advance.

SAULT STE. MARIE

Sault Ste. Marie's lively waterfront, downtown businesses, popular locks, and huge casino have made it the hub of the eastern U.P. In addition to the locks, the coastal area west of Sault Ste. Marie is known for its beaches, inland lakes, beautiful stretches of the Hiawatha National Forest, and the historic Iroquois Point Lighthouse. The town is also a gateway to Canada, with its more industrial sister city of Sault Ste. Marie, Ontario, just over the International Bridge. Many visitors travel over the bridge between the two cities every year (just don't forget that you're crossing an international border and will need proof of citizenship).

Of course, Sault Ste. Marie has been a hub of life in the U.P. since long before the locks or the International Bridge were built. Known as Michigan's first city, Sault Ste. Marie, sometimes referred to as just the Soo, has been a developed town since the mid-1600s, when it was a central fur-trading post. For many centuries before that, the majority of Ojibwa lived in and around the area; today, the Sault tribe of Ojibwa remain an important part of the city and is the largest and most vocal of the U.P.'s tribes.

Rooms are almost always available in Sault Ste. Marie, but there is an unfortunate shortage of independent or charming lodging options in the town, as opposed to chain hotels, which abound.

Next to the popular Lockview Restaurant and across from the locks' visitors center, the 47-room Askwith Lockview Motel (1-800-854-0745; www.lockview.com; $) couldn't really be any better located. The motel looks as though it has been haphazardly added on to at various points, with a main building and then several cottage units, but there is plenty of parking for all guests, and the rooms themselves are more pleasant than the drive-up motel layout would suggest. Most have antique beds, many have refrigerators, and all have cable TV. Hanging flowerpots around the exterior give the place some charm. A free continental breakfast is served every morning in the lobby, and the motel provides a free shuttle to the Kewadin Casino.

Just up the street, Longships Motel (906-632-2422; www.long shipsmotel.net; $) also offers a view of the locks. The nautically themed motel fits right in with its surround-

Ojibwa, Chippewa, and Anishinaabeg

It can get very confusing for non–Native Americans to understand the various tribal names and distinctions in the U.P. Here is a quick and easy breakdown: The Ojibwa, who are the most prevalent tribe in the U.P., are the largest of a group of tribes that share a similar group of languages (Algonquian), referred to collectively as the Anishinaabeg. Chippewa is an Anglicization of Ojibwa that has been widely accepted by the Ojibwa. The two are now used interchangeably.

ings on pleasantly retro Portage Avenue. Its location is ideal, and rooms are basic but clean and well kept, with big windows and cable TV.

Some of Sault Ste. Marie's best lodging options are located at its most popular entertainment venues—casinos. The waterfront location of the 142-room Bay Mills Resort (1-888-422-9645; www.4bay mills.com; $$) puts it automatically ahead of its main competition— Kewadin Casino—as an overnight lodging option. Bay Mills's waterfront, 6,988-yard, 18-hole, par-72 golf course helps strengthen that lead, as does its popular restaurant. Though it might feel a bit removed,

Bay Mills is a short drive to both Sault Ste. Marie and Tahquamenon Falls, and its proximity to a beautiful, largely undeveloped stretch of Lake Superior's shoreline makes it very desirable. The hotel is still relatively new, so the rooms are in good shape. The suites all have Jacuzzi tubs—although the tubs are oddly placed in the bedroom instead of the bathroom. The 15,000-square-foot casino is Michigan's only waterfront casino.

The Kewadin Casino in Sault Ste. Marie (1-800-539-2346; www .kewadin.com; $$) is the flagship casino of the Sault Ste. Marie tribe of Chippewa's empire. Rooms are similar to what you'd find at most Holiday Inn franchises—large, clean, comfortable, and reasonably priced. For about $20 extra a night, you can upgrade to a whirlpool room with an in-room Jacuzzi. In addition to the large casino downstairs, which is a popular destination throughout the U.P., guests have access to an indoor pool, hot tub, and weight room. The casino also often hosts live entertainment.

TAHQUAMENON FALLS

By far the most visited falls in the U.P., with around 750,000 visitors a year and growing, Tahquamenon Falls State Park does actually live up to the hype. And those who take the time to explore beyond the centerpiece Upper and Lower Falls will be rewarded with beautiful hikes and little to no crowds.

On the southern side of the falls, Newberry is the only town in the area large enough to support grocery stores year-round, thanks to its lumber industry, its prison, and its popularity with snowmobilers. Newberry also offers more lodging options than any other town near the falls and thus draws the bulk of the park's overnight visitors. Newberry landmark The Falls Hotel (906-293-8621; www.thefallshotel .com; $) actually predates the prison; its brick façade has watched over downtown Newberry since 1915. Rooms are outdated, but large, clean, and comfortable, with 12-foot ceilings and plenty of windows. And the owners did renovate the lobby and expand the restaurant relatively recently. The lobby looks fantastic—like something out of a John Wayne movie—and the relatively new restaurant has quickly become a local favorite, as has the adjacent lounge with its full bar and occasional live music.

Another restored beauty, The MacLeod House (906-293-3841;www.superiorsights.com/ macleodhouse; $) was built by a local lumber tycoon in 1898, then faithfully restored and turned into a B&B in 1988. In addition to the charming Queen Anne exterior, the parlor is large and pleasant, with a copper fireplace, inlaid parquet floors, and a large red-oak staircase. The three guest rooms are beautiful, with large four-poster beds, hardwood floors, and Victorian-style striped wallpaper. Each room is equipped with a private bath, and the suite includes a whirlpool tub for two. The grounds are lovely, with unusual gardens and a large Chinese gazebo in the back. Tahquamenon Falls is 30 miles away.

Less than an hour's drive directly south from the falls (just west of the MI 123–US 28 junction), Hulbert Lake Lodge (906-876-2324; www.exploringthenorth.com/hulbertlk/hulbert.html; $$) rents five adorable red and white cabins, plus lodge rooms, all overlooking Hulbert Lake. The lake is known for great trout, pike, and bass fishing, and the surrounding 1,000 acres are crisscrossed with excellent hiking trails. Tahquamenon and Whitefish Point are both less than an hour's drive away, and the lodge's onsite restaurant serves home-cooked breakfast and lunch specials every day but Tuesday during the summer, and just breakfast Wednesday through Sunday during winter, when only two of the five cabins are available.

WHITEFISH POINT

The white New England–style lighthouse at Whitefish Point is a favorite with photographers, its prim appearance belying the fact that the waters it watches over are known as the Graveyard of the Great Lakes. A popular shipwreck museum here tells the tales of the countless ships sitting on Lake Superior's floor near Whitefish Bay,

and scuba divers love the area for its amazing shipwreck dives. The Whitefish Point Light Station (1-888-492-3747; www.shipwreckmuseum.com; $$) also offers a handful of lovely rooms, the fees for which go toward keeping the station in shape and buy you entry to the Shipwreck Museum. On remote Whitefish Point, it's absolutely delightful to burrow under a blanket and read in the lighthouse, particularly if you're there during a storm. Rooms, located in the 1923 Coast Guard Lifeboat Station crews' quarters, are small but cozy and nicely decorated with wooden beds and homemade quilts. All rooms have private baths and TV/VCR, and guests are given a complimentary deluxe continental breakfast every morning.

In addition to being a popular tourist attraction, the Whitefish Point Light Station is a cozy and unique B&B. Matt Girvan

Local Flavors

Taste of the town—restaurants, cafés, bars, bistros, etc.

Although there are large swathes of undeveloped land throughout the eastern U.P., between Mackinac Island and Sault Ste. Marie there are probably more restaurants to choose from in this part of the peninsula than in any other. All of the large Mackinac resorts take pride in hiring top-tier chefs from around the world to prepare inventive, delicious meals for island guests. Mackinac tourism also supports a number of stand-alone restaurants, each with its own theme and culinary focus, from comfort food to Mexican and Middle Eastern specialties.

Meanwhile, throughout Les Cheneaux and St. Ignace, the U.P. classics—whitefish, pasties, and apple dumplings—are done as well or better than anywhere else in the peninsula. Whether you're in the mood for a four-course meal or just a good old-fashioned fish fry, you'll find it here.

DRUMMOND ISLAND

The crown jewel of the Drummond Island Resort, Bayside Dining (906-493-1014; www.drummond island.com; $$$) stands out among the area's seafood restaurants for two reasons: its serious attention to the wine list and the addition of several fresh fish entrées that don't include whitefish. Of course, local fish has a spot on the menu as well, but the management has made a point of flying in harder-to-find tuna, swordfish, and halibut fresh every morning. The original owner (Tom Monahan, CEO of Domino's Pizza) designed the Bayside in the style of his hero, Frank Lloyd Wright, and had it built overlooking Potagannassing Bay. Though seafood is the star, Bayside's menu includes aged beef, spring lamb, and homemade pastas.

GRAND MARAIS

The only place that's consistently open for dinner in Grand Marais is the Lake Superior Brewing Company at the Dunes Saloon (906-494-2337; $, no credit cards accepted), so it's a good thing the place serves up great beer and food. On Lake Avenue, right in the middle of downtown Grand Marais, the brewing company offers a great beer sampler, perfect for newcomers unfamiliar with the brewery's beer. The brewpub also sells growlers of beer for those who want to take some back to their cabin or room. On the food front, pizza is the go-to here, but the fresh fish is very good in the summer, and homemade soups are hearty and warming in winter.

LES CHENEAUX

Every U.P. town has its local Friday fish fry spot, and the Dockside Café

(906-297-3051; $) is it for the little lakeside village of DeTour. In fact, the restaurant stays open for dinner only on Friday to serve its popular all-you-can-eat fish fry. During the rest of the week, the Dockside is a favorite breakfast and lunch destination, where the old-timers head for coffee every morning. The huge omelets and crispy hash browns are popular, and the Dockside is where most people in DeTour head when they're in the mood for a burger.

Northwest of DeTour, the one-horse town of Raber only really has one tourist attraction and that's the Raber Bay Bar & Grill (906-297-5701; $$). People make the trek out to the Raber Bay for superfresh fish, homemade soups, and fantastic views of Lime Island and the St. Mary's River with gigantic freighters passing through its shipping lanes. Some argue that this is actually a better place to see the freighters than the restaurants near the locks in Sault Ste. Marie. The restaurant and bar are located in a well-preserved 1931 saloon. All-you-can-eat fresh fish dinners, accompanied by a trip to the salad, soup, and dessert bar are a local favorite; diners polish off plate after plate of delicious local perch, whitefish, and walleye. Steaks, burgers, and ribs are also available, but the main draw here is definitely the seafood.

Traveling west along the 134 from DeTour, hungry drivers often stop in Cedarville to hit Pammi's (906-484-7844; $), a favorite local coffee shop turned restaurant. What started out as a great place to get a decent espresso and fresh-baked pastries has blossomed into one of the area's best restaurants, serving three meals a day. Lunch baskets with your choice of fish and fries are fantastic, particularly the superfresh local perch. Homemade soups and sandwiches are good too, with lots of creative combinations plus a killer Reuben. All sandwiches and wraps are served with one of Pammi's famous deviled eggs, which has the effect of making every lunch here feel like a summer picnic.

Continuing west on 134, Hessel is home to a couple of decent dining options as well. The Hessel Bay Inn (906-484-2460; $$) is a great little family restaurant prized for its whitefish, perch, and water views. In addition to the superfresh fish specials, the menu includes several soups and pastas made from scratch by chef James Romanuk. For lunch, the fresh whitefish makes a great sandwich, and the popular Friday fish fry features all-you-can-eat whitefish. Breakfast includes the usual assortment of pancakes and omelets, with a better-than-average eggs Benedict and a Sunday morning breakfast buffet. During the summer, diners can eat outside on the deck, with a pleasant view of the water.

In downtown Hessel, the Islander Bar (906-484-3359; $) is a local institution. Great fun for a burger and a beer on a sunny summer day—or a frozen winter night, for that matter—the Islander has long been a central meeting place for locals and a spot regular visitors look forward to returning to each year. Easily found by its huge kitschy pirate-ship sign, this place is lively all year-round, with a jukebox, live music some nights, and a friendly crowd.

MACKINAC ISLAND

Most Mackinac Island visitors will take at least one bike ride while on the island. When they do, they're always pleasantly surprised to stumble upon Cannonball (906-847-0932; www.cannonballmackinac island.com; $), a fantastic find halfway around the island from Main Street at British Landing. Cannonball serves seriously good, reasonably priced food on a pleasant, pet-friendly outdoor patio. It's one of the Mackinac Island places that the local residents eat at regularly, which means visitors can trust that the food is good and well priced. Cannonball is famous for its fried pickles, which are far, far better than they sound. The Angus beef burgers are large and juicy and pair nicely with fresh, handmade potato chips. Located along the bike path at the halfway point around the island, Cannonball also sells disposable cameras, batteries, film, and souvenir clothing. The staff is very friendly and helpful here as well. Cannonball is owned by a family that lives on the island year-round, and they are full of good advice for visitors.

Back on Main Street, the Carriage House at the Iroquois Hotel (906-847-3321; www.iroquois hotel.com; $$$$) is not only widely considered one of the best splurge restaurants on the island, but it also affords diners one of the best dinnertime views on Mackinac, including the straits and the light-house. All of which does actually make it worth the exorbitant amount of money you'll spend to eat here. Though it's tempting to always order whitefish everywhere in the U.P. because you know it will be really fresh, given the prices here, you might want to try something that's not so easily available at other restaurants: try the delicious and tender filet mignon with béarnaise sauce, roast prime rib with a ridiculously good blue-cheese bread pudding, the perfectly cooked oven-roasted lamb chop, or the pan-seared diver scallops. The restaurant offers outdoor seating as well, which is worth reserving if you plan ahead.

The only restaurant that gives the Carriage House a run for its money is the dining room at the Grand Hotel (906-847-3331; www .grandhotel.com; $$$$). During the day, nonguests have to pay $10 to get a peak at the stately old hotel, where presidents have lolled on the porch and Esther Williams has strolled in the gardens. After five, however, anyone is welcome for dinner or a drink, provided they are

Who Has the Best Fudge?

It's an age-old question on Mackinac, but unfortunately it's really up to you. All we can say is that the best fudge shops are those that focus on fudge (in other words, not the hotel fudge shops) and answer a question with a question: Is there such a thing as bad fudge? That said, here are some of our favorites:

Joann's (906-847-3707; 2 Main St.) We like the variety (25 different flavors) and the creamy consistency.

Murdick's (906-847-3530; Main St.) The first fudge shop on Mackinac, Murdick's boasts a recipe that dates back to 1887.

Ryba's (906-847-6324; multiple locations downtown and in the Island House) There's no way to walk past, see the candy makers, smell the fudge cooking, and not pop in here for a slab.

dressed in accordance with the hotel's dress code—coat and tie for the gents, dresses or pantsuits for the ladies. Although it is the most expensive place to eat on the island, and probably in the whole U.P., if you're going to dine at the Grand Hotel it seems fitting to be, well, grand. The five-course prix fixe menu ($75 a person) changes every season and offers several choices for each meal (three meals a day are included in the Grand Hotel's room rates, and you can imagine it would get pretty old to have the same five courses for dinner every night). Dinner is served in the hotel's large, opulent dining room by posh tuxedoed and gloved Jamaican waiters. For the record, I'm not entirely sure why the waiters, or for that matter the entire Grand Hotel staff, are *all* Jamaican and honestly feel a bit strange

about it. Odd staffing choices notwithstanding, it's hard not to feel giddy dining here. Service is attentive in that perfect way that's neither cloying nor aloof, and the food is absolutely superb, though almost self-consciously fancy in a very un-Yooper sort of way—I'm pretty sure that the words *jalapeño mint reduction* don't show up on any other U.P. menus. Nonetheless, the dishes are truly creative and so good you'll be willing to overlook a little fussiness. If dinner sounds like too much of a splurge, the dining room's lunch buffet is terrific, with a variety of roasted meats, salads, cheeses, fruits, and desserts for $30 a person. The Grand Hotel also runs the food service at the Tea Room at Fort Mackinac (906-847-3331; www.mackinacparks.com; $$). For lunch, assorted salads, soups, and burgers are simple, good, and reasonably priced (a nice surprise, given the fact that the words *Grand Hotel* are involved). The burger is particularly good, made with prime beef and topped with cheddar cheese and bacon. Buffalo chili and PEI mussels in a dip-worthy herb-laden white wine lemon broth are also good choices. For dinner, the menu expands a bit to include steak, surf and turf, roasted chicken, and grilled white-fish, all of which are very good. The view from the patio here is absolutely incredible, particularly at sunset. In the evening, the fort offers guided tours and stages rifle and cannon demonstrations, which add to the fun of dining here, par-ticularly for the little ones.

For more of a normal meal, try the Island House Hotel's casual restaurant, the Ice House Bar & Grill (1-800-626-6304; www.the islandhouse.com; $$). A small pub tucked behind the hotel, the Ice House is literally and figuratively in the shadow of its larger, fancier, more publicized cousin, the Island House's 1852 Grill Room. The 1852 is great, but for an affordable outdoor lunch with a view of the straits, the Ice House is ideal. Hand-cut fresh potato chips accom-pany every sandwich and are deli-cious as an appetizer served with warmed blue cheese. Homemade soups change daily, and sandwiches range from simple classics like the sirloin burger to new and delicious creations like the BLT with smoked Gouda and the steak Sicilian—

shaved rib eye with sautéed mush-rooms and onions and provolone cheese, served au jus on a crusty baguette.

A former bank on Main Street that was built in the 1800s has been transformed by two local sisters into the popular, cozy Seabiscuit Café (906-847-3611; $$). There's always a wait for a table in the busiest summer months (July and August), but it's worth it. In addi-tion to the atmosphere—exposed red brick walls, dim lighting, cav-ernous booths, a horse-racing theme—the food is outstanding and inventive, from delicious salads like the Michigan Chop Cherry Cob to grilled sandwiches and wraps (the smoked whitefish wrap is a favorite) and a wide variety of dinner entrées that includes some of the best whitefish on the island and ribs roasted so long the meat is falling off the bones. A full bar with a good wine list, a number of spe-cialty cocktails, and excellent bar snacks (macaroni and cheese balls, Guinness cheese dip, hot wings) make this a great place to grab a drink as well. Beer lovers take note: The barman pours a perfect pint of Guinness.

Just around the corner, The Yankee Rebel Tavern (906-847-6249; www.yankeerebeltavern.com; $$) is one of the only places in the entire U.P. where you can find good sushi. The tavern also serves up amazing home-cooked classics, including an incredibly moist and tender pot roast and the famous

Rebel Back Ribs, rubbed with brown sugar and spices and roasted for hours. Whitefish is on the menu too, of course, but The Yankee Rebel mixes it up a bit with their pistachio-encrusted whitefish. Their version of chicken potpie—something that seems to show up on every Mackinac menu for some reason—is also delicious, with a light and flaky pastry crust and fresh roasted chicken. Lunchtime standouts include the Walnut Summer Salad with dried cherries, blue cheese, candied walnuts, and pears, the tavern burgers, and a sinfully delicious prime rib melt. The lunch menu also includes an omelet option that changes daily in case you're on the lookout for a late breakfast. The dessert menu is the same for lunch and dinner, and the best thing on it is the chocolate bread pudding. In addition to a wide variety of beer, wine, and other liquors, the bar has a 1919 old-fashioned root beer on draft that is refreshing and delicious on a warm summer day.

ST. IGNACE

On the other side of the straits, the dining scene in St. Ignace is decidedly more low key. Bentley's B-n-L Café (906-643-7910; $) is a favorite. A charming 1950s diner right across the street from the ferry docks, Bentley's checkered floor, red booths, and yellow walls are a perfect fit for the time warp that is St. Ignace, and it just hap-

pens to be the best breakfast spot in town, to boot. Seating is limited, so you may have to wait for a table in the high season, but it's worth it. Serving up some of the area's best homemade pasties, along with pies, old-fashioned malts and shakes, and the perfect grilled cheese sandwich, Bentley's is a favorite among visitors and locals alike. It's a rare morning when the town's old-timers aren't seated along the counter sipping coffee and trading tall tales.

Just up State Street about five minutes, Java Joe's (906-643-5282; $) isn't entirely different from Bentley's. It, too, is a bright yellow establishment, serving traditional American fare with a bit of a diner feel. Where Java Joe's stands out is in its insanely extensive menu and the number of truly unusual items on it. It's fun to be puttering along the road in St. Ignace and happen upon a breakfast of homemade granola pancakes with warm syrup, or the perfect hash browns, or a piping hot, fresh pasty. And the décor and staff at Java Joe's (including Joe himself, who's a character) make it even more fun. From the kitschy décor to the giant menu to the cast of characters, this is one of those places that just makes people happy.

There are two Village Inn restaurants (906-643-3364; www .viofmackinac.com; $$)—one on Mackinac and one in St. Ignace— and both stay open year-round. The menu is the same at both; the only real difference is that the Mackinac

Island outpost is quite small, while the VI in St. Ignace is pretty roomy. The food is all over the place, in terms of both content and quality, but there are plenty of stars to keep you from going hungry if you find yourself in the area during the off-season or are looking for a decent, reasonable meal in summertime. The house specialty, planked white-fish—a huge piece of superfresh local whitefish, baked and served on a maple plank, surrounded by loads of fluffy duchesse potatoes and a heaping portion of sautéed fresh vegetables—is certainly worth its slightly higher price tag. Other entrées are a bit disappointing (especially pastas), but burgers and pizzas are always a safe bet, and the whitefish-and-chips is excellent, as are the VI's various bar snacks (potato skins, jalapeño poppers,

awesome onion rings, and buffalo wings). The bar at both locations is a favorite local hangout and a good place to meet friendly Yoopers at the end of a workday.

SAULT STE. MARIE

Sault Ste. Marie may just have more quirky restaurants per square mile than any other town in the country. First, there's The Antlers (906-632-3571; $), which, as you may have guessed from its name, boasts walls littered with hundreds of antlers. In 2009, the local owners of popular Patrick Sinclair's Irish Pub, on Mackinac Island, took over The Antlers and set about ensuring that its customers would come for more than just a peek at the 100 or more antlers gracing its walls. The Antlers still serves straightforward

The namesakes of The Antlers Restaurant in Sault Ste. Marie.   Shawn Malone

American food, but the Szabo family has put the emphasis on top-quality local ingredients, and that commitment to quality shows in items like the buffalo burger made with buffalo from Circle K Buffalo Ranch in Rudyard. In addition to its famed antler collection, The Antlers is known for its past incarnation as the home of a bootlegging operation during prohibition and the backdrop for several episodes of *Gunsmoke.* Having improved the menu, the new owners are set to renovate the restaurant itself, with an emphasis on preserving and restoring its history.

Then there's **Clyde's Drive-In** (906-632-2581; $), one of only a handful of fully functional drive-ins left in the U.S. Located on Riverside Drive, Clyde's is a local institution, which makes it a great place to get a feel for the town and meet some locals. The giant, tasty C-burgers are just icing on the cake. If you're not in the mood for a burger, the chili's decent, as is the fried whitefish. Clyde's also serves a good greasy-spoon breakfast, perfect for fueling up before a drive around Sugar Island (the ferry dock is right next door).

While **Freighters** (906-632-4100; $$$) restaurant may not be quirky in and of itself, the fact that one of the city's nicest restaurants is in a Ramada is certainly a bit unusual. Nonetheless, Freighters provides a great dining experience. One wall of the restaurant is made entirely of windows, which look out onto the Soo Locks and provide a spectacular view any time of day and an especially beautiful sunset. On the food front, standouts include gumbo and, of course, whitefish. Seafood specials are always great, and breakfast is popular here with locals and visitors alike. One complaint the restaurant gets often—the service is a tad on the slow side, so don't plan on eating here if you've got to be somewhere else at any particular time. The Captain's Pub & Grill next door is a good spot to grab an after- or before-dinner cocktail.

Down on kitschy Portage Avenue, the two-story, 1950s-style **Lockview** (906-632-2772; $) also delivers great views of the locks. The Lockview is known far and wide for its delicious whitefish, which are caught in the morning and served up any way you like for lunch or dinner. The restaurant is also open for breakfast, which consists of hearty American standards, although a few heart-smart options are also available. In addition to the whitefish, folks come here for the views. It's pretty cool to enjoy a meal while an enormous ship goes floating by the window right next to you.

Combining the great Portage location without the kitsch, **Karl's Cuisine Café & Winery** (906-253-1900; www.karlscuisine.com; $$) offers up gourmet takes on local comfort foods such as pasties and quiche, as well as Karl's famous stromboli and an assortment of

The Lockview Restaurant is popular for whitefish and views of the Soo Locks. Matt Girvan

salads, sandwiches, and small pizzas. The restaurant pairs its dishes
with wine from its winery, Superior
Coast Winery. It's lovely to sit by
the window, sipping wine and
munching on lunch while those
giant freighters pass by.

A hole-in-the-wall tucked into
a tiny side street, Penny's Kitchen
(906-632-1232; $) serves the best
sandwiches and possibly the best
breakfast in the Soo. Penny started
out catering but grew her business
into this small and always busy café.
Lunch consists of gourmet deli
sandwiches (try one of the croissant
sandwiches on Penny's homemade
croissants), soups, and a variety of
delicious salads. Penny's also operates as a bakery, a fact that is obvious at breakfast when the perfume

of freshly baked pastries, cookies,
croissants, and breads fills the air,
and Penny's staff serves up moist
coffee cake, muffin tops stuffed
with fruit and nuts, sourdough pancakes, cinnamon French toast,
stuffed morning croissants, and
delicious French boules—fresh
sourdough bread bowls filled with
eggs, cheese, and your choice of a
variety of other toppings. If you're
looking for a place to stock up on
goodies for a road trip or a picnic
lunch on the beach, this is it.

TAHQUAMENON FALLS

The only sit-down restaurant on-
site at Tahquamenon Falls also happens to be one of the best state park
food concessions in the country.

Tahquamenon Falls Brewery & Pub (906-492-3341; $$) is operated by the grandchildren of Jack and Mimi Barrett, who sold the large swath of land next to Tahquamenon Falls to the state in order for the current parking lot and entrance trails to be built. The Tahquamenon Falls brewpub was built on the last two acres of the Barretts' land in a large, handsome log building. The dining room is dominated by windows looking out into the park and a large stone fireplace that keeps the place warm in winter. Microbrews are decent—the brewery sells a wide range of beers, but only four are available at any given time. The menu includes both lunch and dinner items and is served all day. Fresh whitefish—either as an entrée or in a sandwich—is a standout, as are the pasties, entrée-size salads, and beer-battered french fries. Between the setting, the history, the microbrews, and the food, this is the best restaurant available for several miles.

Down the MI 123 in Paradise, Brown Fish House (906-492-3901; $) is a tiny restaurant run by a local commercial fisherman who only opens up when he gets a good catch. While the schedule may be a bit unreliable, this policy ensures that Brown's consistently delivers the freshest fish around. A smoker in the back makes smoked whitefish for an outstanding homemade chowder, and the restaurant operates a small fish market as well (when there's fish available, naturally).

Extend Your Stay

If you have more time, try these great places to see and things to do . . .

As with the rest of the U.P., there's a lot of history in this region. Long before Mackinac was a Victorian island enticing celebrities and presidents, it figured into the Ojibwa creation myth. Similarly, more than a hundred years before St. Ignace became a good low-cost alternative to the lavish hotels on Mackinac, the town was a key meeting place between the native Ojibwa and the new Europeans, with French fur trappers and missionaries like Father Marquette brokering a cultural truce far more honest and powerful than any subsequent treaties. It was here that the British defeated the French, and the Americans in turn defeated the British, taking Fort Mackinac. Much of this history is preserved today through various monuments and museums throughout the area, as well as through ongoing celebrations and rituals.

One important contrast between the eastern U.P. and the rest of the peninsula is the near-total lack of mining influence in this part of the U.P. This region was not affected by the closing of any mines, but by the downturn of the lumber industry. Unlike the iron and copper mining companies,

Fort Mackinac was built by the British during the American Revolution and wasn't turned over until long after the war. Matt Girvan

however, the lumber companies didn't spend a lot of money building up towns or donating libraries and theaters. While the abandoned mining towns were able to carry on or at least left some trace of their history, most people can't tell that a town ever existed on the site of former logging towns like Deer Park and Bay Mills. Other towns, like Grand Marais—which was left isolated and abandoned when its lumber company hightailed it out of town and took its railroad tracks with it—have been able to make use of their scenic locations to become tourist draws.

The ups and downs of lumber aside, in general this area has historically been economically depressed, routinely posting Michigan's highest unemployment and poverty numbers. Recently, however, thanks mostly to the local Ojibwa, the economy has been on an upswing as the area's tourism numbers surged, thanks to the popularity of the Sault tribe's Kewadin Casinos and the Bay Mills tribe's Bay Mills Resort & Casinos, which also includes a scenic golf course.

Sault Ste. Marie, at the Lake Superior end of the St. Mary's River, has always been a little hub of industry in a sea of inactivity. When the Ojibwa lived predominantly on Sugar Island, the rapids of the St. Mary's provided a constant flow of fish, and eventually the name for the town—the rapids—which is *sault* in French and *bawating* in Ojibwa. Later, as European settlers filtered in, the river retained its importance, becoming a major hub of the fur trade. As the fur trade began dying out in the 1800s, the success of other industries made it increasingly important for ships to be able to travel from one lake to the next, and the river again became a focal point, this time of the shipping industry and, eventually, the tourism industry.

HISTORIC BUILDINGS AND SITES

Mackinac Island

One of the best ways to be immediately swept up in the history of Mackinac is to enjoy a trip around the island with **Carriage Tours** (906-847-3307; www.mict.com). It's a tradition that has been on the island since 1869, according to Mackinac Island Carriage Tours, the company formed by the island's carriage men in 1948. The tour covers all the major Mackinac sights—Main Street, the Grand Hotel, Fort Mackinac, Arch Rock—as well as some sights cooked up by the carriage company, seemingly to make more money. Their butterfly conservatory is very pretty, but it can feel a bit like they just picked you up and now they want more money. Still, the horses are lovely, the carriage men are generally knowledgeable about the island, and it's a pleasant way to get a brief overview.

Up on the hill, away from the bustle of Main Street, the **Grand Hotel** (906-847-3331 or 1-800-334-7263) is the picture of 19th-century elegance,

Carriage rides are one of the best ways to tour Mackinac Island. Eli Duke

The Grand Hotel is Mackinac Island's most famous hotel.   Matt Girvan

a majestic white structure with a mammoth porch sweeping around huge columns. Everything about the hotel is extreme. The gardens aren't just lovely, they're prize winning. The pool isn't just refreshing, it once enticed Esther Williams for a swim. And that huge porch? Several U.S. presidents have sat on it. Though some might bristle at the idea of a hotel charging an entrance fee to nonguests, it is both worth it and probably necessary. Without the fee, the hotel would very likely be completely overrun with tourists, making it hard to justify the astronomical room rates to guests. Once inside, it's like walking into the past: This is as close to time travel as you can get.

The Grand Hotel sits at the entrance to West Bluff, a neighborhood full of 19th-century cottage mansions for the well-to-do, including the ornate Queen Anne–style

Somewhere in Time

Mackinac Island was further immortalized by the film *Somewhere in Time*, starring Christopher Reeve and Jane Seymour. The chamber of commerce actually hands out maps to the various filming locations for interested visitors. Even if you're not interested in the film, the map can be a handy guide to the Grand Hotel, where much of the film was shot.

Paging Doctor Crain

Thought not a Mackinac Island native, Doc Crain has been an island resident for several years and has made it his goal to learn as much as he can about Mackinac. His lust for life and boundless enthusiasm quickly endeared Doc to the locals, and once he began his "Doc Crain's natural and human history tours by foot and bike," he developed a loyal following among visitors as well. Doc started his tours purely to help people discover that there was more to Mackinac than fudge and horse-drawn carriages, and his tales of Native American legends and how the wildflowers bloom here have inspired many, many people to learn more about the island and to treat it with respect, as more than just a tourist destination. Doc's Web site says it all: "I am a father and grandfather and remember when my children were smaller often having to make hard decisions about what our family could afford to do on vacation. There is no charge for my tours. No tickets required. All are welcome all the time. I have been doing this for a decade and find that people are naturally generous enough with tips and gratuities. Bring your family. Give what you can—if you can. 'Nuff said." For information about Doc and his tours, visit www.mackinac islandhikebike.com.

Cudahy Mansion, once the governor's summer residence. It's fascinating to stroll through this neighborhood and see how the wealthy lived back then. As the road turns along the bluff, curious visitors can continue on to another neighborhood of cottages, Hubbard's Cove, which are not as ornate but still very beautiful.

Back down the hill, several of Mackinac's historic buildings stretch to the east of where people congregate now, toward Mission Point from Main Street, in an area known as Historic Downtown Mackinac. The walk is beautiful and should be done regardless, but the story behind some of these buildings is very interesting as well, including the Indian Dormitory, a three-story white building with black shutters that once housed the American Indian Agency. Though the building was once open to public tours, the Mackinac Island State Historic Park has closed it in recent years while preparing a new exhibit focused on the impact of the agency and its founder, Henry Schoolcraft. Also included in this stretch of the island are the Protestant Mission Church, which is a charming New England–style chapel, bright white with a tall steeple, and St. Anne's Catholic Church, which dates to colonial Michilimackinac days.

Closer to what is now downtown, Market Street on Mackinac (906-847-3328) is also worth a wander. The white clapboard buildings at the head of Astor Street, which now house the island's city hall, community center, fire hall, police department, and courthouse, were warehouses for John Jacob Astor's American Fur Trade Company back in the early 1800s. Down the street, four of Market Street's historic structures, including Michigan's oldest house, the McGulpin House, are part of the Mackinac State Historic Park. Entry to them is included with admission to Fort Mackinac.

St. Ignace

The Mackinac Bridge, or Big Mac as it's affectionately called, turned 50 in 2007 with many celebrations statewide. Until it was built, the only way to the U.P. from the Lower Peninsula was by car ferry, which took 45 minutes. During the summer and hunting season, when there were more cars wanting to get across than there were ferries to take them, people often waited for several hours for their turn to cross. The completion of the bridge really introduced the two parts of the state to each other and provided the U.P. with a new industry—tourism—just in the nick of time. The third-longest suspension bridge in the world, this is one of those great bridges to cross, with Lake Huron off to one side and Lake Michigan to the other and great,

Crossing into the U.P., you'll see Lake Huron glistening on the eastern side of the Mackinac Bridge.   Wikimedia Commons

arching spans above. The idea of a bridge had been broached numerous times beginning in the late 1800s, but plans were always thwarted for some reason or another—money, wars, and bad publicity from other bridge disasters among them. In 1954, former U.S. senator Prentiss Brown from St. Ignace, Michigan's then governor G. William "Soapy" Williams, and W. Stewart Woodfill, the owner of the Grand Hotel, joined forces to help get the bridge up. It took them a long time to get enough support and funding for such a large project, and eventually it was bridge designer David B. Steinman's willingness to eat the cost of preparing plans for the bridge, should the funding have fallen through, that got him the design job. The bridge was the highlight of his career. At the time, it was the largest bridge-construction project ever undertaken, and the whole state was fascinated by it. The Bridge Authority hired one photographer, Herman Ellis, to document the construction, and he did an extraordinary job. Unfortunately, the museum that contained the bulk of his photographs burned to the ground in 2005, leaving behind only reproductions of the images in numerous books.

Long before the bridge was built, intrepid explorers still made their way into the U.P. One of the best of them was French missionary Father Jacques Marquette, who built several missions throughout the U.P. and was widely respected by the Ojibwa and the U.P.'s early settlers. Marquette's life and work are commemorated by **Marquette Mission Park**, in St. Ignace, a great little park that surrounds the Museum of Ojibwa Culture. In addition to his missionary work, Marquette was a skilled cartographer and was responsible for helping to map the river network that leads from the U.P. all the way down to the Mississippi. Unfortunately, it was that exploratory trip that eventually did him in. He died on his way back to St. Ignace, most likely near present-day Ludington, according to historians. A fountain and a plaque paying tribute to Marquette are placed at the center of

Although he spent most of his time in St. Ignace, the statue commemorating Father Marquette is on Mackinac Island.
Wikimedia Commons

Marquette Mission Park, on the spot that some believed to be his grave when they found a limestone slab there in 1877. A nearby plaque entitled "Black Robes of the Wilderness" explains the basic beliefs of the Jesuits and the role they played in the region. A subsequent panel, "Priest, Missionary, Explorer," delves into Marquette's own history, tracing his route from France to Quebec and eventually to the U.P. in "New France." Finally "A Gathering Place" details what was going on in the area and between the tribes during the time Marquette was here. Though Marquette spent most of his time in Sault Ste. Marie and then here in St. Ignace, the famous Father Marquette statue is on Mackinac Island in the park in front of Fort Mackinac.

Sault Ste. Marie

The historic center of the Bay Mills Ojibwa tribe, Bay Mills Township (Lake Shore Drive/MI 123 west of Sault Ste. Marie, on the waterfront) was also at one point a smoking, lurching factory town. Evidence of those days are long gone, but the Bay Mills Ojibwa are currently thriving in this small town, and pieces of their history have been preserved at the Mission Church and Bay Mills Indian Cemetery on lovely Lake Shore Drive. The Bay Mills tribe has since gone into the gambling business, building the first

In addition to a resort, casino, and golf course, the Bay Mills features stunning waterfront views. Wikimedia Commons

Built in 1877, the Chippewa County Courthouse is one of Sault Ste. Marie's landmarks.
Bobak Ha'Eri

casino to take advantage of the area's natural beauty by incorporating a golf course into its plans. Though more remote than the Kewadin Casino near Sault Ste. Marie, the Bay Mills casino is equally as popular.

Back in town, the Chippewa County Courthouse (corner of E. Portage Ave. and Bingham Ave., Sault Ste. Marie) is a sight not to be missed, particularly for architecture buffs. In 1877, this beautiful rambling building of limestone trimmed with Jacobsville sandstone was erected on the site of one of the area's first missions, built in the early 1820s. The courthouse is now listed on the National Register of Historic Places. Designed in the Second Empire style, the courthouse is composed of four bays, highlighted by a large central bay capped with clock and bell towers. The building is topped with a wooden statue of Lady Justice. Four clock faces above the four main bays light up at night.

Down on the waterfront, in Brady Park, the site of the first Fort Brady in 1823, a historic walkway between Water Street and the St. Mary's River, called Riverfront Walk (E. Water St. between Ashmun St. and Soo Locks Park, Sault Ste. Marie), is marked with various plaques and monuments commemorating different times in the town's history. A bust of Chase Osborn, Michigan's only U.P. governor and the former publisher of the *Sault Evening News,* is displayed alongside various scenes depicting the

highlights of his entertaining career and an obelisk monument commemorating the locks' 50th birthday (they're now over 150 years old) looks out
over the park. The monument was designed by Charles McKim of the
renowned New York architecture firm McKim, Mead and White.

Nearby, the Water Street Historic Block (Water St. west of George
Kemp Marina, parallel to Portage Ave.) is home to several historic houses,
two of which are fully on display, inside and out, with artifacts from their
original owners. The John Johnston house is the home of one of the first
European settlers to the area, an early fur trader from Ireland. Johnston
immigrated to Canada in 1785 and met with early success in the fur trade.
He married Ozhahguscodaywayquay, daughter of Waubojeeg, the leader of
the Ojibwa, in 1793, after which the couple moved to Sault Ste. Marie and
built this house. During the War of 1812, Johnston helped the British take
Fort Mackinac, and his house was burned in retaliation. He rebuilt what he
could, and this is what is left. The Henry Rowe Schoolcraft Office was the
home and office of Henry Schoolcraft, the area's first Native American
agent and Johnston's son-in-law. Schoolcraft compiled a book of the history
and legends of the Ojibwa that Longfellow eventually used to write his celebrated narrative poem "Hiawatha." Though not open to the public, the
home of Bishop Baraga, one of the first and most influential Catholic missionaries in the U.P., is also included in this block.

Also on the waterfront, Soo
Locks Park (906-632-3311)) is one
of the main attractions in Sault Ste.
Marie. To get to the park from I-
75, take either of the I-75 business
loop exits to Ashmun Street; at
the T-intersection, turn left onto
Portage Avenue, and you'll see the
locks in a block. Built in 1855,
the Soo Locks really brought the
Industrial Revolution to bear in the
U.P. In addition to the money spent
on the locks, the government
invested heavily in several lighthouses throughout the Great Lakes
to keep up with the increased shipping traffic. The St. Mary's River,
which connects Lake Superior to
Lake Huron, was the obvious shipping route when engineers first
started looking at how to get big

Each winter the St. Mary's River freezes
over.   Courtesy U.S. Coast Guard

The Cranberry Capital

In 1876, a farmer named John Clarke bought a farm on Whitefish Point and began growing cranberries, mimicking the processes he had seen the local Ojibwa use to grow blueberries and cranberries here, and selling them. As the year marked the nation's centennial, he called his farm **Centennial Cranberry Farm** (1-877-333-1822; www.centennial cranberry.com), and it is still in operation today. The current farmers have opened up the farms to self-guided tours and set up a gift store and picnic tables to attract tourists on their way to the Shipwreck Museum. It makes for an interesting pit stop, if only to check out a farm that's over 200 years old, and the cranberries make for a good emergency snack break for those who forget that Whitefish Point is isolated and without stores or restaurants. To get to Centennial Cranberry Farm from Paradise, take Whitefish Point Road 10 miles north to Wildcat Road, then turn left at the big cranberry farm sign and head west 2 miles.

ships from up north out to the rest of the world. The problem, however, was a well-known stretch of rapids that dropped over 20 feet, which no commercial freighter would be able to navigate. The locks—four in total—solved that problem. Of course as boats continue to get larger and larger, some of the largest have outgrown the older locks. The only lock able to handle the giant 1,000-foot freighters is the Poe Lock, farthest away from the docks. There is always talk of building another lock to keep up with the big ships. Standing in the viewing area at the docks and watching one of the big ones roll through is amazing. It's easy to see why this spot attracts boat fans from all over the world. Note: Shipping season closes in winter when the lakes freeze. The date varies every year but is generally around the end of January to mid-March.

There are plenty of spots to grab a good view of the locks in Sault Ste. Marie, but one of the best is the Tower of History (326 E. Portage Ave., Sault Ste. Marie; $6 adults, $3 children). At 210 feet tall, the sculptural tower provides visitors with not only terrific views of the locks, but also of the St. Mary's River, nearby Canadian towns and surrounding wilderness across the river, and the town of Sault Ste. Marie directly below the platform. Originally built by the Catholic Church in 1968 as a shrine to the U.P.'s early missionaries, the tower was donated to Sault Historic Sites in 1980 and has been the Tower of History ever since. Enclosed within the tower are exhibits about local and Native American history, which do still include some mention of the missionaries the tower was initially built to honor. The exhibits are actually pretty interesting, but most people take the express elevator to the viewing platform and miss them altogether.

LIGHTHOUSES

Thanks to the brisk shipping business, there are a number of lighthouses around this part of the U.P., but of course not all lighthouses are created equal.

West of Sault Ste. Marie, on Lake Shore Drive, Point Iroquois Lighthouse (906-437-5272; Lake Shore Dr., 5 miles west of Brimley) is perched on Point Iroquois, a strategic point for the Ojibwa as a gateway to the St. Mary's River—a place they battled with the Iroquois over and won. The lighthouse was built in 1870 and decommissioned in 1963. Visitors can climb to the top and use the telescope there to see broadly across the channel.

Farther west lies the region's best-known lighthouse, Whitefish Point Light Station (1-888-492-3747; www.shipwreckmuseum.com). Not only can you rent a room in the lighthouse, but you can also tour the adjacent Great Lakes Shipwreck Museum (free for overnight guests, $10 for nonguests). This stretch of Lake Superior's coast is known alternately as the Graveyard of the Great Lakes and Lake Superior's Shipwreck Coast, and the Shipwreck Museum is full of evidence of the dangers of sailing on the Great Lakes. Exhibits include historic diving equipment used to investigate early shipwrecks and various artifacts from the hundreds of ships that have met with untimely ends in the Great Lakes, including the bell from the *Edmund Fitzgerald*. A guided tour of the 1861 light keeper's quarters is included in the museum admission fee and delves into the personal stories of the various keepers who manned Whitefish Point. Outside, paths leading to Lake Superior pass through the Whitefish Point Bird Observatory, where several species of migratory birds stop every fall and spring.

Au Sable Point Lighthouse, near Grand Marais, is also well worth a visit. From Grand Marais take H 58 to the Hurricane River Campground to catch the trail out to the lighthouse. Built atop red sandstone cliffs, the red-brick Au Sable Lighthouse, with its white tower, was restored earlier this decade to its original 1910 state, including the Fresnel lens. The lighthouse can be accessed only on foot, requiring about a 3-mile round-trip hike. From the top of the tower the Grand Sable Dunes are spectacular. Just down the beach are the remnants of two shipwrecks poking out of the sand, an interesting, if slightly jarring, reminder that lighthouses like this one were built to help cut down on the large amount of wrecks occurring in Lake Superior.

Grand Marais

For such a small town, Grand Marais has a lot of art galleries and museums. Housed in a little green house with yellow trim, the Gitche Gumee Agate and History Museum (906-494-2590; www.agatelady.com; $1) is a fantastic little place full of reverence for history and the land and for the museum's founder, Axel Niemi. A large display of agates, many of them Lake Superior specimens gathered by Niemi over 71 years, is the centerpiece of the museum, but there are also a few great historical exhibits delving into how Grand Marais was formed, what happened when lumber came and went, and how the town's people survived it all. The current owner spent childhood summers visiting the museum constantly, and she has boundless enthusiasm for her two subjects: agates and local history. Impromptu classes on agate hunting are not uncommon, and the museum also schedules longer workshops for those who really want to get into it.

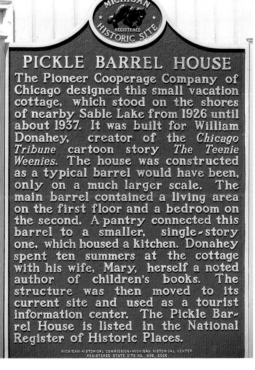

The Pickle Barrel Museum in Grand Marais is one of the U.P.'s more interesting landmarks.   Wikimedia Commons

The town's other quirky museum is the Pickle Barrel Museum (906-494-2404; open June through September, 1–4 PM; donations gladly accepted). The Teenie Weenies comic strip, popular from 1914 to 1970, was created by William Donahey, who along with his wife, Mary, used to spend summers in Grand Marais. In addition to the comic strip, the Teenie Weenies showed up in children's books, toys, and advertisements throughout their career, including regular ads for Monarch food products, a line that included popcorn, pickles, and toffee. One of the ads, depicting the Teenie Weenies in a tiny pickle barrel, was so successful that the Monarch owner decided to build the Donaheys a summer home in Grand Marais to show his thanks. The home was built in the shape of a pickle barrel, naturally—or rather, two pickle barrels. The large barrel housed a living room/dining room, bedroom, and work areas, while a smaller barrel enclosed the kitchen.

The house became such a tourist attraction that the couple found it difficult to work in, so they moved it into town as a souvenir shop and visitors center. It was eventually abandoned and fell into disrepair, but the Grand Marais Historical Society purchased it in 2003 and restored it, opening it to the public in 2005 as a museum commemorating the Donaheys, their funny little cabin, and the Teenie Weenies.

Mackinac Island and Environs

On Mackinac Island, the imposing Fort Mackinac (906-847-3328; www .mackinacparks.com/fort-mackinac; open May through October; $10 adults, $6 children), overlooking the harbor, was built by the British in 1780 during the American Revolution. Within 14 of its original buildings, visitors can explore various history exhibits, see how a military hospital operated back in the early 1800s, visit the old officers' quarters, which are furnished as they would have been during the late 1700s and early 1800s, or have lunch or dinner in the Tea Room (see "Local Flavors"), all the while enjoying incredible views of the island and the straits. A large interactive exhibit for kids lets them play a giant fife or "fire" a pretend cannon, among other things. The museum's largest exhibit, a tribute to Mackinac Island as a whole, is ironically sponsored by Ford, whose cars are not allowed on the island! In addition to the exhibits, the fort offers three guided tours a day, two cannon firings, and various other informational tours, including A Soldier's Life and a reenactment of a court-martial. There's a *lot* going on at the fort. You could easily spend all day there, but most people would rather spend the whole day biking around the island, eating fudge, or hanging out at the

Mackinac Island: Home of the Spirits

Mackinac Island holds a sacred place in the Ojibwa tradition. Because of its shape—not unlike a turtle's back—the Ojibwa named the island Michilimackinac, or Land of the Great Turtle. They believed the first people lived on the island and that it was home to Gitche Manitou, the Great Spirit. Located in the center of the Great Lakes, Mackinac became a tribal gathering place, where celebrations were held, offerings to Gitche Manitou were made, and chiefs were buried to honor the Great Spirit. Not unlike today, spring was a time for the Ojibwa to gather together on the island, relax after the long winter, celebrate the Great Spirit, and hunt, fish, and spend time with their families. Ojibwa legend has it that the arrival of the Europeans scared Gitche Manitou off; the Great Spirit fled the island to dwell in the northern lights.

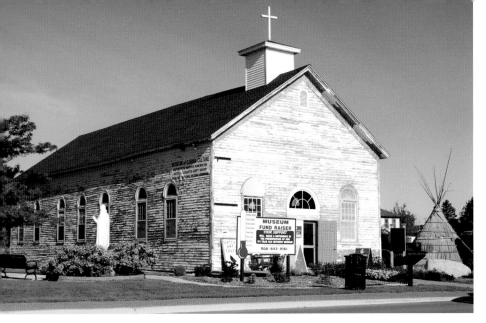

The Museum of Ojibwa Culture in St. Ignace stands on the same spot where Father Marquette founded his Jesuit mission in 1671. Andrew Jameson

beach. To make the most of your time, take the fort's guided tour to see almost everything. It's followed by the cannon firing, which you can enjoy from the Tea Room patio while grabbing a bite to eat or a cup of coffee. Finish up with the giant Ford exhibit, which is very interesting and well produced. If you've still got burning unanswered questions or you're a military history buff, carry on and visit the specific exhibits that interest you. One thing to note: There are many, many stairs leading up to the fort, but you're rewarded with terrific views for all that climbing.

Back on the other side of the straits, near Mackinaw City, Colonial Michilimackinac Historical State Park (231-436-4100; www.mackinac parks.com/parks/colonial-michilimackinac; open May 3 through October 8, 9 AM–4 PM; $9.50 adults, $6 youths 6–17, under 6 free) features a recon-structed 1715 French fur-trading village and military outpost, which was later occupied by British military and traders. Park staff put on reenact-ments of native life, the French fur trade, and the 1761 British takeover, along with a surprisingly interesting archaeological tunnel exhibit entitled Treasures from the Sand. Those planning to visit either of the other two sites making up the Mackinac State Parks (the nearby Historic Mill Creek State Park or Fort Mackinac on Mackinac Island) can buy a combination ticket that allows them into all three for $20 (adults) or $12.50 (children).

In nearby St. Ignace, The Museum of Ojibwa Culture (906-643-9161; open Memorial Day weekend through early October; $5 adults) is small but well done and housed, interestingly, in a former Catholic church built on the site of Father Marquette's original Jesuit mission, which was erected in 1671 and burned down in 1701. The front gallery of the museum focuses on the precolonial history of the Ojibwa people and how they survived those early harsh winters. The back gallery deals with the arrival of other tribes (the Huron and the Ottawa) and of French fur traders in the 17th and 18th centuries. The exhibit depicts a camraderie between the Ojibwa and the French as they joined together against their common enemy, the British. A park surrounds the museum, with a memorial to Father Marquette, a Huron longhouse, and various outdoor exhibits related to the Ottawa and Huron cultures.

Sault Ste. Marie

Those with an interest in the locks and in the area's shipping history will love the **Museum Ship *Valley Camp*** (906-632-3658; www.thevalleycamp .com; open mid-May through mid-October; $10 adults, $5 children). This 20,000-square-foot maritime museum is housed in an old Great Lakes freighter. It's fun to visit the *Valley Camp* just to get onboard the ship, but the exhibits are fairly interesting as well, ranging from a crew's quarters, to an *Edmund Fitzgerald* memorial complete with the salvaged lifeboats from the infamous wreck to four 1,200-gallon aquariums holding various fish found in the Great Lakes.

The large beaux-arts building on Portage Avenue that houses the **River of History Museum** (906-632-1999; www.thevalleycamp.com; open mid-May through mid-October; $6 adults, $3 children) is often overlooked by people who assume it's still the post office it was built to be. In fact, it is now a large and impressive local history museum, taking visitors through the history of the local people vis-à-vis the St. Mary's River. Some 8,000 years of history are captured in 11 galleries through various life-size dioramas and a guided tour (a motion sensor plays the soundtrack when people enter each room).

NIGHTLIFE

Nightlife in St. Ignace, Mackinaw City, and Les Cheneaux is relatively sleepy, with the exception of the nearby **Kewadin Casinos**. Mackinac, however, is a hotbed of nighttime activity, with live music at several venues, and Sault Ste. Marie offers a handful of fun bars plus a new brewpub.

On Mackinac, the old-fashioned **Cupola** at the Grand Hotel (906-847-3331 or 1-800-334-7263; www.grandhotel.com) is a piano bar that feels like something out of *The Great Gatsby*. The ambience, coupled with phenomenal views of the bridge, make it a popular cocktail spot, particularly for couples on a romantic weekend away.

Downtown, one of the more popular bars on the island, Horn's Gaslight Bar & Restaurant (906-847-6154; www.hornsbar.com) is known for its nachos, its margaritas, and its live rock and roll. Just down Main Street, Patrick Sinclair's Irish Pub (906-847-8255) is one of the few places on Mackinac to stay open year-round (usually trading off with the Village Inn and/or the Mustang so that there's always at least one bar open). Sinclair's is beloved by everyone on the island—locals and visitors alike. With various beers on tap and pretty decent pub grub, it's always a good bet, but it gets especially lively when there's an Irish band playing.

For a slightly different Main Street experience, the Pink Pony Bar and Grill (906-847-3341) in the Chippewa Hotel is a celebrated Mackinac bar, restaurant, and entertainment venue. The deck is a great place to hang out for the night, and there is almost always live music playing, plus a pool table and darts.

Around the corner, Mustang Lounge (906-847-9916; 8 Astor St.) is a favorite hangout for locals and summer workers. The Mustang is a pleasantly divey bar, good for beer and greasy snacks and open year-round.

Back on the peninsula proper, the 200 block of Portage Avenue, facing the locks in Sault Ste. Marie, is home to several pubs. The block recently had the honor of celebrating the opening of the 10th microbrewery in the U.P. Opened in April 2011, the Soo Brewing Company (223 W. Portage Ave.) occupies a prime spot on Portage Avenue, across from the locks, and serves up four original microbrews (an English ale, an amber ale, a stout, and an IPA) plus handcrafted rootbeer and ginger ale.

Ray Bauer, owner and brew master of Soo Brewing Company. Shawn Malone

Portage Avenue, in Sault Ste. Marie, is filled with kitschy 1950s-style restaurants and hotels. Matt Girvan

A few doors down from the brewpub, Maloney's Alley (227 W. Portage Ave.) is a favorite local hangout with a number of local beers on tap and a simple bar menu. On the corner, the Palace Saloon (200 W. Portage Ave.) has surprisingly good Mexican food and dynamite margaritas, in addition to the brews and pub grub you might expect from a spot called the Palace Saloon.

SHOPPING

As with the rest of the U.P., shopping is not the reason that people visit this region. That said, the large numbers of Mackinac Island visitors support the existence of more shops here than you would expect in such small towns, although the region lacks the bookstores and antiques stores common in the rest of the U.P., where a greater number of year-round residents can keep such businesses afloat. Gifts unique to the area include Mackinac Island fudge and both local and traditional Native American art.

Housed in a historic Grand Marais frame building, built in 1881 as a lumber company office, Maeve Croghan's Campbell Street Gallery (906-494-2252; www.maevecroghan.com) sells her own paintings as well as crafts and artwork from a select few Grand Marais artists. Croghan's Mackinac Island gallery is well known, and her work has gained some level of recognition nationally, particularly her vineyard paintings, some of which have been turned into labels for vineyards in Paso Robles, California.

Casino Country

The Sault Ste. Marie area is home to two huge casinos—Kewadin and Bay Mills—that have recently revived the area's economy. The two casinos attract visitors from all over the state for gambling in their Vegas-like game rooms. Both have also taken a page from Vegas's book and added additional entertainment options to their facilities. Country music star Loretta Lynn, comedian Roseanne Barr, and the 1980s rock band Poison have all played at the 1,500-seat theater at Kewadin, and Bay Mills built a highly acclaimed 18-hole waterfront golf course and opened a comedy club to keep gamblers entertained. Most of the hotels in Sault Ste. Marie offer free shuttle service to the Kewadin, and some will take guests to Bay Mills (farther away) as well. To sweeten the deal, Bay Mills has started offering free drinks to gamblers, one of the Vegas standbys that none of the other U.P. casinos has adopted. Both casinos also have restaurants and a couple of bars, featuring live music, a DJ, or karaoke every night of the week. In addition to the Sault Ste. Marie casino, Kewadin operates casinos in St. Ignace, Manistique, Hessel, and Christmas.

Bay Mills Resort & Casinos. 1-888-422-9645; www.4baymills.com; 11386 W. Lakeshore Drive, Brimley

Kewadin Casino. 1-800-539-2346; 2186 Shunk Road, Sault Ste. Marie

Another Grand Marais historic frame building is home to The Marketplace (906-494-2438; open daily in July and August, weekends in May, June, and September, closed October through April), which sells the work of 20-some local artists and craftspeople collectively known as Grand Marais Cottage Industries. Merchandise ranges from needlepoint to original watercolors to incredibly beautiful wood carvings, and all of it is made in Grand Marais.

In Sault Ste. Marie, Alberta House (906-635-1312), part exhibition gallery and part shop, is the nonprofit arts center of the Sault Area Arts Council. Located in a former railroad hotel built in 1903, Alberta House now contains the Olive Craig Gallery, the Alberta House Shop, and the arts council office on the first floor. Artist studios and a growing art library are housed on the upper floors. The shop is a place for local artists to showcase and sell their work. Generally staffed by the artists themselves, the shop contains everything from photographs and oil paintings to more gift-oriented items like clocks made from old Michigan license plates.

Cedarville's Creekside Herbs and Art (906-484-2415) is a unique place comprising a renovated barn with an art gallery, a kayak shop, nature trails, and display gardens. Owned by two local sisters who strive to introduce visitors to local and Native American arts and culture, this place feels more like a community center than a store, which is exactly the desired effect. That said, the items for sale here are interesting too, especially Native American arts and crafts, handblown glass items, unique pottery, beads, and jewelry. There is a lot to see here, and plenty of unique items to take home for yourself or loved ones. And the "herbs" part of the name isn't just a reference to the herb gardens in back; the sisters sell hundreds of herbal remedies and delight in passing on their knowledge.

John Herbon Pottery and Ceramics Studio (906-643-8196), in St. Ignace, produces and sells very beautiful handcrafted ceramics, all with subtle touches and allusions to the surrounding nature that make them distinctly North Woods, but not in a touristy way. It's worth stopping in here just to have a look.

Native Expressions Ojibwa Museum Store (906-643-9161), a great little shop in the Ojibwa Museum in St. Ignace, sells a large selection of Native American books and music and a very high-quality assortment of locally made Native American arts and crafts. It's worth a visit even if you're not going to the museum.

The Great Outdoors

Outdoor adventures and activities in eastern U.P.

BEACHES

Driving along Lake Shore from Bay Mills, hugging the shore of Lake Superior, pull off at Big Pine Picnic Area, 1 mile east of Bay View Campground and 9 miles northwest of Raco. From this popular and scenic Hiawatha National Forest beach, visitors can see big freighters entering the St. Mary's River from afar. In addition to its sandy strip, the beach offers some pebbly areas that are good for rock hunting.

Going west toward Grand Marais, head into the Muskallonge State Park a few miles west of Deer Park to access the North Country Trail, which can be reached through the trails in the park. The North County Trail will take you to Lake Superior Campground Beach, which is hidden and beautiful, with sand on one side and agate on the other.

Once you reach Grand Marais, just to the west of the harbor is Grand Marais Agate Beach, a well-known agate beach where the colorful stones are often found. The mouth of Sable Creek is at one end of the beach, with a path to Sable Falls.

Grand Marais beach is littered with beautiful agate stones.   Wikimedia Commons

Right at the harbor in Grand Marais, **Grand Marais Harbor Beach** is a crescent of sand that provides access to a protected swimming bay and terrific surrounding views of Grand Marais.

BICYCLING

This is one of the best regions in the U.P. for road cycling—through the Hiawatha National Forest and the Lake Superior State Forest, around little waterfront towns like Hessel and St. Ignace, and everywhere on Mackinac Island. Many visitors bring their bicycles, but you can also rent a bike from **Arnold Transit Co.** (906-847-3351; www.arnoldline.com), **Mackinac Island Bicycle Shop** (906-847-6337; Hoban St., Mackinac Island), or **Mackinac Wheels** (906-847-8022; 1800 Huron Rd., Mackinac Island).

The **Mackinac Island Circle Tour** is an easy ride around the island that will take about an hour and a half with no stops, but there are plenty of sights worth pulling over for, and even a tasty snack stop along the way. The bike path starts right next to the ferry docks and follows the coast around the island.

The lovely stretch of **MI 134** between Cedarville and DeTour affords views of pleasant bays and hushed forests, as well as access to sandy beaches and marshes that are excellent for bird-watching (see below). The road is quite flat, with large, paved shoulders, which makes it ideal for a lazy bike ride. Mountain bikers can take any number of more rough-and-tumble trails off the main road.

The Big Sand

The **Grand Sable Dunes** (*grand sable* is French for "big sand") are not only interesting to see and fun to walk, they provide some of the only high ground around these parts, affording spectacular views of Lake Superior and the coastline. To reach the dunes, take H 58 out of Grand Marais and follow the signs for Sable Falls.

The Grand Sable Dunes provide some of the best Lake Superior views in the region.

Matt Girvan

BIRD-WATCHING

About 2 miles west of Hessel, the Birge Nature Preserve is a peaceful 275-acre preserve that is home to several eagles and ospreys.

Also along the MI 134, near the intersection of MI 48, the Michigan Department of Transportation maintains a popular birding site as a rest stop along the highway. Strange as it may sound, it's an excellent place to spot warblers, vireos, and flycatchers, as well as raptors in September and gulls and cormorants offshore.

Neebish Island, in the St. Mary's River (ferry service available from Barbeau), is a largely undeveloped wilderness island, home to a number of unusual birds, including various owls—great gray, snowy, and northern hawk owls—as well as red- and white-winged crossbills, northern shrike, and rough-legged hawks. Be careful going in off-season unless the ice is frozen solid or melted entirely. The Coast Guard cuts through the ice bridge that forms with the mainland every year in late March, but ice often reforms, not thick enough to walk on but too thick to allow the small ferry through, essentially stranding people on the island. Don't worry too much, though; although there are no stores on Neebish, there are a handful of residents. In addition to watching the birds, visitors to the island can get a close-up view of the big freighters as they pass by on their way to the St. Mary's River and the Soo Locks.

Part of the Lake Superior State Forest, St. Vital Point, near the DeTour State Forest Campground (see "Camping") is home to large flocks of warblers during the late spring and late summer.

Because of its location in the northeast and the fact that it juts out into Lake Superior, Whitefish Point Bird Observatory (906-492-3596; 16914 N. Whitefish Point Rd., Paradise) is a phenomenally popular landing spot for migrating birds. Before heading out to the wetlands or low dunes near the point, birders should check in with the folks manning the observatory gift shop for tips on where to see what.

Scenic Route: Tahquamenon to Sault Ste. Marie via Lake Shore Drive

Lake Shore Drive, running from MI 123 at Tahquamenon Falls east to Sault Ste. Marie, passes by several scenic vistas and worthy stops, including, from west to east, Whitefish Bay, the Hiawatha National Forest (especially pretty during the fall color season), Mission Hill views of the Lake Superior shipping lanes, Point Iroquois Lighthouse, Monocle Lake, Bay Mills Native American community and Bay Mills Casino, and the scenic and popular Bay Mills section of the North Country Trail with its panoramic views and swinging bridge.

CAMPING

Much of the undeveloped forestland in this region belongs to the state, and camping is almost always allowed with a backcountry permit.

On Drummond Island, about 15 miles from the ferry dock, off the main interior road, Glen Cove (open May through October) provides backcountry camping with no permit required and easy access to the water for kayakers. For camping that's a little less rough, H&H Resort and Campground (906-493-5195; www.diyachthaven.com; open year-round, water and electrical; $15) run by the Drummond Island Yacht Haven, offers conveniently located (if tightly spaced) sites with easy access to the marina for kayakers and boaters.

In Les Cheneaux, just 5 miles west of DeTour Village via MI 134, DeTour State Park (906-635-5281; open May through October; $15) has 21 first-come, first-served sites in the woods on Lake Huron. This is a dynamite spot—great fishing on-site in Lake Huron and nearby at Caribou

Lake and the St. Mary's River, hiking trails through the Cranberry Lake Flooding area 1 mile north, wetlands and marshlands that attract various birds and wildlife, easy boat access to the lake via DeTour Passage.

Government Island (906-387-3700; open May through October), a beautiful, uninhabited island just off La Salle Island, is part of the Hiawatha Forest and allows backcountry camping with a permit. The island features a sandy beach and a number of pleasant forest walks.

For an island camping experience that's a bit less rustic, Lime Island (906-635-5281; open Memorial Day through mid-September; $15 for camp-sites, $65 for cottages) is ideal; it even offers cottages, showers, and flush toilets for those who can't deal with backcountry wilderness. Lime Island is also a great place to fish, hike, lounge on the beach, watch the freighters in the St. Mary's River, and just get away from it all. Rustic cottages and camp-sites are maintained here by the state park system, but to get to the island, you'll need to have your own boat or charter a boat. It's only 3 miles across from DeTour, but the channel is too rough to kayak over.

Farther west, in the Hiawatha National Forest, just a half mile west of the Bay Mills Native American community off Lake Shore Drive, Monocle

Almost the entire circumference of Drummond Island is easily navigated by kayak, which makes the island a real paddler's paradise.   Charles Dawley

Lake campground is something special. Set in a hardwood forest around beautiful Monocle Lake and within walking distance of the Point Iroquois Lighthouse, the campground is well placed for exploring this section of Lake Superior's coast as well as nearby Bay Mills. Hiking is great here, particularly to the lighthouse or the Monocle Lake overlook.

A half hour's drive from Tahquamenon Falls, Muskallonge Lake State Park (www.midnrreservations.com; open May through October; $14 for tents, $16 for RVs) is the perfect home base for a week of exploring. It's hard to believe that Muskallonge was once the site of the Deer Park lumber town. Now it is a peaceful lake, surrounded by deep, quiet forests full of deer, numerous rivers and other inland lakes, sand dunes, and the nearby Lake Superior shore. The North Country Trail passes through this park, and there are various short loop trails that lead hikers to it, as well as to a particularly beautiful stretch of Lake Superior's coastline. Despite the large number of sites, Muskallonge fills up fast, so be sure to reserve early.

Also close driving distance to Tahquamenon, just 8 miles north of Seney on MI 77, the East Branch of Fox River is a popular camping spot for those who want to fish for trout in the famed Fox River. Sites are first-come, first served and cost $15 a day.

CANOEING AND KAYAKING

Paddling is great throughout the U.P., but the east side offers a particularly great selection of routes. Rent a kayak or canoe at Mark's Rod & Reel Sports Shop (906-293-5608; 13951 E. CR 462, Newberry), or book a guided canoe trip at Rainbow Lodge, located at the mouth of the Two Hearted River (906-658-3357; 32752 CR 423, Newberry).

For an easy paddle, try Blind Sucker #2 (906-293-5131; 33 miles northwest of Newberry via MI 123 and CR 407). It promises 6 miles of pleasant, easy canoeing from the boat launch at the river's mouth to its source, meandering through marshlands, forests, and wild blueberry patches.

Canoeing down the Tahquamenon River (906-492-3415) can be really beautiful, particularly on a nice summer day. The park's only canoe livery does two-hour, half-day, and full-day trips starting at the Lower Falls and heading toward the river's mouth.

Local canoe liveries (see above) will also take paddlers up the Two Hearted River to the Reed & Green Bridge for an all-day paddle back to the river mouth.

Kayaking is amazing all the way around Drummond Island and betwixt and between Les Cheneaux, as well as around the St. Mary's River and Lime Island. For newcomers, it's a good idea to book a guide, particularly to get a handle on the bays and marshes of Les Cheneaux. Les Cheneaux

Water Trail leads from the Carp River near St. Ignace along the north shore of Lake Huron through Les Cheneaux to DeTour Village. It's 75 miles in total, almost all of it a stunning coastline paddle.

Woods & Water Ecotours (906-484-4157; www.woodswaterecotours .com) is a one-woman operation that leads kayak trips through Les Cheneaux and Drummond Island—hands-down the best way to see the shorelines of these islands. Woods & Water also rents boats to those who prefer to go it alone but requires that you first take their introductory safety course or prove knowledge of the basics covered in it. Maps of the area and rights-of-way maps are provided, and it offers delivery anywhere around the area for an extra $5.

CROSS-COUNTRY SKIING

The 9.3-mile groomed Algonquin Pathway (906-635-5281; 20th St. West and 16th Ave. West, Sault Ste. Marie; take I-75 north from Sault Ste. Marie and exit at 3 Mile Rd.) is part of the Lake Superior State Forest. The first loop is also lit for those out at sundown or early morning.

The large Chi Mukwa (Big Bear) Community Recreation Facility (906-635-7465; 2 Ice Circle Dr., Sault Ste. Marie), operated by the Sault Ste. Marie Tribe of Chippewa Indians, includes a groomed cross-country ski trail in addition to a public skating rink, in-line skating, and various other activities open to the public.

A short drive southwest of Sault Ste. Marie, Pine Bowl Pathway (906-635-5281; 19 miles southwest of Sault Ste. Marie via I-75), also part of the Lake Superior State Forest, includes over 7 miles of secluded groomed cross-country ski trails over rolling terrain.There are spectacular views on DeTour Pathway (5 miles west of DeTour Village on MI 134). This 4-mile groomed, marked trail leads through the woods to St. Vital Point on the shores of Lake Huron.

Several miles of groomed trails cut through the trees and around the shores of Drummond Island. The trails are publicly accessible, but trailheads are in the woods near the Drummond Island Lodge; trail maps are available at the lodge as well.

All roads and trails are open to cross-country skiing on Mackinac Island. The back of the island is reserved for cross-country skiing and snowshoeing, with no snowmobiling allowed.

Sand Dunes Cross Country Ski Trails (11 miles west of St. Ignace on US 2) features marked and groomed trails along the sand dunes in the Hiawatha National Forest; there are five trails, 1.5 to 6.2 miles (2.4 km to 10 km).

Two groomed cross-country ski loops known collectively as St. Martin

Cross-Country Ski Trail (6 to 7 miles west of Hessel) take skiers through the woods and wetlands near Search Bay.

FISHING

The Two Hearted River (35 miles northeast of Newberry via MI 123 and CRs 500, 414, 412, and 423) is probably Michigan's best-known trout stream. The river is buzzing in spring and fall, but even with all the attention, it's nowhere near overfished. The most popular spots are the river's mouth and Reed & Green Bridge, but all of the river has good fishing.

The East Branch of Fox River (906-452-6227; 8 miles north of Seney via MI 77) may be the best-known and -liked brook-trout stream in a region full of great trout streams. Like the Two Hearted, there's no bad spot to fish here. Interestingly, many people believe that the Fox, and not the Two Hearted, is the river Hemingway was really talking about in his Nick Adams stories.

Fishing is also amazing all throughout the shores and dozens of inland lakes of Les Cheneaux, as well as in Lake Huron and the St. Mary's River, with the local favorite prize being yellow perch. Bass, salmon, pike, herring, smelt, musky, walleye, and splake are all also found in the waters surrounding these 36 tiny islands. A guide can be extremely helpful in and around Les Cheneaux, and there are several knowledgeable local guides to choose from.

Doing business as Dream Seaker Sport Fishing Charters and Guided Tours (1-888-634-3419; www.dreamseaker.com), Les Cheneaux resident and longtime captain Jim Shutt leads visiting fishermen to the northern Lake Huron area and the St. Mary's River system, departing from Hessel, St. Ignace, Cedarville, DeTour, Drummond Island, or Mackinac Island. If you don't catch a fish, Captain Shutt will keep taking you out until you do.

Les Cheneaux Islands Water Tours and Charter Service (906-484-3776; www.fishingwithnorm.com), also known as Fishing with Norm, is another local operation that offers fishing charters and boating tours throughout Les Cheneaux. Norm has 31 years of experience fishing these waters and guarantees that you'll catch a fish or next time's free.

Lifelong Drummond Island resident Captain Ivan Gable runs Sturgeon Bay Charters (906-493-6087; www.sturgeonbaycharters.com). Captain Gable knows the island and its waters like the back of his hand. He sticks to what he knows—Drummond Island and its environs—and leads fishermen to perch, salmon, walleye, trout, and herring.

If you'd rather go it alone, head to Caribou Lake, 3.5 miles west of DeTour Village off MI 134. Caribou Lake is a popular local fishing lake, known for smallmouth bass, rock bass, walleye, yellow perch, northern pike, pumpkinseed sunfish, brown bullhead, and white sucker.

Family Fun

The U.P. is one of America's most family-friendly destinations. Here are a few great options for families in the eastern U.P.:

The **Agawa Canyon Tour Train** (1-800-242-9287; www.agawacanyon tourtrain.com) runs on an old railroad that used to haul lumber and iron ore from Canada's interior to the industrial port of Sault Ste. Marie, Ontario. Today, the Agawa runs railway treks into the Canadian wilderness. The trains are much nicer than those old lumber trains, with large picture windows and comfortable seats, and the ride into the dense wilderness is pretty amazing, especially when the train dips and shoots down to the canyon floor, where visitors can get out for a couple of hours and hike or walk around the canyon, which contains the Agawa River and a handful of waterfalls. The trip takes one full day and is especially beautiful during fall color season, or in the winter when it's referred to as the Snow Train.

The very well organized **Great Lakes Shipwreck Museum** (1-888-492-3747; www.shipwreckmuseum.com; $10) has become increasingly popular over the years. In addition to the museum, which tells the stories of some of the better-known wrecks and gives the general background of Lake Superior, the bird observatory is fantastic, and the **Whitefish Point Light Station** exhibits do a great job painting a picture of a lighthouse keeper's life as it really was. To get to the museum, take MI 123 north to Paradise, then follow N. Whitefish Point Road to its end.

A fantastic ranchland home for 30 rescued American black bears, **Oswald's Bear Ranch** (906-293-3147; www.oswaldsbearranch.com; $10

You can also access Lake Huron via DeTour State Forest Campground, 5 miles west of DeTour Village on MI 134. It's a prime spot on Lake Huron for fishing for walleye, bass, pike, and musky.

Fishing is also decent right off the shoreline rocks of Mackinac Island, especially on the backside of the island, away from the crowds. Fishermen catch perch, salmon, walleye, musky, steelhead, pike, and whitefish here.

GOLF

The Bay Mills Sault tribe really upped the ante for U.P. casinos when it built a waterfront championship golf course: Wild Bluff Golf Course at Bay Mills Resort & Casinos (1-877-229-6455; www.4baymills.com; 18 holes,

per car) invites visitors to walk through its four large habitats. The bears are enclosed, for the safety of visitors, but their enclosures are very large, and the Oswalds have made a real effort to provide a natural habitat. Viewing platforms provide the perfect angle for pictures of the bears playing or lounging. Many of the bears have been raised here, as people and the Michigan Department of Natural Resources (DNR) bring rescued cubs here every year.

See the locks and the freighters up close and personal on a **Soo Locks Boat Cruise** (906-632-6301; www.soolocks.com; $22.50 adults, $10.50 children 5–12, under 5 free).

The **Tahquamenon Falls Riverboat Tour and Toonerville Trolley** (906-876-2311 or 1-888-77-TRAIN; www.superiorsights.com/toonerville) is a great combination of trips all wrapped into one. Visitors take a narrow-gauge train through dense forests to the Tahquamenon River, then disembark from the train and hop on a riverboat for a 21-mile cruise down the river, ending a half mile above Upper Falls.

Kids get a kick out of the interactive children's museum, and the cannon and rifle demonstrations as well at **Fort Mackinac** (www.mackinac parks.com).

While purists will point out that totem poles aren't indigenous to this region, the man who carved the totem poles at **Totem Village Museum** (906-643-8888; $5 family, $2 adults, $1 children, under 5 free) had nothing but a deep reverence for the local Ojibwa, and they in turn took a liking to him. Kids love to wander around the village and pick out gifts like fur hats and minitotem poles in the gift shop.

7,022 yards, par 72). Rated four and a half stars by *Golf Digest*, it's a challenging but very playable course, featuring rolling hills, wild rivers, and large natural ravines in addition to its wooded surroundings and lake views.

The Rock at Drummond Island Resort (906-493-1000; www.drum mondisland.com; 18 holes, 6,830 yards, par 71) lists deer and geese as regular course obstacles. In addition to the local wildlife, The Rock boasts challenging long, tree-lined fairways and water obstacles, earning a four-star rating from *Golf Digest*.

Wawashkamo Golf Club (906-847-3871; www.wawashkamo.com; no metal spikes allowed) is a charming nine-hole course on Mackinac Island, where golfers can still use classic Scottish hickory sticks if they choose.

Blueberry Bonanza

Wild blueberries grow unchecked in much of the land surrounding this area, and everyone is allowed to pick those found in national forest-land. Blueberries are in-season from the end of July to the end of August. Following are some good spots to find them:

Blind Sucker River. In Deer Park, the south banks of the Blind Sucker River.

Muskallonge Lake State Park. Along the section of the North Country Trail that runs through the park.

Raco. Near the old missile base off MI 28 between Brimley and Raco.

Wawashkamo (Ojibwa for "walk a crooked trail") is the oldest continuously played course in Michigan and offers visitors a truly unique experience.

Expanded to 18 holes by Jerry Matthews in the mid-1990s, The Jewel at the Grand Hotel (906-847-3331; www.grandhotel.com; 18 holes, 5,500 yards, par 67) is a fantastic course that mixes long, open fairways near the hotel with tougher, tree-lined fairways on the back nine in the woods. A special horse-drawn carriage takes golfers between the front and back nine.

HIKING

Lake Superior Nature Sanctuary (517-655-5655; www.michigannature.org) is a wild, undeveloped piece of Lake Superior shoreline that is currently under the protection of the Michigan Nature Association. Visitors are welcome in the sanctuary, but chances of getting horribly lost are high, which is why the Nature Association began training volunteer guides to take people around.

Michigan's other car-free island, Lime Island (906-635-5281), is as rustic as Mackinac is Victorian and prim. Visitors need to bring their own boat or charter a boat to get here, but once they do, they have access to 980 acres of wilderness, surrounded by the St. Mary's River. Wilderness hikes, or walks through an abandoned company town, with the river's huge freighters in the background, are one-of-a-kind.

On the eastern shore of Drummond Island, Marble Head features a path along 200-foot-high dolomite cliffs that leads down to the North Channel, with breathtaking views of the water and Cockburn Island, Ontario.

Tahquamenon Falls State Park has more to offer than just the falls. Surrounded by forests, marshes, bogs, and other wetlands, the park features a half-dozen or so hiking trails that connect them all. Hikers can take the Giant Pines Loop from Upper Falls, follow it to Wolf Lake, and catch the Wilderness Loop, which connects to a 16-mile section of the North Country Trail that passes through the park. With everyone focused on the falls, these trails are usually empty and quiet, making them prime wildlife viewing areas.

At **Birge Nature Preserve** (off MI 134 west of Hessel on Point Brulée Rd.), vibrant wildflowers run riot over this 275-acre preserve at the base of Point Brulée about 2 miles west of Hessel. Its wetlands and forests also provide prime wildlife viewing, including regular sightings of eagles, beavers, and ospreys.

HUNTING

Both the deer and bear populations in this region of the U.P. have decreased in recent years, which has made some locals criticize the Michigan DNR for not regulating hunts more in the region. That said, it remains a popular sport, and as in other regions, land located in the Hiawatha National Forest (much of the land around Hessel and Les Cheneaux Islands) and the Lake Superior State Forest is open to hunters. See www.fs.fed.us/r9/forests/hiawatha for details on hunting in the Hiawatha Forest, and www.michigan.gov/dnr for information on hunting in Lake Superior National Forest. For information about state hunting regulations and hunting seasons for various game, see chapter 7.

Guided and Private Hunting

In Barbeau, **Antler Bay Trophy Whitetail Ranch** (906-647-2018; www.antlerbay.net) offers whitetailed-deer hunts on a 1,700-acre private hunting preserve.

Public Land Hunting Locations

The campground area at Monocle Lake is closed to hunters, but elsewhere in **Monocle Lake Recreation Area**, visitors can hunt for deer, beaver, and waterfowl in-season. To get to the recreation area from Brimley, take Lakeshore Drive north about 6 miles; the park is on the left.

Although hunting is not allowed in **Muskallonge Lake State Park**, duck and goose hunting is allowed on that portion of Muskallonge Lake not within the park's boundaries, as well as on the nearby section of Lake Superior outside the park confines. To get to the lake from Newberry, take MI 123 north toward Tahquamenon and turn west onto CR 407. Muskallonge Lake is 30 miles northwest of Newberry on CR 407.

No hunting signs are clearly posted in those areas of **Tahquamenon Falls State Park** (906-492-3415; 41382 W. MI 123, Paradise) that restrict hunting. The rest of the 50,000-acre park is open to hunters, who visit annually in search of deer, bear, fox, beaver, and grouse in-season.

SNOWMOBILING

Ice bridges between the islands are one of the biggest draws of snow-mobiling in this area. Particularly popular is the International Ice Bridge to Canada on Drummond Island. Near Christmastime, when the ice has frozen solid, snowmobilers bring Christmas trees to outline an ice highway from Drummond over to the nearest Canadian island. As winter progresses, another tree-lined bridge opens up to mainland Canada, giving access to a whole new network of trails.

Sunday Drive on Sugar Island

Sugar Island, the ancestral home of the Ojibwa, is a lovely place to visit, both for its views of the St. Mary's River and beyond and for the profound sense of history felt upon its shores. Covered in sugar maple (hence the name), it's also a fantastic place to see fall color. The Sugar Island Ferry (906-635-5421; $6 per car) leaves from the dock at the end of Portage Avenue in Soo Locks Park in Sault Ste. Marie twice an hour all year long.

In addition to the ice bridge, Drummond Island has over 100 miles of groomed snowmobiling trails. The popular St. Ignace Snowmobile Trail leads east to Hessel and Les Cheneaux, where it meets up with several more miles of groomed trails.

Farther west, Falls Trail begins in Newberry and heads northeast to Paradise, Whitefish Point, and Tahquamenon Falls, where it meets up with the Grand Marais Trail. The Grand Marais Trail is a long trail that stretches from Grand Marais all the way east to Tahquamenon and finally south to loop around Hulbert Lake.

Snowmobiles are available for rent at The Country Store (906-493-5455) on Drummond Island and at the Quality Inn (1-800-906-4656) in St. Ignace. Near Tahquamenon Falls, Gallagher's Windy Corners (1-888-491-8808) also rents snowmobiles, as does North Shore Lodge (906-494-2361) in Grand Marais.

WATERFALLS

There are dozens of worthy falls in this part of the U.P., but the most magnificent are Sable Falls and Tahquamenon Falls. Just east of Grand Marais on H58, Sable Falls is often overlooked in favor of larger, more powerful falls. Power or not, you can't beat the absolutely perfect composition of

Sable Falls, outside Grand Marais, is just one of hundreds of waterfalls throughout the Upper Peninsula. Matt Girvan

these falls—water cascades down the middle of centuries-old black rocks, bordered by bright green moss and hemlock and cedar groves.

Just under 200 feet wide, the Tahquamenon Falls (906-492-3415) are by far the largest in Michigan, sending up to 50,000 gallons of water per second hurling nearly 50 feet into the canyon below. There are two prime viewing spots in the park for both falls—Upper Falls and Lower Falls—and

Tahquamenon's Upper Falls gets more than 200,000 visitors every year. <small>Matt Girvan</small>

Fossil Hunting

Fossils are abundant in this part of the U.P. and especially so on Drummond Island's north shore. **Fossil Beach** is obviously known for its fossils, and the **Maxton Plains**, best known for their protected alvar grasses, are also a decent place to spot fossils. The folks at the Drummond Island Chamber of Commerce are very helpful. They're happy to plan out a fossil-hunting trip for visitors, depending on whether they have four-wheel drive or not or whether they want to deal with hiking in. Call 906-493-5245 for more information.

a great 4-mile loop hike (8 miles round-trip) between them that follows the river. The Lower Falls, while not as tall and thundering as the Upper Falls, are no less beautiful. The river gets very wide here and the water comes stumbling along several rock shelves. In addition to hiking between the two, visitors can rent canoes to paddle the river, being very careful, of course, not to get sucked into the rapids.

South Central

BEACHES, GHOST TOWNS, BIG SPRING, ESCANABA, AND MANISTIQUE

THIS LARGE SWATH OF THE UPPER PENINSULA running along the coast of Lake Michigan, from Brevort to Escanaba, is known for its fantastic fishing and beaches in the summer, hunting in the fall, and ski-worthy mountains in the winter. During much of its past the westernmost county in this region (Menominee) was also part of what was called Iron Country—one of the largest American iron ranges, the Menominee Range, is here, and iron production dominated the area around it for decades.

Remnants of that past are still visible, particularly in the area's ghost towns. One such town—Fayetteville—has been preserved and is now part of the state's park system. Visitors can tour through the old ironworks, the town's hotel, and examples of various living quarters, and marvel at how a town of several thousand was depopulated virtually from one day to the next.

In addition to its numerous sandy beaches and lovely lake views, the shores of Lake Michigan are home to one of the U.P.'s largest cities, Escanaba. Escanaba made an appearance in the 2001 Jeff Daniels comedy *Escanaba in Da Moonlight*, which folks up here don't like to talk about much. In fact, the real Escanaba is far more citified than the movie version. It's one of the few towns in the U.P. where you don't feel like absolutely everyone knows each other, and its restaurants are well respected throughout the state.

This area also boasts hundreds of beautiful, clear inland fishing lakes, as well as the U.P.'s largest deer population, making it a popular vacation spot

LEFT: Sand Point Lighthouse is walking distance from downtown Escanaba.   Henryk Sadura

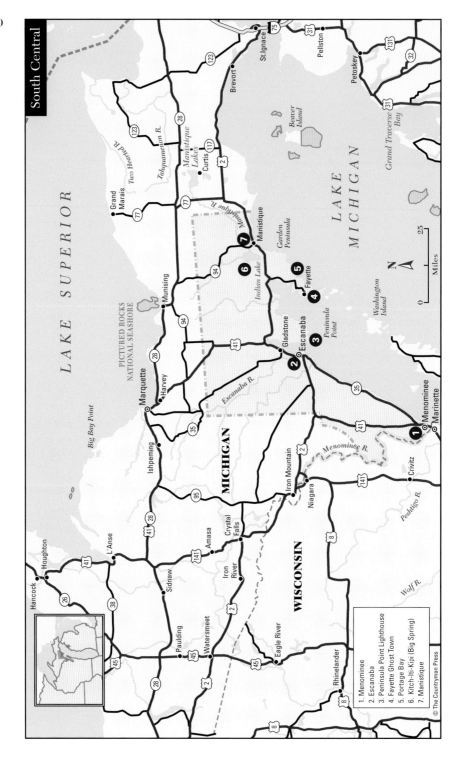

LAKE SUPERIOR

LAKE MICHIGAN

MICHIGAN

WISCONSIN

PICTURED ROCKS NATIONAL SEASHORE

1. Menominee
2. Escanaba
3. Peninsula Point Lighthouse
4. Fayette Ghost Town
5. Portage Bay
6. Kitch-Iti-Kipi (Big Spring)
7. Manistique

© The Countryman Press

Seney Wildlife Refuge is one of the best wildlife viewing spots in the country.
Wikimedia Commons

for avid hunters and fishermen. And birdwatchers and other nature lovers return time and again to the world-famous Seney Wildlife Refuge, a 96,000-acre protected wetland habitat with 50 miles of trails and endless opportunities to view local wildlife, particularly the many unusual migratory birds that call this spot home.

Pick Your Spot

Best places to stay in south central U.P., and nearby . . .

LAKE MICHIGAN BEACH, BREVOORT LAKE, AND THE MANISTIQUE LAKES

Eighteen miles west of St. Ignace along US 2, the Lake Michigan Campground in the Hiawatha National Forest offers one of the best slices of summer living in the country. Between the town of Brevort—once a popular overnight stop before the Mackinac Bridge was built and visitors from the Lower Peninsula had to ferry across the lake—and the town of Pointe aux Chenes, Lake Michigan Beach offers 8 miles of sandy shores, giant dunes, and wild blueberries. Just inland from the beaches, also in the Hiawatha National Forest, Brevoort Lake is a beautiful and popular summertime destination, with 4,000-plus acres of prime fishing and boating and reliably warm water for swimming.

Northwest of Pointe aux Chenes, and strangely more than 20 miles from the town that bears their name, the Manistique Lakes are popular in winter and summer alike. The charming town of Curtis sits along the isthmus between Big Manistique Lake and South Manistique Lake and offers dozens of cabins, cottages, and resorts for visitors. Located on South Manistique Lake and Portage Creek in downtown Curtis, Gordon's Resort (906-586-9761; www.gordonsresort.com; open year-round; $$, credit cards not accepted) has two-, three-, and four-bedroom cabins for rent, overlooking either the creek or the lake. Cabins 1 and 2 are the newest and thus in the best condition, but are two-bedroom cabins. Cabin 3 offers three bedrooms, and cabin 4 offers four; both could use a new couch and carpet but are perfectly clean and comfortable. All four cabins have knotty pine interiors, full kitchens, cable TV, decks, and spacious rooms. The resort offers picnic tables and gas grills, plus the use of several 14-foot rowboats. The only things not provided for some reason are towels. In addition to being on one of the Manistique Lakes and near the others, Gordon's is walking distance to Curtis, which is a small but charming waterfront village located on a narrow isthmus between South Manis-

tique Lake and Big Manistique Lake.

Big Manistique Resort (906-586-9828 or 1-800-880-9828; www.bigmanistiqueresort.com; open year-round; $$) offers six two- and three-bedroom cottages on a sandy strip of shoreline surrounding Big Manistique Lake have hardwood floors, knotty pine interiors, full kitchens, new TVs, and North Woods country décor (lots of quilts and overstuffed chairs). Each cottage comes with its own 14-foot rowboat for exploring the lake. The resort also rents canoes, kayaks, and bikes, but if you bring your own, there's plenty of room to park your trailer. In the winter a heated shop provides a warm spot to fix sleds and snowmobiles. Pets are welcome for a small deposit, making this an ideal spot for family vacations.

In the summer the lakes are full of fishermen and swimmers, in the fall the fall colors and prime hunting make it a popular weekend destination, and in the winter the area's well-groomed cross-country ski and snowmobile trails are popular as well, so most of the resorts stay open year-round.

A few miles north of Curtis, Interlaken Resort and Burnt Island (906-586-3545; www.interlakenresort.org; $$) is a popular family resort with cute, funky little cabins featuring knotty pine interiors and dark wood exteriors on a huge section of Big Manistique Lake. For the slightly more adventurous, in addition to the eight main resort cabins, Interlaken offers two rustic cabins out on Burnt Island in the lake, easily accessed by boat, and also allows visitors to camp and picnic on completely undeveloped "Virgin Island." The main cabins are fully equipped with kitchens, microwaves, TV/VCR units, towels, and linens; the Burnt Island cabins have built-in bunks and wood-burning stoves. All guests have free access to canoes, paddleboats, motorboats, and pontoon boats, and the resort sits on several well-groomed cross-country ski trails and snowmobile trails for winter fun.

For more of a full-service hotel option, the lovely Chamberlin's Ole Forest Inn (906-586-6000 or 1-800-292-0440; www.chamberlins inn.com; $$) in Curtis offers five-star accommodations for two-star prices. A historic railroad hotel-turned-B&B, Chamberlin's was originally built in the late 1800s, then moved to its present-day location overlooking Big Manistique Lake in 1924 and remained a hotel until the early 1970s. When Bud Chamberlin stumbled across it in 1989 on a snowmobile ride, it had been sitting empty for over 10 years. Chamberlin bought the hotel, spent nearly two years refurbishing it, and opened it as a bed & breakfast in late 1990. Much of the original 1800s woodwork remained intact, and the house is furnished predominantly with antiques left over from the hotel's early days, although Chamberlin has updated the 12 guest rooms with large bathrooms, placing a Jacuzzi tub in one. While the majority of the rooms

Chamberlin's Ole Forest Inn, near Curtis, has both great rooms and good food.   John Natiw

have private baths, a few do not—they are obviously priced lower, but be sure to ask for a private bath if you want one. In 1992 Chamberlin opened a restaurant in the inn, which is very popular, especially in the evening when diners can enjoy beautiful sunset lake views from the dining room or the wraparound porch. The porch is also a fantastic spot just to sit and marvel at the colors in fall. A wonderful spot for couples, Chamberlin's isn't a great fit for families with young children.

ESCANABA

Escanaba's downtown actually feels larger than Marquette's, although Marquette is a much larger city. Once you get past the unappealing strip malls and fast food joints on the city's outskirts, the historic downtown is very attractive, with beautiful old buildings and numerous galleries, cafés, restaurants, and retail stores. At the east side of downtown, where the land juts into the lake, is lovely Ludington Park, with benches looking out over Little Bay de Noc on Lake Michigan, paths, bike trails, and grassy areas just crying out for a picnic. Just across the street is the House of Ludington (906-786-6300; www.houseofludington.com; $), which is not only close to the park, but also within walking distance of downtown Escanaba's shops, art galleries, and cafés. This landmark Queen Anne–style hotel, built in 1865, is in an ideal location from which to explore all that Escanaba has to offer. The location also provides

House of Ludington.   Matt Girvan

easy access to the highway, making it a nice home base for exploring the rest of the area as well. Half of the Ludington's 25 guest rooms boast Lake Michigan views, and all have cable TV and private baths. Rooms are decorated according to a variety of themes—Lighthouse, Stars & Stripes, Log Cabin, Honeymoon, Country Meadows, Garden, or Victorian—and come with one double bed, two double beds, or two separate rooms with an adjoining bath. The hotel also houses two restaurants—a more formal dining room with lake views, and a casual restaurant with home cooking at reasonable prices—as well as a pub that resembles an Old West watering hole.

MENOMINEE AND MARINETTE

Menominee and its neighbor across the river, Marinette, are charming little towns, but both my favorite B&Bs are in Marinette. The bright red Lauerman House Inn (715-732-7800; www.lauermanhouse.com; $$$) is a huge and beautifully restored Colonial-revival building complete with grand white columns that looks cheerily out over Riverside Avenue on the Marinette side of the Menominee River. The original wood and detailed light fixtures have been restored to their past splendor, but the rest of the décor is fairly modern, with art deco furniture, clean lines, and bright colors, not to mention Egyptian cotton

sheets. All of the Lauerman's rooms are large and include a private bath and sitting room, and its two suites also include two-person Jacuzzi tubs. The Red Room and the Green Room both boast excellent river views, as do most of the inn's common rooms. A full breakfast, including a hot entrée, fresh fruit, and fresh pastries, is served every morning. The Lauerman House Café bakes bread and pastries daily and serves soups, salads, and sandwiches for lunch Monday through Friday. Less formal than its sister inn, the M&M, the Lauerman House feels like a lovely old family home, and the rooms are large and comfortable for families traveling with children.

An absolute stunner of an inn in downtown Marinette, just over the Menominee River from Menominee, the Queen Anne–style M&M Victorian Inn (715-732-9531; www.mmvictorian.com; $$$) has had every ornate detail lovingly restored. It might actually look better now than it did when it was built in 1893 by a local lumber baron. Rooms strike a nice balance between Victorian and modern, with antique beds covered in Egyptian cotton and goose-down duvets. Suites include two-person Jacuzzi tubs, and all rooms have high-speed wireless Internet access, cable, private baths, and phones. The common rooms are as lovely as the guest rooms, with lots of polished wood antiques, stained-glass windows, and brightly painted walls that make all that vintage finery seem fresh and modern. In addition to its five guest rooms, the M&M houses the popular La Grappe D'Or restaurant, which specializes in French bistro fare, as well as two bars and a well-stocked wine cellar. Breakfast is a lavish affair, featuring a hot entrée, fresh-baked pastries and muffins, fresh fruit, and Starbucks coffee. The M&M's sister inn, the Lauerman House (see above) welcomes families with open arms, but the M&M is more of a couple's getaway, and children under the age of 10 are not allowed.

Local Flavors

Taste of the town—restaurants, cafés, bars, bistros, etc.

LAKE MICHIGAN BEACH, BREVOORT LAKE, MANISTIQUE LAKES

As with the rest of the U.P., you cannot go wrong with whitefish in this area, but the dozens of inland lakes provide numerous other fresh seafood options as well, including walleye, trout, and perch.

Thirty miles west of St. Ignace on US 2, which runs along the shore of Lake Michigan, the Cut River Inn (906-292-5400; closed December; $) is just a mile from the picturesque Cut River Bridge. The Cut River Inn has been popular with summer visitors for years, but the simple dining room is also a local favorite, with folks driving from far and wide for its broiled or fried whitefish and perch, and delicious apple dumplings with ice cream and rum sauce. Fairly tasty, if bland, breakfast burritos and filling lunchtime wraps and sandwiches make it a good bet no matter what time of day you happen to be passing through.

Chamberlin's Ole Forest Inn (1-800-292-0440; www.chamberlins inn.com; $$) in Curtis, is not just a great place to stay, but also a nice spot to grab a meal. The food is decent at Chamberlin's (especially the planked whitefish—yum!), but the reason people come here is the view—a spectacular panorama of Big Manistique Lake from the dining room windows and the porch of the restored 18th-century railroad hotel. This is also one of the few games going in town. Curtis is home to a number of cabins and resorts, but restaurants are in short supply. Breakfast and lunch here are solid as well, particularly the homemade biscuits and gravy at breakfast, and homemade soup at lunch.

If you're not in the mood for fish, head for the Pizza Stop (906-586-6622; closed Fridays; $) in Curtis, where you can either grab one of a handful of tables or order a pie to go. The tiny Pizza Stop's chef-owners make the sauce and the dough fresh every day, churning out delicious pizzas that are generally considered the best within a number of miles. Locals and regular summer visitors call ahead to order and run over to pick up their pies or grab one of a handful of tables to eat in. Toasted sandwiches and salads are also on offer, as are specialty coffee drinks, and ice cream in the summertime. Located in tiny "downtown" Curtis, the Pizza Stop is the only casual restaurant within walking distance of the town's resorts and residential areas, so the owners make an effort to provide whatever the community wants, resulting in a well-loved and popular spot.

MANISTIQUE AND THE GARDEN PENINSULA

For a small, one-tower town, Manistique has some surprisingly great dining options. The Upper Crust Bakery & Deli Café (906-341-2253; www.wix.com/lsmith09 /upper-crustclosed Sundays in winter; $), for example, is a fantastic place flooded with natural light and blessed with pleasant river views from its many windows and its outdoor deck. Occupying the same space as the popular Tamarack Books, Traders' Point Antiques, and the River Shack Antiques Annex, the café features a handful of salads and 40-odd sandwich choices, all made with bread baked on the premises every morning. Two soups are made fresh daily as well, and could include chicken noodle, Wisconsin cheese, or the popular

Friday Fish Fry

If you didn't grow up in the Midwest, or you're not Catholic, Friday fish fries might seem a touch unusual, but it's a widespread tradition in the U.P., and nearly every restaurant worth its salt has a version of it. The custom sprang out of the Catholic tradition to avoid meat on Friday, particularly during Lent, and it remains popular, especially in Michigan, Wisconsin, and Minnesota—more so up north than in the southern regions of those states. Irrespective of religion, everyone loves the fish fry tradition in the U.P., where whitefish, walleye, and perch are caught locally and fried to perfection.

potato bacon. The bakery portion of the Upper Crust churns out tasty pies, cookies, pastries, and cakes daily. Aside from its wall of windows, the Upper Crust is decorated simply, with wooden café tables on hardwood floors, and Tamarack Books on one side, which lends the place a pleasant literary vibe. In the summer the café serves dinner on Saturday, offering a surprisingly large and varied menu for an establishment that serves dinner only one day a week for three months out of the year. Homemade pastas are a favorite, as are the delicious, fall-off-the-bone country ribs.

For dinner every other night of the week, head to **Three Mile Supper Club** (906-341-8048; 8555 W. CR 442, Manistique; $, no credit cards accepted). Don't let the somewhat institutional feel scare you off. This spot has some of the best whitefish around, and a surprisingly good salad bar to boot. In fact, this may be the only Manistique restaurant that is consistently recommended by locals. Soups and salad dressings are all homemade, and the BBQ items and steak are also very good if you're not in the

Manistique's landmark water tower.

mood for whitefish. Steaks are cut to order and always cooked perfectly. The restaurant was a roadside disco of some kind at some point, and the full bar is still there, which can be good or bad. Because the dining room and the bar are in the same big room, and smoking is allowed in both, it can get very smoky, which can put a bit of a damper on dinner for nonsmokers.

Down the Garden Peninsula, the **Garden House Bar & Grille** (906-644-2844; $)—in Garden, naturally—was once a rowdy bar and local hangout, but has become more of a real restaurant in recent years. The all-you-can-eat Friday fish fry is popular, and the homemade chili is tasty, as are the homemade soups, but my favorite is the prime rib sandwich with grilled mushrooms, onion, and cheese—not at all healthy but very tasty. The Garden House still features a full bar as well, and what a bar it is—an antique wooden beauty stocked with various microbrews and a supertasty old-fashioned root beer.

ESCANABA

The mix of French, German, Scandinavian, and Italian immigrants in the town of Escanaba has created a delicious dining scene known throughout the peninsula. The bulk of the town's restaurants are located on Ludington Street, either in the downtown area, or farther out on the outskirts.

You wouldn't expect to find the

finest dining in town at the Best Western on the highway, but that is exactly what has happened here. With a respected chef and a very solid Italian menu built around daily fresh seafood specials, inventive pastas, and perfectly cooked steaks, **Pacinos Food & Spirits** (906-786-0602; www.pacinosfood andspirits.com; open June through October, closed Sundays and Mondays; $$$), in the Best Western on Ludington, is a popular spot for special-occasion dining. The décor is a bit over the top—more like the Italy you might find at Epcot Center than the old country—but the service is great and the food is consistently good. The daily specials take advantage of local fresh seafood and are always a good bet. Dinner is really the star here; at lunch, entrée-size salads and pasta dishes are tasty and filling but nothing spectacular, and the breakfast buffet is downright bad, with undercooked bacon and biscuits with lumpy gravy.

A few blocks closer to town, **The Stonehouse** (906-786-5003; www.stonehouseescanaba.com; 2223 Ludington St.; $$$) feels like a throwback to the 1960s, when going out to dinner meant shrimp cocktail and a steak. The Stonehouse's extensive menu includes a page each of meat, seafood, and chicken entrées, each served with your choice of soup or several salads, plus vegetable, potatoes, mac 'n' cheese, or linguine and clams. If you're not feeling that hungry, The

Stonehouse also offers a half-dozen entrée-size salad options, including the popular honey pecan salad.

Known for its friendly service, its jumbo margaritas, its pork enchiladas, and its tasty salsa (sold in jars at the restaurant's gift shop), **Ferdinand's** (906-786-8484; 1318 Ludington St.; closed Sundays; $$) has been an Escanaba favorite for decades. The food is surprisingly good despite the near-total absence of Mexican immigrants in this part of the state. For those in your group not ready to venture beyond meat and potatoes, Ferdinand's menu includes a few midwestern standards such as hamburgers and steak as well. If you've still got room after a plate of enchiladas or fajitas, the Mexican fried ice cream is definitely worth a try. Watch out—the fresh fruit margaritas are dangerously delicious, and it's easy to forget that they're packed with alcohol.

Escanaba is home to the first of three **Hereford & Hops Steakhouse & Brewpub** (906-789-1945; www .herefordandhops.com; 624 Ludington St.; $$) restaurants, a combination grill-your-own-steak restaurant and microbrew pub started by two local couples. The restaurant, brewery, and pub are housed on the ground floor of a former hotel in downtown, built in 1914 and restored when the restaurant's owners purchased the building in 1994. The dining room is pleasant and simple, with white tablecloths and lots of exposed brick. In addition to the grill-your-own steaks (your choice of sirloin, rib eye, filet, T-bone, or New York strip), which are incredibly popular, the restaurant offers an expansive menu, including its take on the blooming onion, pork chops, pastas, pizzas, slabs of delicious BBQ ribs, prime rib, and a wide selection of seafood dishes that includes fresh walleye from nearby Fayette and a popular Friday fish fry. All the grill-your-own dinners come with a trip to the restaurant's legendary salad bar, plus baked potato and Texas toast. The brewery's microbrews are good and go really well with the steaks. In fact, its Whitetail Ale was a gold-medal winner at the 2006 World Beer Cup. In the summer, diners can sit outside on the patio, grill their own steaks, and enjoy some microbrews—almost like having a BBQ at home, except without the cleanup.

Just two blocks away is the delightfully kitschy Swedish Pantry (906-786-9606; www.swedishpantry .com; 819 Ludington St.; $) almost always as filled with people as it is chock-full of clocks from the motherland—none of them is set to the right time or even the same time, so at least one clock's chimes are usually ringing. The clocks and the bustle only make the place more fun, and the fact that the food is terrific only adds to the draw. From Scandinavian classics such as Swedish pancakes or Swedish meat-balls with lingonberries to down-home American standards such as pot roast and meatloaf, absolutely

everything here is homemade and delicious. And cheap! The restaurant hasn't raised its prices in years. Though breakfast is served all day, the restaurant is very busy most mornings and absolutely crammed on Sunday. If you're in a hurry, consider opting for something from the attached bakery—everything in it is oversize for some reason, from the muffins to the cookies, but it's all good, and the Swedish *limpa* bread is great for sandwiches.

Just a few miles north of Escanaba on the US 2, The Buck Inn (906-786-7453; $) is a longtime local favorite, especially during the hunting season. This is a good ol' all-American steakhouse with thick juicy cuts and seriously good burgers. Don't be afraid to bring non-meat-lovers here, though, at least not on account of the menu; the game heads decorating the place may be a different story. The expansive menu includes an assortment of salads, soups, wraps, seafood dishes, and even a few Mexican favorites. That said, the best thing going at The Buck, and what the restaurant has built its reputation on, are the steaks and the burgers, both of which are on offer with a wide selection of top-pings and sides.

Continue northeast on US 2 toward Gladstone to reach Delona Restaurant (906-786-6400; 7132 US 2; $). Very popular for hearty, delicious breakfasts, Delona has an atmosphere as warm and comfort-ing as its food. Located in an old house overflowing with charm, Delona also has a bakery that churns out delicious pies that people drive miles for.

MENOMINEE

A favorite family restaurant on the water overlooking Green Bay, in Menominee, Schloegel's (906-863-7888; 2720 10th St.; $) specializes in the local classics—walleye, whitefish, pasties, and brats—with some popular Swedish favorites, like Swedish pancakes and Swedish meatballs, thrown in. The bakery bakes delicious pies fresh daily, as well as bread and a number of giant pastries. The restaurant is a sort of stand-in for the U.P. itself: The atmosphere is friendly and casual, and the views are great.

A 145-year-old house across from the park on First Street is home to one of Menominee's favorite eateries, the Serving Spoon (906-863-7770; 821 First St.; $). With its porch, windows looking out on the waterfront, old hardwood floors, and charming quirks, the house feels more like an old friend than a restaurant. Despite its strict no-fryer policy, the Serving Spoon has become a popular spot for breakfast, lunch, and increasingly dinner. Though it places an emphasis on healthy cooking, the restaurant always puts taste first, and it shows. Cakes, pastries, and pies are baked daily, as are breads and soups. Lured by veggie sandwiches and traditional Reubens, Greek gyros, a popular portobello mushroom sandwich (sliced, seasoned portobellos grilled on tomato focaccia with sun-dried tomato pesto and fresh parmesan cheese), and arguably the town's best burgers, the Serving Spoon's loyal fan base always returns for more. Breakfast options include breakfast burritos, omelets, and a tasty veggie Benedict, as well as Menominee's best coffee. In the summer, when it stays open later, the café also serves pasta dishes and at least one special entrée per night, typically a fresh seafood dish.

Extend Your Stay

If you have more time, try these great places to see and things to do . . .

Although the U.P. is prized today for its natural beauty and vast array of outdoor sporting options, it is not a land devoid of museums or libraries. In fact, the U.P. is surprisingly diverse, culturally, for a region that is a bit removed and not incredibly developed. Owing to its industrial past, a lot of money was spent at one point on architecture in various parts of the peninsula. In the south central region, lumber, iron, and fishing barons built mansions on the waterfront and contributed to picturesque downtowns complete with well-designed libraries and city halls.

The industrial era also brought immigrants to this part of the U.P. from all over the world, which resulted in a lively ethnic mix that continues to color the cultural landscape, as descendants of Italian, Scandinavian, German, and Eastern European iron and lumber workers celebrate their heritage today with museums, restaurants, events, and traditional folk music. And of course before industry or immigrants shaped the local culture, a large Native American population called the shores of Lake Michigan home. Their rituals, celebrations, and artwork continue to have a prominent place in the region today.

HISTORIC BUILDINGS AND SITES

Now a private home, the Escanaba Carnegie Library (First Ave. and Seventh St., Escanaba) was originally built in 1902, one of the over 2,000 public libraries donated by Scottish industrialist and philanthropist Andrew Carnegie. Visitors are not allowed inside, but there's no law against gawking at its neoclassical columns from the street and wondering what it would be like to live in a 106-year-old library.

Southeast of Escanaba, down the Garden Peninsula, Fayette Historic State Park (906-644-2603; 13700 13.25 Lane, Garden) is a fossilized ghost town. The preserved and restored buildings of this one-time iron boomtown are a fascinating glimpse into life as it was. See "Family Fun" sidebar for more details.

The Upper Peninsula's boom-and-bust mining industry resulted in the creation and abandonment of several towns. Today, ghost towns like Fayetteville, pictured here, are tourist attractions. Matt Girvan

LIGHTHOUSES

At the Peninsula Point Lighthouse (from US 2 east of Rapid River, take CR 513 south approximately 18 miles to Stonington) visitors can climb the spiral staircase to the top for terrific 360-degree views of the lake, the bay, various islands, and the nearby Garden peninsula. In August and September, thousands of migrating monarch butterflies stop here to rest on their way to Mexico. It's also a good spot for migrating birds to take a breather, which makes bird-watching here spectacular in the spring.

In Escanaba's Ludington Park, Sand Point Lighthouse is a picturesque New England–style lighthouse, painted bright white with a red roof. The

Escanaba boasts one of a handful of Carnegie Libraries in the U.P.   Andrew Jameson

Sand Point Lighthouse was decommissioned in 1939 and completely restored by the county historical society in the 1980s. Now, summertime visitors can check out the restored keeper's quarters and climb the stairs to the top of the tower for a view across Little Bay de Noc that includes Escanaba's marina and a glimpse of the Peninsula Point lighthouse across the bay.

MUSEUMS AND GALLERIES

Downtown Escanaba features two great galleries. Housed in a pleasant red-brick building, **East Ludington Gallery** (906-786-0300; www.east ludingtongallery.com) is a co-op gallery that showcases the work of 35 local artists, including everything from photography to painting, wood carving, pottery, glass, jewelry, and ceramics. Although pleasant just to browse through, this is also a great place to look for unique gifts from the area, priced in a wide range from completely affordable to big splurge.

Located in a former church school and gymnasium donated by the Irish-born widow of William Bonifas, a lumberman from Luxembourg who made his fortune in the U.P., the **William Bonifas Fine Arts Center** (906-786-3833; www.bonifasarts.org) hosts a rotating schedule of exhibits focused predominantly on local artists, with the occasional international exhibit thrown in. The center also offers numerous art classes, ranging from beginning-level classes in a variety of media to youth art classes to advanced classes for working artists. Members of the center get a discount on classes, but they're very reasonably priced to begin with. The design of the center itself is reason enough for a visit—the original Romanesque-style exterior of the church school and gym has been restored, and the interior has been completely renovated and modernized to house the center's administrative offices, climate-controlled galleries, artist studios, a pottery studio, and a theater.

Farther south, in the more populated Wisconsin border town of Menominee, the Menominee County Heritage Museum (906-863-9000; www.menomineehistoricalsociety.org; 904 11th Ave.) features ornate eaves and stained-glass windows that seem better suited to a church than a museum. It makes sense—the building, which is on the National Register of Historic Buildings, was formerly St. John's Catholic Church. Today this large red and white structure houses the summer-only museum's collection of photographs, paintings, artifacts, and ephemera. Popular exhibits include an animated model circus, dugout canoes from the Menominee Indians, and photos of early Polish, Scandinavian, and German immigrants to the area.

NIGHTLIFE

If you leave the Infinity Coffee House (906-553-4179; 815 Ludington St.) feeling anything short of enchanted, go back inside awhile—you need some more of their medicine. In addition to fantastic coffee that puts Starbucks to shame, Infinity is a buzzing, happy hub for everyone from local retirees to young artists and writers. On weekends and Tuesday nights, the coffee shop is also a live music venue, and in fact with so many local musicians hanging out here, it's not unusual to hear live music that hasn't been scheduled. The café keeps a well-stocked game shelf as well, and the service revolves around the motto "Come as a stranger, leave as a friend."

SHOPPING

Antiques and Books

Traders' Point Antique Mall (906-341-7500; www.traderspointantiques .com; 375 Traders' Point Dr., Manistique) is a high-quality antiques mall in Manistique, adjacent to a bookshop and the popular Upper Crust Café, Traders' Point is just as jam-packed full of stuff as the average antiques mall, but it's smaller and feels less cluttered. You get the feeling that everything here has been placed where it is for a reason, not just thrown together

Mines to Wines

Three new wineries in this region—one in Manistique and two on the Garden Peninsula—make for a pleasant little wine trail that gives the better known wineries in the Traverse City area a run for their money. **Mackinaw Trail Winery** (www.mackinawtrailwinery.com) is located on the waterfront, next to the marina, in Manistique. The tasting room pours generous tastes of the winery's reds, whites, fruit wines and

Threefold Vine Winery is one of a handful of new wineries worth exploring in the U.P.

Courtesy Pure Michigan

dessert wines; they're all good, but this region is particularly well suited to producing ice wines, so make sure you give it a try.

Fruit wines are also a specialty of the region, particularly those from the vineyards on the Garden Peninsula, where loam soil, cool springs and warm autumns make for great fruit. Stop by **Garden Bay Winery** (www .gardenbaywinery.com) and **Threefold Vine Winery** (www.exploringthe north.com/threefold/vine), both in Garden, to try lovely raspberry, strawberry, blueberry, and honey wines.

in the usual antiques jumble. And the prices are generally very good. Traders' Point also sells a number of antiques available only in this neck of the woods, including local artwork and Munising woodenware.

In Escanaba, the small, independent, locally owned Canterbury Bookstore (906-786-0751; 908 Ludington St.) sells new books in a variety of categories. Canterbury is a good stop if you're looking for a regional history or nature book. The shop also carries a number of regional hiking and nature guides and a unique assortment of Scandinavian books.

In the southwest corner of the region, Timeless Treasures Antique Mall in Menominee (906-864-2412; 902 Second St.) occupies a groovy 1920s theater, which seems fitting. A trip to Timeless Treasures is worth it just to check out the building, but you're bound to find at least some small trinket in the mountains of collectibles for sale here from dozens of dealers.

One of the best bookshops in this part of the peninsula is also in Menominee. Aurora Books (906-863-5266; www.aurorabooks.com; 625 First St.) is a fantastic independent bookstore housed in a charming old brick building on the waterfront in downtown Menominee, Aurora sells both new and used books and a few collectible rare books as well. Even if you're not in the market for a new book, the store is worth a visit just to check out the local art and historical photographs lining its walls.

Gift and Specialty Shops

It is highly unlikely that you've ever set foot in a store similar to the Noc Bay Trading Company (906-789-0505; www.nocbay.com; 1133 Washington Ave., Escanaba). A regular stop for local Native Americans in preparation for the regional powwows, the shop is full of everything that goes into the dance costumes, music, and revelry of a powwow, from buckskin and beads to drum parts to traditional Native American music, with plenty of history and information to make it an absolutely fascinating shop. The store's "Learning Circle" has compiled detailed instructions for various costumes and items and made them available to its customers both in the store and on its Web site. Visiting the store is an experience not to be missed!

Nearby, in downtown Escanaba, Sayklly's Confectionery and Gifts (906-786-1524; www.saykllyscandy.com; 1304 Ludington St.) offers a completely different experience. A local tradition since 1906, the shop's hand-dipped chocolates and chewy saltwater taffy are popular gifts both locally and beyond. Although you can get the same quality sweets at the family's other location in the Delta Plaza Mall, shopping at the original storefront downtown is a far more enjoyable affair.

Occupying a historic building on a corner of downtown Menominee, Art & Décor (906-864-7243; 601 First St.) is a spacious, light-filled gallery and home gift shop that is full of unique finds, from local and international painting, sculpture, ceramics, and photography to cool home finds like recycled glass tumblers, unusual lamps, and handmade candles.

The Great Outdoors

Outdoor adventures and activities in south central U.P.

The U.P. is as much a nature lover's dream as it is an outdoorsman's paradise, equal parts wildlife refuge and hunter's haven. This particular region is especially popular with sportsmen for its dozens of inland lakes, which are incredible for fishing in the summer, and its large deer population, which makes for excellent hunting in the fall. Meanwhile, bird-watchers love the Seney National Wildlife Refuge, home to numerous species, many of them rare. Of course Lake Michigan's beaches are always popular as well—a day spent lying on the lake's shores and dipping into its cool blue waters is just about perfect.

Beware of the Blackflies

One word of caution—when the snow finally melts away and the ground defrosts, the U.P. is home to legions of blackflies, which are extremely unpleasant. And we're not just talking annoying, buzzing flies—these guys bite. And swarm. Though it shifts a bit from year to year, depending on how long the winter was, a general rule is that if you're going to the U.P. from mid-May to mid-June, bring insect repellent, leave your cologne and perfume at home, and wear long pants and sleeves in light colors. The popular mosquito repellent DEET doesn't really work on blackflies, but some people swear by Avon's Skin So Soft and B vitamins. The blackflies tend not to bite indoors, and they disappear at night, but staying inside all day and coming out at night isn't why most people come to the U.P.

In the fall visitors flock to view the beautiful colors as the leaves turn and to hunt various deer and fowl; and in the winter the well-groomed cross-country ski trails, mile after mile of snowmobile trails, and family-friendly ski resorts bring almost as many visitors in December as the summer sun brings in July.

BEACHES

Thanks to its assortment of inland lakes, islands, and peninsulas and its long, unbroken stretch of Lake Michigan shoreline, this region of the U.P. offers more beaches than any other. The beach fun begins in the easternmost part of the region, with Lake Michigan Beach, off the US 2 near Brevort. This long stretch of perfect white-sand beach is backed by low dunes, with Hiawatha National Forest in the background. The beach is also part of the national forest—to get to it you need to pay the $5 day-use fee.

Traveling west, you'll hit Cut River Gorge, off US 2, just a few miles down the road. This is an excellent spot for a picnic and a swim. Turn off and park by the charming Cut River Bridge. Pathways on the east and west sides of the bridge lead down into the Cut River Valley, to the mouth of the river, and then out to Lake Michigan. The river has carved out a beautiful limestone gorge on its way to the lake. The walk out to the beach on Lake Michigan takes about 15 minutes.

Back on US 2, west of Naubinway, turn south onto Gould City Road, which dead-ends at Scott Point. About 10 miles off US 2, Scott Point feels a million miles away from anywhere, and because it's not an obvious turnoff, you've got a good chance of having this beautiful, seemingly endless white-sand beach all to yourself.

Continuing on US 2, just past Manistique, you'll pass Rogers Park, another great, sandy Lake Michigan swimming beach, surrounded by pine forest.

If you turn off US 2 and head south down the Garden Peninsula, there's a fantastic, secluded little beach right next to the Fayette Historical State Park, a well-preserved ghost town.

Nearby, east of Garden, turn east on Portage Bay Road. It's a bumpy ride, but you'll be rewarded with an afternoon at Portage Bay, a lovely white-sand beach surrounded by low dunes and shade trees; the bay is calm and pleasant for swimming, and in spring, the area is awash with wildflowers.

Ludington Park encompasses several miles of beachfront property adjacent to downtown Escanaba.   Matt Girvan

Walking distance from downtown Escanaba, Ludington Park (off Ludington St.) is a fantastic 120-acre lakeside park with lots of bright green grass, a jogging trail, shade trees, playgrounds, tennis courts, concert area, and benches and picnic tables overlooking the water. The bridge to Arnson Island leads to an idyllic sandy swimming beach.

BICYCLING

Ludington Park and the city of Escanaba are perhaps best explored by bicycle, and you can rent bikes at the Escanaba Marina, located within the park. Five miles of concrete bike paths swerve through the 120-acre lakeside park at the end of Ludington Street, downtown Escanaba's hub. This is an easy, scenic ride.

BIRD-WATCHING

The U.P. is world-renowned for bird-watching, thanks in large part to the Seney National Wildlife Refuge. With its thousands of acres of protected woodland, there are few places on earth better suited to bird-watching. In addition to the Seney Wildlife Refuge, the Hiawatha National Forest and a number of smaller parks attract numerous species as well. The region's many inland lakes are also home to the notoriously edgy loon, as well as osprey, bald eagle, and sandhill crane.

Thanks in part to their remote location, the flooded woodlands known as Gene's Pond (north of Felch, off CR 581; after about 5 miles turn left at PUBLIC ACCESS sign and follow the road to parking lot), created by the Sturgeon River, are a fantastic place to spot rare large birds. Loons and cormorants hover near the shore and make quick dives for fish in the shallow pond, while bald eagles and ospreys make big powerful plunges from high above, and great blue herons nest in the tops of nearby trees. Beyond the main pond, a large cedar and pine swamp hides numerous warblers and other songbirds. Be careful venturing too far into the swamp, as it is also home to bobcat, bear, and the occasional gray wolf.

With its historic lighthouse and remote location, Peninsula Point, in Stonington (from US 2 east of Rapid River, take CR 513 south approximately 18 miles), is a favorite resting spot of various migrating birds, and permanent home to gulls, duck, geese, heron, and various other shorebirds and songbirds. Though a bit off the beaten path, this spot is especially popular with birders in the spring and fall when migrating owls, hawks, and eagles land here. Thousands of migrating monarch butterflies also stop here every fall on their way to Mexico. Between the fall colors, the lake, the various birds, and the huge swaths of beautiful butterflies, it's hard not to be completely enchanted by this spot in autumn.

Near Escanaba, the protected bay and interconnected network of

The trumpeter swan is one of several birds that call the Seney Wildlife Refuge home.
Wikimedia Commons

coastal wetlands created by Portage Creek are known as Portage Marsh. The marsh provides shelter to a huge variety of shorebirds, songbirds, waterfowl, and migratory birds. According to the Michigan Department of Natural Resources (DNR), state-threatened birds like bald eagles and Caspian and common terns are commonly spotted here.

At the Rainey Wildlife Viewing Area, 5 miles north of Manistique (off MI 94 in Thompson), wooden boardwalks lead into a quiet maple and birch forest, then over Smith Creek and surrounding wetlands to an observation plat-

The majestic osprey is one of many birds seen often in the Upper Peninsula.
Wikimedia Commons

form. Songbirds are plentiful here, especially warblers, and a nearby bald eagle nest makes for prime viewing in the spring and early summer.

CAMPING

In this part of the U.P., the Hiawatha National Forest provides a variety of camping options, as do numerous smaller parks. Whether you prefer to camp in untouched wilderness, in a shady campground with modern conveniences, or on the beach, you'll find plenty of options here.

A large and popular campground with all the amenities, including water, flush toilets, and even a convenience store on-site, Brevoort Lake Campground (1-877-444-6777; open May through September; $25) has 70 sites scattered throughout the sandy peninsula between Boedne Bay and Brevoort Lake. Most sites have direct water access to the 4,000-plus-acre lake. In addition to several short trails, the North Country Trail

Camping Information

We have listed our favorite campgrounds here. For detailed information about all the campgrounds in the federal- and state-maintained parks of the region, visit the following Web sites:

Hiawatha National Forest:
www.fs.fed.us/r9/forests /hiawatha

Ottawa National Forest and Sylvania Wilderness Area:
www.fs.fed.us/r9/ottawa

and the Route of the Sand Dunes pass through the campground, providing two excellent hiking opportunities. Fishing is fantastic here—a walleye-spawning reef in the lake ensures a near-constant supply of walleye, but smallmouth bass, crappies, sunfish, perch, northern pike, and muskellunge are also caught here.

In addition to a sandy swimming beach with access to the usually warm waters of Brevoort Lake, campers can take an easy 2-mile hike to nearby Lake Michigan Beach.

Lake Michigan Beach (open May through September; $16) also has a popular campground, featuring several large campsites and spectacular views of the lake. Some sites are placed between 20- to 30-foot-high stabilized dunes for maximum privacy. Sites are available for RVs and trailer tents as well. Swimming is allowed in the lake, but the water can be cold, and when the wind picks up, the surf can get rough. The wind has actually been known to produce surf-worthy waves, but with no lifeguard on duty and a strong undercurrent, it's not a good place for beginners.

Farther west, past Manistique, Flowing Well (from US 2 at Nahma Junction, take FR 13 north for 3 miles; open mid-May through November; $9) offers 10 large sites along the banks of the Sturgeon River. This spot is ideal for fishermen—the river is known for trout fishing (brook and steelhead) and salmon—and for travelers looking to avoid the crowds but still stay within reasonable driving distance of the U.P.'s big attractions. Sites are extra large, and there are plenty of trees and space between them, so

Lake Michigan Beach is one of the best beaches in the U.P. EPA

The Sturgeon River is known for great trout fishing.   Robert Emperley

privacy is not a problem here. Some sites are on the bank, overlooking the river, others are placed farther back in the forest. In the springtime, wildflowers take over the forest, making the site even prettier than usual.

Located between Manistique and Escanaba, Little Bay de Noc Recreation Area (www.fs.fed.us/r9/forests/hiawatha; open May through September; fees from $11) provides a fantastic waterfront camping in the Hiawatha National Forest, with large rustic sites arranged around the shore of Little Bay de Noc, on the north end of Lake Michigan. Each site has a view of the water and a trail to the shore, and sites are separated by trees for privacy. Fishing in the bay is excellent, particularly for walleye, and sunsets here are spectacular. The campground can get very busy in summer, and reservations are accepted only for group sites.

South from Manistique, down the Garden Peninsula, Portage Bay Campground (take MI 183 south past Garden, turn on Portage Bay Rd.; open May through November; $15) is a lovely secluded campground in a state forest, with sites placed throughout the forest surrounding dunes, wetlands, and a quiet cove. Arriving at Portage Bay down a long dirt country road feels like discovering a beautiful new corner of the world. In the spring, the wildflowers and birds are a sight to see. Swimming is pleasant at the sandy cove, and two walking loops through the forest explain the significance of the surrounding plants to Ojibwa life. Although a popular spot, Portage Bay's remote location keeps it from getting overcrowded, even in the summer.

In addition to Lake Michigan, the region's vast network of inland lakes and rivers makes it ideally suited to canoeing and kayaking, whether you're an expert paddler or just testing the waters. To rent a canoe and connect with a guide, head to **Big Cedar Campground and Canoe Livery**, on the banks of the Manistique River, near the **Seney Wildlife Refuge** (906-586-6684; 7936 MI 77, Germfask). From there you can paddle down the Manistique (an easy-to-moderate paddle) and into the refuge.

Rentals are also available on-site at **Brevoort Lake**, which promises easy paddling over a serene 4,000-plus acres.

Manistique River (Germfask, along MI 77 north of US 2) is an easy-to-moderate paddle. Launches are near Germfask; the river flows into Seney National Wildlife Refuge.

CROSS-COUNTRY SKIING

As in the rest of the U.P., cross-country skiing is a popular way to get through those long stretches of winter. **Rapid River National Cross Country Ski Trail** (Hiawatha National Forest, off US 41, 6 miles north of Rapid River) is one of the best cross-country ski trails in the entire U.P., mostly because it is the most varied, both in the skill level of the various trails and in the scenery and topography. Five Nordic ski loops and two skating loops are available, and the trails meander in and out of dunes, lowland swamps, and pine forests.

FISHING

As you might suspect, with all its lakes and streams, this region boasts some absolutely phenomenal fishing spots. Whitefish are plentiful in Lake Michigan and several of the inland lakes, trout abound in the rivers and streams, and fishermen come from far and wide to catch salmon, bass, perch, pike, and muskellunge (musky) as well. To fish in the state parks and national forests, you must have a Michigan fishing license if you're over the age of 17. Visit www.michigan.gov for details.

It's easy enough to fish on your own at any of the lakes or rivers in the region, but a guide who really knows these waters can't hurt. **Delta Dawn Charters** (906-428-9039; www.deltadawnchartersup.com; Escanaba Municipal Marina, Loren W. Jenkins Memorial Dr.) operates a comfortable 24-foot 232 Gulfstream Grady-White, captained by avid local fisherman Bill Myers, who focuses on catching walleye, salmon, and trout. Charters leave out of Escanaba, Manistique, and Gladstone.

Places to Fish

Roughly east to west:

Brevoort Lake (from US 2 turn north on the Brevort Camp Road [FR 3108], then right at FR 3473 to the campground entrance) Large managed and stocked lake with walleye, smallmouth bass, crappies, sunfish, perch, northern pike, and muskellunge.

Big Manistique Lake (east of MI 77, near Curtis) Large, deep lake best known for yellow perch. Also good for ice fishing in winter.

South Manistique Lake (east of MI 77, near Curtis) Smaller, shallow lake, great for muskellunge, walleye, and bass.

Flowing Well and Sturgeon River (from US 2 at Nahma Junction take FH 13 about 3 miles north to Flowing Well) River fishing for trout and salmon.

Haymeadow Creek (US 2 east from Rapid River 1.6 miles, then turn left on CR 509 and go north 9.4 miles to the entrance) High-quality trout stream known for brook trout.

Big and Little Bays de Noc (Escanaba) The "walleye capital of the world" and home to numerous professional walleye fishing competitions, the Bays de Noc are also full of salmon, bass, perch, and pike. Little Bay de Noc has made numerous top-10 fishing lists.

GOLF

Golf has really taken off in the U.P. over the last several years, and visitors are typically just as surprised by the quality of the courses up here as they are by the low greens fees. Many of the 18-hole courses here today started out as 9-hole courses, and there are still several public 9-hole courses in the region, including the Country Meadows Golf Course in Escanaba.

Also in Escanaba, the Escanaba Country Club (906-786-4430; www.escanabacc.com; 12th Ave. South, Escanaba) has the honor of being the oldest course in Delta County. It was built in 1915 as a 9-hole course and expanded to a full 18-hole course in 1991. It now includes tree-lined fairways as well as several challenging water holes.

Highland Golf Club (906-466-7457; www.highlandgolfclub.net) is Escanaba's more casual 18-hole course. Wide-open fairways and a mellow atmosphere make this a great course for beginners, with a few challenges thrown in for good measure.

Northeast of Escanaba, in Gladstone, Terrace Bluff Golf Club at

Terrace Bay Inn (906-428-2343; www.terracebay.com) is one of the most respected courses in the area and has been rated number 1 in the U.P. more than once. Terrace Bluff is a championship course cut into the woods on a bluff overlooking Terrace Bay. The course is both scenic and challenging, with narrow fairways bounded by beautiful birch and maple forests and panoramic views of the bay below.

HIKING

The U.P. is full of hiking trails that are both challenging and beautiful. The 40-mile Bay de Noc–Grand Island Trail, from Bay de Noc near Rapid River all the way up to Grand Island near Munising, is no exception. The trail roughly follows the route historians believe the Ojibwa used to portage goods between Lake Superior and Lake Michigan. Although there are no loops, there are three trailheads, and views of the Whitefish River Valley coupled with pretty streams and mature forests make the trail interesting enough that hiking just a section of it back and forth is well worth doing. North of Manistique, in the Hiawatha National Forest, Pine Marten Run is a 26-mile system of hiking and horseback-riding trails with five distinct loops. Although all the trails are lovely, my favorites are the Triangle Lake Trail (7.2 miles), which passes by active Indian River beaver communities, and Ironjaw Lake for its lake views. Still, the Swan Lake Trail passes close enough to the water for an afternoon swim, making it the obvious choice on a warm summer day.

North Country National Scenic Trail

The North Country National Scenic Trail is the longest scenic trail in the United States; to date only four hikers have completed successful end-to-end trips. The trail spans 4,600 miles and seven states, from New York to North Dakota. You can hike the North Country Trail across the entire breadth of the U.P., from the Mackinac Bridge in the east to Ironwood in the far west, before heading down into Wisconsin. The trail was first envisioned in the late 1960s as part of the National Scenic Trails program, was eventually completed in the early 1970s, and finally officially designated in the early 1980s. While trekking across the entire peninsula may sound like a bit much, many hikers take advantage of pleasant sections of the trail running through both the Hiawatha and Ottawa National Forests. For information on the trail, visit www.northcountrytrail.org.

Family Fun

One of the peninsula's favorite spots is only a few miles from Manistique: **Kitch-iti-kipi** (Ojibwa for "Big Spring") in **Palms Book State Park** (906-341-2355; www.michigan .gov/palmsbook). This thunderous sulfur spring bubbles up into a crystal-clear, turquoise pond surrounded by silvery logs and bright green moss. Kitch-iti-kipi, Michigan's largest freshwater spring, is 200 feet across and 40 feet deep. According to the state's DNR, over 10,000 gallons a minute

Large trout congregate around the viewing boat at Big Spring, waiting to be fed by families. Matt Girvan

gush from fissures in the underlying limestone, and the flow continues throughout the year at a constant 45 degrees Fahrenheit. The fun begins with a big wooden barge, self-propelled by a wheel in the back. Stay to the back right if you want to play captain, but make sure someone in your crew gets a spot around the center viewing area—a big hole cut in the center of the barge. As the barge creeps out over beautiful turquoise waters, giant brown trout swimming by will garner the first "wow!" followed soon thereafter by "oh wow!" as the barge approaches the bubbling spring below. Trout food is available for sale in the convenience store at the park entrance, which is probably why those trout are so big.

Well worth the detour off the beaten path, **Fayette Historic State Park** (906-644-2603; 13700 13.25 Lane, Garden) is a real-live ghost town, or at least as close as you can get to one inside a state park. Much of the former booming iron town has been carefully restored and preserved. Visitors can check out the old mine and ironworks, the former hotel, the town's tiny school, living quarters, and a giant model of Fayette as it once was. The rest of the park is well suited to a picnic: A half-moon bay on one side is bordered by towering cliffs, and there's a pleasant and quiet sandy swimming beach next door.

At the southern end of downtown Escanaba, **Ludington Park** (906-786-4141; the end of Ludington St. to Seventh Ave., Escanaba) is a great place to spend an hour, an afternoon, or an entire day, depending on how much time you've got. The park occupies 5 miles on Little Bay de Noc and includes a large playground, a sandy swimming beach on a charming little island (Arnson), tennis courts, and a marina that rents bicycles. In addition to playing, picnicking, biking, or just hanging out, you might be able to catch a summer concert in the park's outdoor band shell, and the shoreline is a decent fishing spot as well.

For information about state hunting regulations and hunting seasons for various game, see chapter 7.

Guides and Outfitters

U.P. Wide Adventure Guide. 906-430-0547; www.upwideadventureguide.com; W6508 Epoufette Bay Road, Naubinway

Wild Spirit Guide Service. 906-497-4408; www.wildspiritguide.com; N15107 Township Line Road, Powers, 30 miles west of Escanaba off US 2

Public Land Hunting Locations

Hiawatha National Forest. Near Stonington, south of Rapid River, on CR 513 off US 2

Indian Lake State Park. 8970W CR 442, Manistique

Fayette Historic State Park. 13700 13.25 Lane, Garden, 30 miles south on MI 183 off US 2

SNOWMOBILING

The U.P. is extremely popular with snowmobilers. Its trails get written up in snowmobiling magazines, and the sport manages to get people excited about the prospect of a long winter. The state actually maintains over 6,000 miles of groomed snowmobile trails, not out of the goodness of its heart but because the sport generates a lot of tourism revenue. Several areas that are calm lakeside retreats in summer turn into buzzing centers of activity in the winter. Maps of the state-maintained snowmobile trails are available online from the Michigan DNR (www.michigan.gov/dnr). Snowmobile rentals are available at the Fish and Hunt Shop in Curtis (906-586-9531; www.fishand huntshop.com) for $150 to $250 per day.

Nearly every snowmobile trail in the U.P. is accessible from Curtis, and that's no exaggeration. The Curtis Area Chamber of Commerce grooms and maintains 140 miles of snowmobile trails around the Manistique Lakes (www.curtischamber.com and www.curtismi.com; call 1-800-ok curtis for trail report and information). This system of trails connects to the 6,000-plus-mile state snowmobile trail system, as well as other local systems, making it possible to ride between towns and areas.

3

North Central

PICTURED ROCKS AND MARQUETTE

THIS STRETCH OF LAKE SUPERIOR is home to both the U.P.'s most-visited national park (the vividly beautiful Pictured Rocks National Lakeshre) and the U.P.'s largest city (Marquette). Although the area farther south of Marquette is technically Iron Country, this is where iron was truly king, pumping money and people into the area for years and producing some of the world's highest-quality ore. The town of Marquette was once a busy shipping port for both iron and sandstone from local quarries, tinged red by the iron ore and called brownstone when it arrived to builders in Boston and New York.

As with the other mining centers throughout the U.P., Marquette's iron business drew immigrant laborers from all over Europe, with a high proportion of British (mostly from Cornwall), Finnish, Canadian, Scandinavian, and Italian immigrants. The descendants of those miners have created a lively and unique culture in modern-day Marquette.

And, though the mines are mostly closed, this is one of the few areas of the

LEFT AND RIGHT: Striking Pictured Rocks along the shore of Lake Superior is one of Michigan's most visited sights.. Matt Girvan

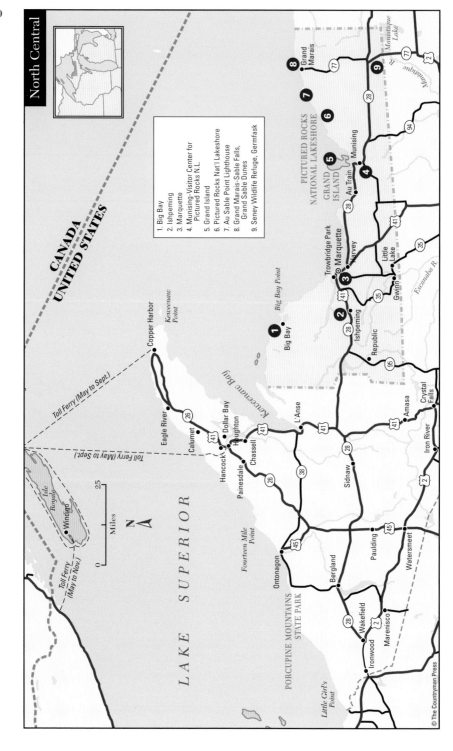

North Central

CANADA
UNITED STATES

1. Big Bay
2. Ishpeming
3. Marquette
4. Munising-Visitor Center for Pictured Rocks N.L.
5. Grand Island
6. Pictured Rocks Nat'l Lakeshore
7. Au Sable Point Lighthouse
8. Grand Marais-Sable Falls, Grand Sable Dunes
9. Seney Wildlife Refuge, Germfask

LAKE SUPERIOR

PORCUPINE MOUNTAINS STATE PARK

© The Countryman Press

U.P. that has remained economically prosperous. Northern Michigan University's campus in Marquette draws just under 10,000 young people to the town every fall. As in most college towns, the students keep a number of bars, cafés, restaurants, and stores open in downtown Marquette.

The campus isn't the only draw. The area's lakeshore is one of the loveliest in the U.P., with 3-billion-year-old rock outcroppings and long stretches of white sand backed by large forests and rolling dunes, plus world-class trout fishing in Au Train, world-famous wildlife viewing in the Seney National Wildlife Refuge, and the unparalleled beauty of Pictured Rocks National Lakeshore.

Of course, because of all its charms, this area is inundated with visitors in the summer, but even still there's plenty of space. In winter, a number of cross-country and snowmobile trails bring a second tourism season to the area, and those same trails are popular with mountain bikers in the summer months.

Pick Your Spot

Best places to stay in north central U.P., and nearby . . .

AU TRAIN, MUNISING, AND PICTURED ROCKS

In the heart of Au Train, Pinewood Lodge Bed & Breakfast (906-892-8300; www.pinewoodlodgebnb.com; open April through November; $$$) is a lovely log cabin resort on the shores of Lake Superior. The resort is not especially kid-friendly, catering instead to couples looking to get away. In addition to seven rooms, all with knotty pine interiors, large and comfy pine-log beds, private baths, and TV/VCR units and most with lovely Lake Superior views, the resort boasts a bright and cheerful garden full of flowers, adjacent to a gazebo on the bluff overlooking the lake. There are few better places in the area to watch the sun set over the lake. Even hammocks and pillows are supplied. Pinewood is also in the enviable position of being spitting distance from the deservedly famous Brownstone Inn, the best restaurant for several miles.

The Rock River Beach Resort (906-892-8112; open April through November, two-night minimum; $$$, no credit cards accepted), down the road, is more of a family-friendly spot, with eight large and pleasant summer cottages framing a small beach where the Rock River flows into Lake Superior. All but one of the cottages face Lake Superior, with terrific views, and a large shared patio is outfitted with rocking chairs for guests to watch the sunset or the northern lights. The cottages themselves are finished in knotty pine and feature modern country furnishings—very

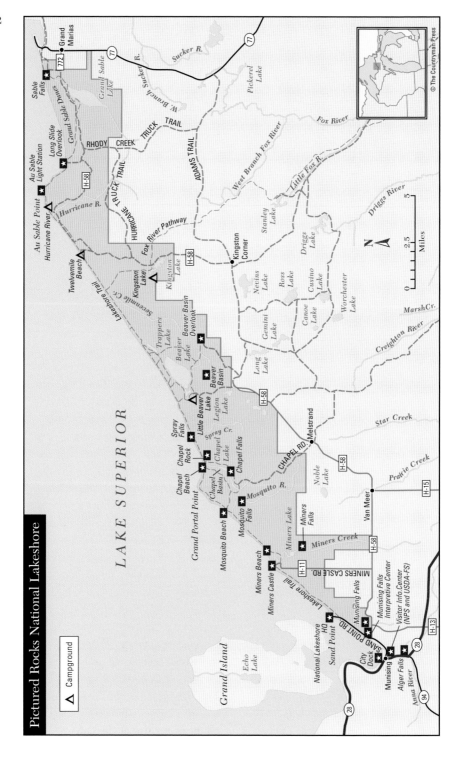

Pictured Rocks National Lakeshore

△ Campground

LAKE SUPERIOR

The beautiful historic buildings of downtown Marquette.   Wikimedia Commons

comfortable, but don't expect things like TV and wireless here. Rock River is all about getting outside. The resort's beach is half sandy, half rocky, with great fishing and kayaking available a few steps out your front door. In addition to immediately available recreation, the resort is conveniently close to Pictured Rocks, Au Train, and Munising.

Near Munising, the Falling Rock Lodge (906-387-1623; open year-round, one-week minimum in summer, two-day minimum rest of the year; $$, no credit cards accepted) is a lovely, newish red cedar two-bedroom with a green metal roof and a deck looking out over spring-fed Powell Lake in the Hiawatha National Forest. Owned and operated by the Dwyers, owners of the popular Falling Rock Café & Bookstore in downtown Munising, the house is as cozy and delightful as the café, with a large picture window overlooking the lake, handmade quilts on all the beds, big overstuffed armchairs, and a delightful tree house in the backyard. The Dwyers have stocked the lodge with bicycles for exploring the forest, along with a kayak, a rowboat, and fishing equipment. Satellite TV, a DVD player, and high-speed wireless Internet will keep anyone from missing the modern world too much, and the lodge comes with a basket full of coffee from the Dwyers' café, along with baked goods for breakfast and coupons for use at the café.

Also in the Hiawatha Forest, Timber Ridge Motel Suites and Lodge (906-387-3790; open year-round; $) was initially built with snowmobilers in mind—it's located on a trail and provides access to over 300 miles of other trails—but these large and comfy suites are a real find during other seasons as well. Called motel suites, the rooms are really more like condos, each with its own private deck overlooking Hovey Lake. The view is pretty spectacular any time of year, but especially when framed by the fiery red and glowing gold leaves of fall. Though the place feels completely cut off from the rest of the world, it's only a quarter mile to the nearest restaurant and 10 miles to Munising, making it an ideal home base for summer travelers looking to take in some of the local sights. In the winter, in addition to snowmobiling, one of the region's best cross-country ski trails is within walking distance, and Timber Ridge provides a heated repair shed, plus a sauna to warm and soothe muscles at the end of the day.

MARQUETTE AND ENVIRONS

There's nothing like spending the night in a lighthouse to make you feel like you're really getting away from it all. Perched atop a cliff overlooking Lake Superior, several miles north of Marquette, the red-brick Big Bay Point Lighthouse Bed and Breakfast (906-345-9957; www.bigbaylighthouse.com; open year-round; $$, no credit cards accepted) is a prime location for a cozy B&B. Sticking with a nautical theme befitting the architecture and location, each of the inn's seven guest rooms is named after a different keeper of the lighthouse or one of their assistants or helpers. Many of the rooms face Lake Superior for fantastic views. Because of the inn's remote location out on the point, surrounded by nearly 50 acres of wilderness, guests are also likely to spot various wildlife, including deer and fox. In addition to sitting by the fire and reading in the inn's shared sitting room, guests can hike from the lighthouse to various sights, including waterfalls. Breakfast includes fresh-baked breads and muffins, fruit, juice, coffee, and a hot entrée every morning.

At the opposite end of the spectrum, the Landmark Inn (906-228-2580; www.thelandmarkinn .com; open year-round; $$$) is smack in the middle of downtown Marquette. Not just cleverly named, the Landmark Inn is the pride and joy of Marquette's lodging industry. Originally opened in 1930 as the Northland Hotel, this was a local hub from the 1930s to the 1960s and a destination for well-known visitors, including Amelia Earhart, Abbot and Costello, Duke Ellington, and Louis Armstrong. After falling into disrepair throughout the 1970s, the hotel closed in the 1980s. A massive renovation started in 1995 and was completed

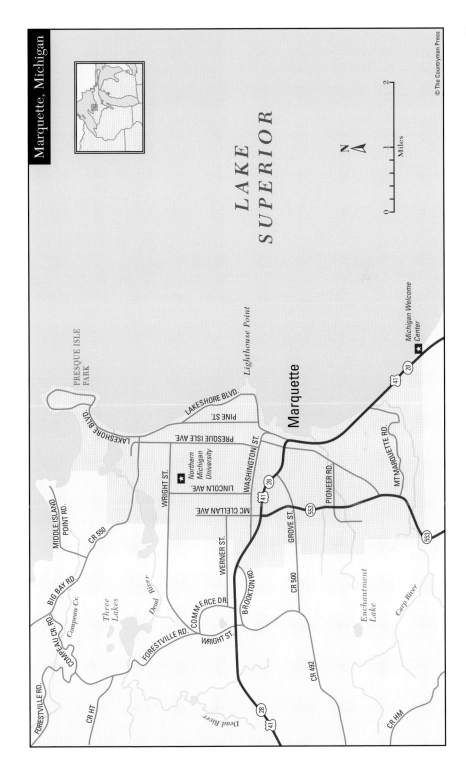

Marquette, Michigan

LAKE SUPERIOR

PRESQUE ISLE PARK

Lighthouse Point

Marquette

Michigan Welcome Center

LAKESHORE BLVD.

LAKESHORE BLVD.

PINE ST.

PRESQUE ISLE AVE.

WASHINGTON ST.

Northern Michigan University

WRIGHT ST.

LINCOLN AVE.

MC CLELLAN AVE.

MIDDLE ISLAND POINT RD.

CR 550

BIG BAY RD.

COMPEAU CR. RD.

FORESTVILLE RD.

CR HT

Compeau Cr.

Three Lakes

Dead River

FORESTVILLE RD.

COMMERCE DR.

WERNER ST.

WRIGHT ST.

BROOKTON RD.

GROVE ST.

CR 500

CR 492

Dead River

Enchantment Lake

Carp River

CR HM

PIONEER RD.

MT MARQUETTE RD.

553

553

28

41

28

41

28

41

N

0 1 2
Miles

in 1997, after which the hotel became Michigan's first to be awarded membership in Historic Hotels of America. Today the Landmark has regained its position in Marquette society. Capers, the lobby restaurant, is popular with guests and locals alike for its American take on Spanish tapas and its inventive Sunday brunch, while the more casual Northwoods Pub draws a beer and nachos crowd most nights, and the upstairs cocktail lounge is popular with Marquette professionals catching up over after-work drinks. Half the hotel faces Lake Superior, giving a fair percentage of the rooms nice lake views. Rooms have been decorated in a pleasant, modern take on Victorian, dominated by bold colors and simple stripes, as opposed to the over-the-top frill you see at many historic inns. Some of the rooms, such as

The Landmark Inn is truly a landmark in Marquette. Naoko McCracken

the Amelia Earhart Room, have private fireplaces and walls dotted with information about the room's well-known guest.

Local Flavors

Taste of the town—restaurants, cafés, bars, bistros, etc.

Dining options vary greatly as you make your way around Lake Superior's shore, dominated by locally available fish, produce, and meats and influenced by the various immigrant groups that flocked to the U.P. to work the mines.

As with the rest of the U.P., restaurants in this region tend to be casual, down-home affairs with friendly service. A few more upscale, special-occasion options exist in Marquette, but even at these spots, it would be strange to see someone in formal wear.

AU TRAIN, MUNISING, AND PICTURED ROCKS

Far and away the best restaurant in Au Train, and for several miles around, The Brownstone Inn (906-892-8332; www.brownstoneinn.net; closed Mondays in off-season; $$$$) specializes in inventive twists on North Woods classics. The owners are California transplants, which could have something to do with the introduction of tropical salsas and Caribbean spices to the usual Lake Superior whitefish. From Mexican quesadillas and burgers to filet mignon topped with crab, The Brownstone covers multiple culinary bases and does it well. Desserts are homemade and delicious, with options changing regularly, and the wine list is also excellent, with several bottles from the California wine country making an appearance alongside local Michigan wines and beers. The inn is not an inn, but it certainly looks like one from the road, with its stonework and chimneys. Built in the 1940s from locally found stones and salvage materials, the Brown-stone sits right on MI 28, beckoning hungry motorists. The interior is cozy and warm, and service is extremely friendly. One night when we were too tired to drive after taking our time and enjoying a two-hour meal, we asked our waitress to recommend a nearby hotel, and she not only called around to get a reservation for us (not easy on Fourth of July weekend at the last minute!) but drew us a map and gave us her phone number to call her if we ran into any trouble.

Nearby Munising, the launch-pad for exploring Pictured Rocks, is almost as well known for having bad restaurants as it is for its proximity to Pictured Rocks. The lone exception is the **Falling Rock Café & Bookstore** (906-387-3008;

The popular Brownstone Inn is known for inventive takes on classic North Woods fare.
Matt Girvan

Falling Rock Café & Bookstore pulls triple duty as a coffee shop, bookstore, and community center for Munising.   Matt Girvan

www.fallingrockcafe.com; 104 E. Munising Ave.; closed Mondays in off-season; $). It's easy to imagine spending many hours sitting in this spot, reading a book on one of the couches or catching up with friends at a table in the café. Falling Rock is the hub of social life in Munising, with outstanding coffee, gourmet sandwiches made fresh on the spot, homemade soups made daily, and an old-fashioned soda fountain of polished chrome that serves the local favorite Jilbert Dairy ice cream. The café also provides free high-speed wireless, although last time we were in they were collecting donations to keep that service going. In addition to deli sandwiches for lunch, the café serves excellent egg sandwiches for breakfast, along with bagels and homemade muffins and pastries. CDs from local musicians are on sale, as are the handicrafts of various local artisans, making Falling Rock a good place to look for gifts as well. This is one of those special places that draws a town together—so much so, in fact, that in 2006, when the owners announced that they were thinking of closing during the off-season because it was just too hard to stay afloat financially as a small bookstore in a feast-or-famine economy like Munising's, the local community banded together to convince them otherwise. The café created a Friends of Falling Rock program, asking local patrons to donate $100 a year to keep the business open, and the public responded enthusiastically, raising over $13,000. It just goes to show how important a community gathering place is to people, especially during the harsh winter months in a remote place like Munising.

South of Munising, in the Hiawatha National Forest (just inside the Wetmore entrance off MI 28), Camel Rider's Restaurant (906-573-2319; lunch and dinner only, closed Mondays), adjacent to Camel Rider's Resort, overlooks a beautiful chain of lakes, which produce plenty of fresh fish for the menu. Perch, trout, whitefish, and walleye are all available in-season, and delicious. The kitchen is big on drawn butter and deep frying, but you can ask to have your fish broiled instead if you like. On the meat front, they serve a decent steak (including one monster that's big enough for two) and offer special extrathick 1-pound stuffed pork chops that are delicious, if entirely unhealthy. The food is consistently good here, but the restaurant is made great by its unique and beautiful surroundings.

MARQUETTE AND ENVIRONS

Downtown Marquette has more dining choices than any other spot in the U.P. For hearty, family-style Italian dinners, locals head to Casa Calabria (906-228-5012; www.the casa.us; 1106 North Third St.; dinner only; $$), where no matter what you order your plate will be

Camel Rider's is as popular with boaters and bikers in summer as it is with snowmobilers in winter. Courtesy Pure Michigan

heaped high with warm and filling pasta, often loaded with cheese. Healthy? No, but one bite in and you won't care. From the giant chunks of homemade, toasty garlic bread dripping with olive oil to the baked pastas bubbling with cheese, Casa Calabria is exactly what you're looking for on a cold Marquette day. Its large dining room is also a good place to head with big groups. In addition to the pastas, this *casa* is known for its steaks—certified Black Angus and USDA prime sirloin, served with garlic bread. Casa Calabria is a good place to try out the *cudighi*, a spicy Italian sausage sub that has been a Marquette staple since it was introduced in the early mining days.

A few blocks down Third Street, **Sweet Water Café** (906-226-7009; www.sweetwatercafe.org; 517 N. Third St.; $$) is a popular spot with the college crowd in Marquette, thanks to its focus on organic, locally sourced foods and tasty vegetarian options. Sweet Water isn't a vegetarian restaurant at all—it just provides lots of options. Breakfast at Sweet Water is hands-down the best in town and possibly the best in the U.P. It's really that good, from the almandine lattes to the fresh juices, farm-fresh eggs, French toast made from fresh-baked bread, and thick-cut bacon from a local butcher. Vegetarian and vegan scrambles are also available, as is a warm and hearty winter cereal composed of oatmeal, wheat berries, brown rice,

millet, dried cranberries, and raisins, topped with toasted almonds. Lunch and dinner are equally as inventive and delicious, with everything from a world-class cheeseburger to the café's Orbit Burger, a grain and lentil patty. While it sounds boring, when served with pesto, tomato slices, and Swiss cheese atop fresh-baked bread, it's absolutely delicious. Lunch sandwiches and salads are available any time of day, but Wednesday through Sunday the café does a special dinner menu that changes weekly but always includes an option from every category: red meat, pasta, vegan, fish, and chicken or pork, each listed with a suggested beer or wine. Desserts are baked fresh daily and well worth saving room for.

Catering more to grad students and young professionals, **Lagniappe** (Creole for "gift") (906-226-8200; 145 Jackson St.; closed Sundays; $$$$) has a great jazz-inspired setting—the brick-walled basement of a nightclub, with low lighting and oversize, private booths—and a delicious menu featuring New Orleans classics such as seafood bisque, crab cakes, crawdad étouffée, gumbo, hot beignets, and bread pudding with Jack Daniels sauce, as well as modern spins on the Big Easy, including crawfish nachos and seafood fondeaux (a Lagniappe creation: fondue made with two types of seafood). Service is very good, and the quality and inventiveness of the food makes it worth the slightly

Tasty Treats

Babycakes Muffin Company (906-226-7744; www.babycakesmuffin company.com; 223 W. Washington St., Marquette) Delicious muffins, scones, croissants, cookies, and breads baked fresh daily.

Dead River Coffee (906-226-2112; 143 Washington St., Marquette) Sustainably sourced coffee roasted on-site in small batches has quickly made Dead River a local Marquette choice for best coffee. Pick up a half pound to take home with you, and your morning coffee is on them.

Donckers (906-226-6110; www.donckersfudge.com; 137 W. Washington St., Marquette) An institution dating back to 1896, Donckers is known for its fudge and its pay-by-the-pound bulk candy. A good stop if you're fueling up for a road trip.

Gophers Café and Bakery (906-226-0900; www.gopherscafeand bakery.com; 910 N. Third St., Marquette) Located in a cute older house in downtown Marquette, this popular lunch spot and bakery is famous for its desserts—especially double-lemon cream cake, cheesecake, and fruit tarts—as well as Belgian chocolates and pralines.

Jean Kay's Pasties & Subs (two locations: 906-774-0430; 204 E. B St., Iron Mountain and 906-228-5310; 1639 Presque Isle Ave., Marquette; www.jeankayspasties.com) Well known throughout the U.P., with a thriving mail-order business, Jean Kay's uses cubed flank steak plus potatoes, onions, and optional rutabagas for the traditional meat pasty and offers a vegetarian version with broccoli, cauliflower, celery, onions, carrots, potatoes, peppers, mushrooms, and low-fat cream cheese in a whole wheat crust.

Jilbert Dairy (906-225-1363; www.jilbertdairy.com; 200 Meeske Ave., Marquette) The U.P.'s favorite ice cream maker is based here in Marquette. The dairy welcomes visitors to its retail store and ice cream parlor, where they can watch the whole operation, test out new Jilbert sundae creations, and pick up a few pints.

higher prices. The bar is also popular with locals looking to grab a martini after work.

Down on Front Street, The Vierling Brewpub & Restaurant (906-228-3533; www.thevierling .com; closed Sundays, open lunch and dinner only; $$) is a refurbished 100-plus-year-old saloon. While the place has been faithfully restored, it's now far more of a proper restaurant than a wild and

Tom Wahlstrom, chef-owner of Elizabeth's Chop House in Marquette and one of the best chefs in the U.P. Shawn Malone

woolly drinking hall, with the possible exception of the popular Friday fish fry. Instead, guests nosh sedately on grilled sandwiches and large salads at lunch and a variety of Italian specialties plus steaks and whitefish done a number of ways (grilled, Cajun, fried, you name it) at dinner. The lunch menu offers a wide variety of tasty salads. The Vierling also brews its own beer, creating English-style ales with modern twists in the downstairs brewery, which is viewable from the street.

Just a few doors down, Elizabeth's Chop House (906-228-0900; www.elizabethschophouse.com; $$$$) is the best restaurant in the U.P. Run by chef Tom Wahlstrom and his wife Elizabeth, who runs the front of house, the restaurant is stylishly upscale (exposed brick, hardwood floors, white tablecloths) and the service and food are superb; so much so that Wahlstrom was named U.P. Chef of the Year in 2010. In addition to wonderful steaks (this is a chop house, after all), Elizabeth's is one of the best seafood spots in the area, with everything from oysters on the half shell to whitefish to a killer olive-oil-poached halibut on offer. The bar is also well worth a visit if you want a nice glass of wine or a well-poured cocktail and a bite to eat from the seafood-focused bar menu.

Extend Your Stay

If you have more time, try these great places to see and things to do . . .

Thanks in large part to the university in Marquette, there is quite a lot going on culturally in this part of the U.P. The area's cultural history has also been influenced by the mining industries and the amount

Henry Ford and Big Bay

When an 80-year-old Henry Ford bought the mill in Big Bay in 1943, it had been shut down for several years and not much was happening in the town. Ford dropped a lot of money into refurbishing the hotel and the area around it, but Big Bay never turned into the model company town he had hoped it would be. A week at the hotel was a perk for Ford execs that were doing well, while Ford himself kept a summer retreat at the Huron Mountain Club, a superprivate fenced-off club for the very wealthy just outside Big Bay where old-money billionaires like the Fords maintain summer wilderness retreats on 21,000 acres of lakes, forest, waterfalls, and mountains.

Overlooking the old sawmill that once produced wood panels for Henry Ford's early station wagons was a building that is now the **Thunder Bay Inn** (400 Bensinger St., Big Bay). The inn, built in 1910, was originally a warehouse and later a lumber company hotel but was purchased and renovated by Ford in 1940 as a vacation retreat for himself and his executives. In 1959, the hotel was the setting for the film *Anatomy of a Murder*, which was based on a novel about a real Big Bay case written by Marquette-area native John Voelker under the pen name Robert Traver. The Thunder Bay's pub was added on to the hotel specifically for the film. The hotel changed its name to the Thunder Bay Inn in 1986 when the present-day owners bought it, turned it into a B&B, and named it after the hotel in the movie. The hotel is full of history, from Ford and his ideas about company towns to the film, which was such a big deal to the area that it is still constantly referenced.

of wealth that was amassed and kept here for several decades. While the rest of the U.P. mining areas suffered continuous boom-and-bust cycles, the Marquette iron range (along with the Keweenaw Copper Country) held on to money for longer, building fancy homes, schools, libraries, museums, theaters, and even opera houses that are still around to be appreciated today.

HISTORIC BUILDINGS AND SITES

Most of Marquette's stately old buildings were either donated by industrial barons or were once their homes. The tony Ridge and Arch Historic District is where all the local barons lived at one point. Their beautiful and enormous old homes are evidence of a time when there was an awful lot of money flowing through this region. The Marquette County Historical

Museum sells maps of the historical homes in the neighborhood, but the highlights include the sprawling Merritt Mansion at 410 E. Ridge Street, two Gothic-revival homes at 430 E. Arch and 450 E. Ridge Streets, and two stunning churches, a Methodist Romanesque revival and St. Paul's Episcopal, a truly amazing Gothic revival on which no expense was spared. A pleasant stroll around the neighborhood will reveal various treasures from the past, as well as a few new beauties that manage to fit in well with the neighborhood.

Although not quite as opulent as the Ridge and Arch homes, the Brewmaster's Castle Home, on Washington Street, is equally worth a peek. The house is all that's left of the former U.P. Brewery. Opened under the name Franklin Brewery in 1873, the business changed its name to the U.P. Brewery in 1886. When the brewery released its popular Castle Brew, it changed the design theme to "Castle" and built a handful of new buildings to meet demand for the beer. In its heyday, the brewery was producing 40,000 barrels a year, but when Prohibition was enacted in 1919, the brewery was forced to close. The German brewmaster who lived in this little sandstone castle eventually left town, and the house is now used as a business office, but the owner has no problem with visitors checking the place out from time to time during normal business hours.

On Main Street, the Delft Theater (130 W. Main St.) is all that remains of Marquette's great old movie houses. An art deco gem, the Delft has been well maintained; its sign still glitters on cold, snowy nights, college students

The Delft is one of several groovy old movie theaters in the U.P. Wikimedia Commons

Marquette County Courthouse was featured in the film *Anatomy of a Murder.* Bobak Ha'Eri

still head here to watch the latest films, and the theater has become one of the most-photographed buildings in town.

Down near the lake, on Front Street, the **Peter White Public Library** (906-226-3571) dominates the landscape. A lovely white beaux-arts building dating to the early 1900s, the library underwent a very tasteful renovation that added to its space without detracting from its style. The library is a great place to escape the cold for a minute if you're walking up Front Street and get hit by a Lake Superior breeze. In addition to plush chairs and a huge collection, the first level of the library includes a community arts center and gallery, as well as a café.

Just a block off Front Street, on Baraga, the **Marquette County Courthouse** (234 W. Baraga Ave.) also dates back to the early 1900s (1902, to be exact). A large and beautiful domed brick building, surrounded by trees and gardens, the building can be seen from blocks away. In addition to its size and stately countenance, the Marquette County Courthouse's big claim to fame is its role in the 1959 film *Anatomy of a Murder*.

What better way to show that your town has money than to build a really over-the-top bank? This seems to have been the thinking throughout the U.P. during the mining boom, with ornate banks popping up throughout the Keweenaw Peninsula and the Marquette Range. This **Wells Fargo** (101 W. Washington St.) was built in 1927, when Marquette needed to show that it wasn't going broke. It was designed in the beaux-arts style, with massive columns, a 25-foot ceiling, and details inside like bronze doors and chandeliers.

Despite being a relatively small area, this stretch of Lake Superior's coast has quite a few lighthouses. You can both tour Big Bay Point Lighthouse (906-345-9957; www .bigbaylighthouse.com; open June through September; $2) and stay the night, if so inclined. The view from the tower is spectacular, and the grounds can be toured anytime for free.

One of the most picturesque and photographed lighthouses in the state, Grand Island's East Channel Lighthouse is unique in its use of wood, and not just brick, for structure. The lighthouse was recently restored, making it lovely for photographs, but its interior is not accessible to visitors.

Another standout in a sea of picturesque lighthouses, the bright red Marquette Harbor Lighthouse (906-226-2006; 300 Lakeshore

Marquette Harbor Lighthouse is an easy walk from downtown Marquette. Henryk Sadura

Blvd.), perched on a bluff overlooking the harbor, looks like it was just made to appear on postcards. Used as a Coast Guard residence up until the late 1990s, the lighthouse is now open to the public as part of the adjacent Marquette Maritime Museum.

MUSEUMS AND GALLERIES

Marquette's first major art museum, The DeVos Art Museum (906-227-1481; www.nmu.edu/devos; open daily; free) opened on Northern Michigan University's campus in 2005 in a brand-new, beautiful modern building designed by well-known HGA architects. With a $1 million programming endowment from the DeVos Foundation in Grand Rapids, the museum has been able to expand the mission of the previous university art museum, bringing in not only local and regional exhibits but artists from elsewhere in the United States and the world, and building up a solid permanent collection as well. The DeVos focuses on contemporary art of various media, exhibited in two large open-plan galleries with hardwood floors, crisp white walls, and lots of natural light. An outdoor concert area and a sculpture garden are also part of the museum, which was designed to flow seamlessly from the rest of the university's art and design buildings. Irrespective of the exhibit, the museum is worth a visit for the building alone. The architects did a really impressive job of integrating the 20th-century modern style of the museum and its Rhine zinc exterior with the 19th-century brick and sandstone of the building it connects to, without making the whole thing seem totally incongruous.

Although nowhere near as grand as the DeVos, the small, private Marquette County History Museum (906-226-3571; www.marquette history.org; closed Sundays; $7 adults, $6 seniors, $3 students over 12, $2 children 12 and under), on Spring Street, does a good job of telling the continuing history of the region, including a look at Native American culture and how it has affected and been affected by Anglo culture, plus the social and economic impacts of the various industries that have come and gone in the U.P., including mining, lumber, fishing, and shipping. The museum currently houses three small galleries, at least one of which is devoted to a revolving exhibit that looks at a different aspect of life in the U.P. Past examples include Anatomy of a Yooper, which delved into the reasons behind various regional foods, slang, and customs, and Person to Person, about the ways people have communicated in the U.P. over time. Early in 2007, the museum purchased a former bus shelter in downtown Marquette, with the intention of renovating it and eventually moving the museum into the much larger space. Currently, only half the museum's collection is on display due to space constraints.

Around the corner, on Washington Street, the Oasis Gallery (906-225-1377; www.oasisgallery.com; closed Sundays and Mondays; free) was founded in 1987 and is an ongoing project by the Marquette Arts Council bringing together 11 artists, each of whom is responsible for curating one exhibit for the gallery per year. Exhibits can center on anything the artist/curator chooses—a particular theme, subject, style—and include the work of both local and international artists. Thanks to the near-total lack of restrictions placed on them, the artists always manage to put together a unique and interesting show, full of surprises. In a recent show entitled Art for Artists: A Show of Artwork from Artists' Collections, artists got to introduce patrons to their favorite artists and share a little something about themselves at the same time. The gallery stays afloat by throwing two popular fund-raisers every year, the annual Dinner by Artists event at which the artists/curators cook for local patrons and host a silent auction for various artworks and door prizes, and the Holiday Sale, from Thanksgiving to Christmas, when the gallery invites all local artists to sell their work through the gallery. The gallery takes a 30 percent commission as a donation. The gallery also sells memberships on a sliding scale. In general, it's one of those great art projects that is wholly embraced and supported by the community.

Away from downtown, in a small blue A-frame house with neat white trim near Presque Isle Park, the **Studio Gallery** (906-228-2466; 2905 Lake Shore Blvd.) displays and sells the artwork of four local female artists. Three of the women are nationally known: watercolorists Kathleen Conover and Maggie Linn and sculptor and jeweler Vicki Allison Phillips. The newest addition to the group is Yvonne Lemire, a sculptor, jeweler, and professional welder whose jewelry and home accents are big sellers. The women maintain a working studio in the back, and at least one of them is always on hand to answer questions or greet patrons.

Less than 20 miles inland from Marquette, but a world away culturally, **Da Yooper's Tourist Trap & Museum** (906-485-5595; www.dayoopers .com), just outside Ishpeming, is a really fun stop. Da Yoopers musical comedy troupe has set up a museum devoted to various aspects of Yooper life. Equal parts comedy and history museum, the Tourist Trap features murals and models of Yooper life, including a deer camp diorama and a model of an iron mining drift, as well as various gag items, from recordings of the comedy troupe's skits—heavy on da Northwoods accent and toilet humor— to oversize models of Yooper tools (Big Gus is the world's largest chainsaw, Big Ernie is the world's largest rifle, etc.) and various Yooper innovations, like a Model A with a bucket on the front for snow removal. The head Yooper also happens to be into rock collecting, so there's a neat little rock shop attached as well, and visitors can buy all sorts of gag gift items in the Tourist Trap store, including the popular Yooper Glossary, which purports to unlock the mystery of "Yoopanese." Some of the exhibits and gags may not be suitable for children.

NIGHTLIFE

The university makes it possible for Marquette to have a bit more of a nightlife than the rest of the U.P. The scene is dominated for the most part by bars and pubs, with nonstudents heading to a handful of cocktail lounges in town. **Lagniappe** (see "Local Flavors"), a Cajun/Creole restaurant on Jackson Street, has a popular martini bar. The **Northland Pub** in the Landmark Inn (906-228-2580; 230 N. Front St.) is a fun and lively pub that really gets hopping on the occasional live music night or when there's a big sports event on. They serve food fairly late as well, in case you suddenly have a craving for nachos.

The **Wild Rover** has been trying, with some success, to fill the hole left by the closure of the Shamrock, serving well-poured pints of Guinness and cranking up the music after 10 pm. The Portside Inn (906-228-2041;

www.theportsideinn.com; 239 W. Washington St.) is a popular pizza joint that attracts a lively crowd of students, other residents, and visitors at night. People like The Portside for its selection of beers on tap, pizza, live music on Thursday, and patio.

Although people have differing opinions about the food, no one disputes the fact that UpFront (906-228-5200; 102 E. Main St.) is a much-loved part of Marquette's nightlife. Located in a restored historic building close to the water, the bar has live music most nights, featuring groups from across the musical spectrum.

Meanwhile, local music on Thursday nights and a good crusty dive vibe keep Marquette locals loyal to Vango's, on Third Street (906-228-7707; 927 N. Third St.).

SHOPPING

Due largely to the university, Marquette boasts a collection of varied and interesting shops, as well as a wide selection of independent bookstores. Antiques are also plentiful, many of them dating to the wealthy mining days.

Antiques

Housed in a 1915 movie theater in Ishpeming, 20 miles south of Marquette, the **Butler Theater Antique Mall** (906-486-8680; 119 S. Main St.) is divided into stalls for 18 different dealers, all of whom sell very well-priced collectibles ranging from costume jewelry and pottery to furniture. The theater itself is a good reason to pop in, even if you're not in the market for antiques. The art deco elements of a 1950 renovation are still intact, and the theater hosted the premiere of *Anatomy of a Murder* back in 1959, making it something of a local landmark. Several of the movie's stars actually came to the premiere in Ishpeming, out of respect for John Voelker, who wrote the novel that the film was based on (under the pen name Robert Traver) and grew up in Ishpeming.

Marquette's classic Butler Theater has been restored and converted into an antiques mall full of great deals.

Marjorie O'Brien

Falling Rock Café & Bookstore (906-387-3008; www.fallingrockcafe.com; 104 E. Munising Ave.) in Munising is a magical little place with vintage chairs and couches spaced throughout the store in just the right places to encourage people to sit down and stay awhile. Comprising two large, rambling rooms full of books plus a popular café, Falling Rock almost feels more like a community center or a library than a retail shop. The books are, in fact, for sale, and there are a number of good ones to choose from, whether you're looking for a hardbound classic, a cookbook, or a brand-new novel.

In Marquette, Snowbound Books (906-228-4448; 118 N. Third St.) is a popular bookshop, with an assortment of new, used, and rare books, that's known for carrying the biggest variety of regional and U.P.-specific books anywhere, as well as an assortment of books by local authors. Which is not to say that they sell only U.P. or Michigan-related books—various categories are well represented in this larger-than-average bookstore.

Gift and Specialty Shops

South of Marquette, in West Ishpeming, is the first brick and mortar outpost of popular Yooper Shirts (www.yoopershirts.com; 1710 US 41), a company making cool graphic T-shirts with various Yooper themes. The shirts sell in the gift shops of a few local museums and online as well, but this is the company's first stand-alone store. It's in a strange location (at a gas station), but I suppose it's sort of convenient to be able to get gas, a pizza, and a cool new T-shirt all in one place.

The Great Outdoors

Outdoor adventures and activities in north central U.P.

In addition to one of the U.P.'s most popular outdoor attractions, Pictured Rocks National Lakeshore, and Lake Superior, the largest of the Great Lakes, this section of the U.P. is absolutely teeming with recreational opportunities. Snowmobilers tear around on hundreds of miles of trails in winter and still don't come close enough to bug cross-country skiers.

Dozens of waterfalls draw hikers and families in the summer; rivers, streams, and inland lakes full of trout, perch, bass, walleye, and whitefish bring anglers from all over the country; and paddlers have hundreds of shoreline miles at their disposal.

In the fall, flaming red and glowing gold leaves light up Lake Superior's shore, providing some of the best fall color views in the country. Fall also brings Michigan's popular deer hunting season, followed by black bear hunts.

It's important to remember that, due to its large size, Lake Superior

takes a very long time to warm up in the summer once the winter ice melts.
August waters are generally warm, and pleasant swimming can be found
earlier in the summer at some of the region's smaller, shallower inland lakes.

BICYCLING

Biking is a great way to get around Marquette, especially if you take the
Marquette Lakeside Path. Looping around the lake from the harbor down
to Presque Isle Park at the north end of town, the path provides a pleasant
5-mile (each way) lakeside bike ride and an easy way to get from one side of
town to the other without dealing with any of the hills.

Above and beyond simple transportation corridors, there are a number
of great rides in this part of the U.P. About a half hour north of Marquette,
the Big Bay Trail is a popular part of the Noquemanon Trail Network that
loops around Big Bay, offering both woods and lake views.

The Hiawatha National Forest has a handful of great paths, the most
challenging of which is Bruno's Run, a section of the Valley Spur cross-
country ski trails that crisscross through the Hiawatha Forest near Munising. It's a great ride that combines views of Pete's Lake and Indian River
with exposed roots and lots of up-and-downhill action.

Rentals

Cross-Country Sports. 906-337-4520; http://crosscountrysports.com;
507 Oak Street, Calumet

Down Wind Sports. 906-482-2500; www.downwindsports.com; 308
Shelden Avenue, Houghton

Keweenaw Adventure Company. 906-289-4303; www.keweenawadventure
.com; 155 Gratiot Street, Copper Harbor

Lakeshore Bike. 906-228-7547; www.lakeshorebikemqt.com; 505 Lakeshore Boulevard, Marquette

Trek & Trail. 906-932-5858; www.trek-trail.com; 1310 E. Cloverland Drive,
Ironwood

BIRD-WATCHING

Home to the northern section of the Seney National Wildlife Refuge
(906-586-9851; www.fws.gov/midwest/seney), this part of the U.P. is a bird-
watcher's paradise. Established in 1935 as a refuge and breeding ground for
migratory birds and other wildlife, Seney today attracts birders from all over
the world, hoping to see glimpses of rare breeds like the yellow rail and the
bald eagle. Check in with the experts at the visitors center when you arrive

One of several state-maintained song trails in the U.P. Wikimedia Commons

for up-to-the-minute advice on where to see what, but as a general rule early morning or evening are the best times to view wildlife.

At the grocery store in Au Train, west of Munising, birdwatchers can check out binoculars and a taped bird guide that describes the markings and songs of 20 common songbirds found along the nearby Au Train Songbird Trail, in the Hiawatha Forest. It's a great way for amateur birders to get up to speed quickly, and the tape itself can sometimes serve as a birdcall. The trail is about 2 miles long, passing through uplands and forest, along a stream, past a bog and a wooden platform overlooking Au Train Lake. May and June are particularly good for viewing, when visitors have a high chance of spotting various warblers, ospreys, bald eagles, and sandpipers, among many others.

CAMPING

Au Train, Munising, and Pictured Rocks

There are many great camping spots in this part of the U.P., but a few really stand out. A fantastic home base for the area, within easy driving distance of Pictured Rocks, Munising Falls, and Miner's Castle, Au Train Lake Campground (Hiawatha National Forest, west of Munising, at Au Train; open May 15 through September 30, first come, first served; $14) is spacious and wooded and also has the benefit of being on the shores of the largest inland lake in the area and right next door to the scenic Au Train River as well. In addition to providing pleasant scenery and swimming, both bodies of water are chock-full of fish, and the lake is popular for water-skiing as well. Located in the Hiawatha National Forest, campsites are large and well spaced throughout the trees for privacy. The Au Train Songbird Trail, popular among birdwatchers, also starts and ends at this campground.

Farther east, located within Pictured Rocks National Lakeshore (12 miles west of Grand Marais), Hurricane River (open May 10 through October 31, first come, first served; $12) is accessible by either kayak or car. The pleasantly woodsy campground has 21 large sites arranged in two loops around the Hurricane River. Picnic tables are set up around the area where the river flows into Lake Superior, and campers can take an easy 1.5-mile hike to the Au Sable Lighthouse. Listed on the National Register of Historic Places, the lighthouse was constructed in 1874 and still operates, now with a solar-powered lamp. Hurricane River provides a put-in point to Lake Superior for kayakers wishing to get a closer look at the Pictured Rocks.

Also in Pictured Rocks National Lakeshore, Little Beaver Lake Campground (open May 10 through October 31, first come, first served; $12) is relatively small and quiet, with just eight large sites well spaced for privacy, each with a view of Little Beaver Lake below. A small boat ramp is available at the site, and fishing in the lake is great for pike, perch, walleye, and bass. Because of its size, the campground fills up quickly, so get there in the morning to score a spot.

Miner's Castle, one of the most photographed rocks in Pictured Rocks National Lakeshore. Charles Dawley

Another popular Pictured Rocks National Lakeshore campground is located on a sandy plateau over Twelvemile Beach (open May 10 through October 31, first come, first served; $12). Three sets of stairs lead to the beach, which is a popular launch point for kayaks heading for the Pictured Rocks. Sites are fairly large and well spaced, with small groves of trees separating sites for privacy. The campground is also located on the North Country Trail, making it popular with hikers.

A 42-mile section of the North Country Trail runs through Pictured Rocks National Lakeshore from Munising to Grand Marais. This particularly picturesque section of the trail is very popular with backpackers and hikers, and the National Lakeshore has graciously provided numerous back-country campsites (906-387-3700; open May 10 through October 31; $19) along the trail to accommodate both trail hikers and kayakers making their way along Superior's shore. Backcountry permits are required for all back-country campers, and reservations can be made for any one of the 12 back-country sites, 7 of which offer group backcountry camping.

CANOEING AND KAYAKING

Between Lake Superior itself, the numerous rivers flowing into it, and the giant Hiawatha National Forest, there are a few really special paddles in this part of the U.P.

For beginners, the Au Train River, in the Hiawatha National Forest, provides a slow and meandering 10-mile canoe trip that starts at the Au Train Lake Campground and leads to a sandy beach on Lake Superior. Paddlers can either get out at the beach or continue on to brave the big lake.

Experienced paddlers can head from the docks at Munising out to and around Grand Island (906-387-3700). There are even beachfront campsites set up on the island, which put paddlers in perfect position for tackling Pictured Rocks National Lakeshore.

Grand Island. Matt Girvan

Streaks of mineral stain decorate the sandstone formations of Pictured Rocks National Lakeshore.   Matt Girvan

The only way to really view Pictured Rocks National Lakeshore (906-387-3700) is by boat, and in a kayak you can land close enough to get a really close look at those vibrant colors. With Lake Superior's erratic weather, however, only experienced paddlers should take on this trip.

A fantastic 120-mile stretch of Lake Superior paddling stretching east from Big Bay to Grand Marais, the Hiawatha Water Trail (www.hiawatha watertrail.org; info@hiawathawatertrail.org) is what Pictured Rocks paddlers generally use. The Hiawatha Water Trail Association provides lots of information about the trail, including a map of the trail with various put-in and take-out points.

For a group with varying skill levels looking for something a bit more challenging than the Au Train River but not quite as ambitious as paddling around Pictured Rocks, Indian River Canoe Trail (906-786-4062), in the Hiawatha National Forest, is a great trip. The river is wide and gentle, but the trail is long (36 miles) if you want to add a little challenge to it, plus trout fishing is decent despite the popularity of the river, and it flows through various woods and wetlands that are good for spotting birds and wildlife.

Canoes and kayaks can be rented at Big Bay Outfitters in Big Bay (906-345-9399; www.bigbayoutfitters.com) or at Northern Waters Adventures in Munising (906-387-2323; www.northernwaters.com;

Family Fun

One of the coolest winter sights in the U.P. is the **Ice Caves of Eben**. Technically located on private property (ask at the Hiawatha National Forest visitors center in Munising about current access and directions), the ice caves are reached through a fairly easy 1-mile trail (2 miles round-trip) through the generous landlord's birch woods. Trails approach from both the top and the bottom of the caves—it's obviously best to approach from the bottom. We found out the hard way one day how slippery

Off the beaten path, the Ice Caves of Eben are a great winter destination near Marquette. Kati Warner

those caves are when trying to scramble down from the top. Though they are referred to as the ice caves, there's really only one big cave. Ice hangs over it and coats the interior in a layer so thick it turns various shades of blue during the day, similar to a glacier. It's a lot of fun to climb in and around the cave, but be very careful not to slip.

Pictured Rocks National Lakeshore. Matt Girvan

Two different types of boat cruises departing from Munising are both worth a shot. The **Munising Bay Shipwreck Tours** (906-387-4477; www.shipwreck tours.com; 1204 Commercial St.; open Saturday before Memorial Day through mid-October; $30 adults, $27 seniors, $12 children 6–12, under 6 free) are really interesting for the whole family—kids will love the glass-bottom boat, with fish sweeping by and pirate-looking shipwrecks rising up below, while parents marvel at the hundreds of boats this seemingly calm lake has sunk. And then, of course, a **Pictured Rocks Cruise** (906-650-2379 or 1-800-650-2379; www.picturedrocks.com; 100 W. City Park Dr., open mid-May through mid-October; $35 adults, $10 children 6–12, under 6 free) is a must, unless your kids are expert kayakers. Although some kids do get bored on the three-hour boat tour from Munising out to the Pictured Rocks and back, most are thrilled by the boat and the unusual colors and formations of the rocks. Waving and hollering at the occasional backcountry hiker is another favorite part of this trip.

A trip to **Munising Falls** is also a must if you're in the area. Set back at the end of a lovely boardwalk through the woods, Munising Falls is fairly large and framed perfectly by the woods and boulders on either side, making it an ideal photographic subject. Popular even in the off-season, when it's lovely to see the occasional rivulet breaking through the frozen falls, this spot can get positively jammed in summer. Head out early to avoid the largest crowds. To get to the falls, take MI 28 north toward Grand Marais and follow the signs.

One of the most popular waterfalls, even in an area dominated by photo-worthy falls, is **Miners Falls**. To get to the falls, head west on H-58 from Munising, then take H13 north toward Miner's Castle. You'll see a sign for Miners Falls about 3.5 miles along H13; turn right at the sign, down a short dirt road to the parking lot. The falls are located a short walk away (about 15 minutes along a flat path through the woods). Large, thunderous, and reasonably accessible, it's a must-see for any family vacationing in the area.

Miners Falls is a must-see for visitors to nearby Pictured Rocks. Wikimedia Commons

129 E. Munising St.), where guided kayak tours of Pictured Rocks, Grand Island, and other local spots can also be booked.

CROSS-COUNTRY SKIING

Dozens of cross-country skiing trails crisscross the Hiawatha National Forest, and a significant chunk of the 75-kilometer Noquemanon Trail System is located in this region as well, making it a popular year-round destination. The groomed 25-kilometer Lower Noquemanon Trail, near Marquette, includes several hills and is rated intermediate to difficult. The trail is part of the Noquemanon Trail System, a 75-kilometer system being developed in and around Marquette and Big Bay.

Beginning at Munising Falls, the Munising Trails (906-387-3700; www .nps.gov/piro/planyourvisit/crosscountryskiing) provide a network of loops that spreads out to Miner's Castle, giving skiers several options depending on their available time and skill level. The trails weave through the trees and are dotted with informative interpretive stations.

In the Hiawatha National Forest, the Valley Spur Cross-Country Ski Trail (6 miles south of Munising on MI 94) is a 38-mile cross-country trail system that is rarely if ever crowded. Valley Spur includes 11 loops of varying difficulty, each of which passes through different scenery, from hemlock groves to inland lakes.

FISHING

While fishing centers predominantly on the inland lakes in the southern U.P. near Lake Michigan, in the north, along Lake Superior's shores, anglers flock to the many rivers and streams rushing toward the Great Lake. Trout and salmon fishing are particularly good here.

The mouth of the Carp River is easily accessible at Marquette Lower Harbor. The river is known for its crystal-clear waters and an abundance of steelhead, king salmon, coho salmon, brown trout, and brook trout.

Licensing

Fishing is abundant in the U.P., but you must purchase a valid Michigan state fishing license before engaging in it, even if you plan to catch and release. Visit www.michigan .gov/dnr for details.

Chocolay River also runs through Marquette County, dumping into Lake Superior at Harvey, a few miles east of Marquette. The Chocolay is known for steelhead trout, but there are also brown trout, brook trout, and salmon in its waters. The river stays free of ice most of the year as well.

Some of the U.P.'s best fishing is to be had in the waters surrounding Grand Island. Trout Bay is excellent for lake trout and coho salmon; Murray Bay has perch, pike, walleye, and rock bass; Echo Lake, in the interior of the island, is known for bass, pike, and panfish. Largely surrounded by woods and sheer sandstone cliffs, this is also one of the area's most picturesque fishing spots.

One of the best-known trout streams in the U.P., the Yellow Dog River draws anglers from all over the country every year, fishing for brown, brook, and rainbow trout. Easily accessible from Big Bay, about a half hour northeast of Marquette, the Yellow Dog runs from Bulldog Lake in the McCormick Wilderness on the border of Marquette and Baraga Counties to Lake Independence in Marquette County near Lake Superior.

GOLF

Greywalls at Marquette Golf Club (906-225-0721; www.marquettegolfclub .com; 1075 Grove St.) is the U.P.'s only 36-hole club (6,828 yards, both par 71), with cart rental, restaurant, and bar. Of Greywalls's two 18-hole courses, one is nationally ranked and has been earning praise and plaudits since its opening in 2005. The club's other course, Heritage, is a good, solid course, but Greywalls is magnificent, with undulating fairways banked by hemlock groves that open up to give sudden and spectacular Lake Superior

Greywalls at Marquette Golf Club, near Escanaba, is one of the best in the state.   Steve Pelton

Chapel rock formation of Pictured Rocks National Lakeshore. Matt Girvan

views every once in a while. In the fall, the color of the trees provides an incredibly beautiful contrast to the green of the fairways, making the scenery all the more appealing.

HIKING

It's hard to call any part of the U.P. the best spot for hiking, but if pressed I'd probably say this was it. There are just so many great and varied trails packed into a small area here. Chapel Basin (906-387-3700; www.nps.gov /piro), located in Pictured Rocks National Lakeshore, for example, offers several choices, depending on the time you have available. A 3-mile hike leads to impressive Chapel Falls, plunging 60 feet over the cliffs. Just a mile and a half or so beyond the falls is Chapel Rock, and hikers can then continue on the same trail to Mosquito River.

Yellow Dog River Falls, between Marquette and Big Bay (off CR 510) is another fantastic, challenging hike. The trail runs between Big Bay and Marquette, following the Yellow River as it dips and drops several times to create a network of waterfalls and pools. You have to climb and dip, so it's not an easy woodland walk, but it's still pretty straightforward, and the scenery is excellent.

HUNTING

Hunting for deer, grouse, and bear is allowed in Pictured Rocks National Lakeshore (906-387-2607), which stretches from Munising to Grand Marais. Hunting areas are restricted, however. Area closure maps are available at the Grand Marais Ranger Station. For information about state hunting regulations and hunting seasons for various game, see chapter 7.

SNOWMOBILING

As is the case throughout the U.P., snowmobiling is quite popular in this area during the winter. When Lake Superior is sufficiently frozen, snowmobilers head out to Grand Island to check out its frozen sea caves and icy cliffs. The Hiawatha National Forest is also quite popular with snowmobilers, as is the L'Anse to Big Bay AAA Trail, which brings snowmobilers on a fantastic ride through the Huron Mountains and the Yellowdog Plains to the town of Big Bay. Once in Big Bay, riders can take advantage of the 148 miles of groomed snowmobile trails around the bay as well.

Snowmobiles can be rented from Grand Island Snowmobile Rentals in Munising (906-387-2132).

Southwest

IRON COUNTRY AND THE PORKIES

PROMOTED AS BIG SNOW COUNTRY in the winter, the westernmost region of the Upper Peninsula is also known, understandably, as Waterfall Country in the summer when all that snow melts. According to the local tourism bureau, the region boasts 22 easily visited waterfalls, the most remarkable of which include the Presque Isle and Black River Falls in the Ottawa National Forest and the Superior Falls on the Montreal River, which forms a border between Michigan and Wisconsin. The sister cities of Ironwood, Michigan, and Hurley, Wisconsin, on either side of the Montreal River, are the most lively towns in the area. Both are populated primarily by the Finnish, Italian, and Eastern European ancestors of various immigrant mine workers. With the mines closed, their offspring have found their livelihoods in restaurants, stores, and cafés that are kept afloat by locals but are more than welcoming to visitors as well.

> **Central Time**
>
> Although most of Michigan is on Eastern Time, the Michigan counties along the Wisconsin border are on Central Time—this includes the length of US 2 from Ironwood almost to Escanaba. Ironwood, Watersmeet, Iron River, Iron Mountain, and Menominee are all on Central Time, so be sure to change your watch, or you might show up an hour early for your dinner reservation.

LEFT: The Copper Peak ski jump is one of only a handful of ski jumps in the world.
Wikimedia Commons

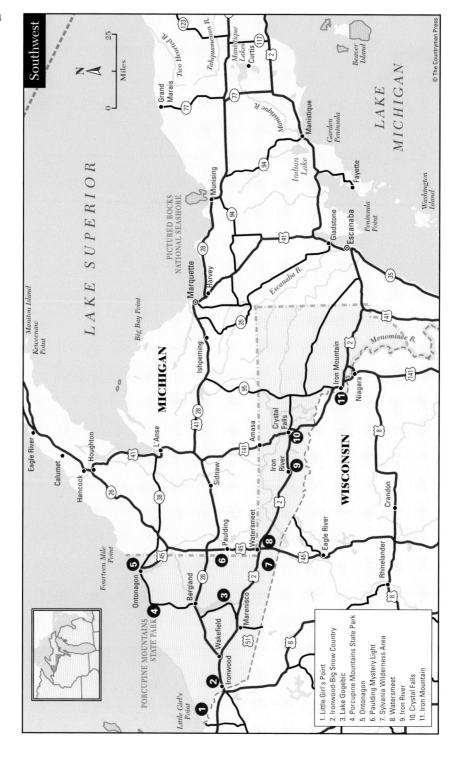

© The Countryman Press

N

0   25

Miles

LAKE SUPERIOR

LAKE MICHIGAN

MICHIGAN

WISCONSIN

Manitou Island
Keweenaw
Point

Big Bay Point

Fourteen Mile
Point

Little Girl's
Point

PICTURED ROCKS
NATIONAL SEASHORE

Garden
Peninsula

Peninsula
Point

Washington
Island

Beaver
Island

PORCUPINE MOUNTAINS
STATE PARK

Eagle River
Calumet
Hancock
Houghton
L'Anse
Ontonagon
Bergland
Wakefield
Ironwood
Marenisco
Paulding
Watersmeet
Sidnaw
Amasa
Crystal
Falls
Iron
River
Niagara
Iron Mountain
Crandon
Eagle River
Rhinelander
Ishpeming
Marquette
Harvey
Munising
Grand
Marais
Manistique
Curtis
Manistique
Lakes
Gladstone
Escanaba
Fayette

Taquamenon R.
Two Hearted R.
Tahquamenon R.
Manistique R.
Escanaba R.
Menominee R.
Indian
Lake

123
117
2
77
77
94
28
94
41
35
35
41
41
28
95
41
28
141
45
45
2
2
2
2
45
8
8
8
8
141
26
38
51

1. Little Girl's Point
2. Ironwood-Big Snow Country
3. Lake Gogebic
4. Porcupine Mountains State Park
5. Ontonagon
6. Paulding Mystery Light
7. Sylvania Wilderness Area
8. Watersmeet
9. Iron River
10. Crystal Falls
11. Iron Mountain

Downtown Ironwood consists primarily of a single main street. Wikimedia Commons

Inland from Lake Superior, Lake Gogebic is the U.P.'s largest inland lake. Warm and swimmable much earlier in the year than Superior, Lake Gogebic is also a prime fishing lake, which explains why it is ringed with cottages and campgrounds that draw regular visitors every summer. In the fall, the colors surrounding the lake rival even those of New England, and in winter, snowmobilers have free rein of hundreds of miles of snowmobile trails.

IRON MOUNTAIN, IRON RIVER, AND THE MENOMINEE RANGE

One of the least developed areas in a region known for its wilderness, the thick forests along this stretch of US 2 west of Escanaba and north of Wisconsin are known for their brilliant fall colors, their rivers, streams, and waterfalls, and their abnormally large wolf and deer populations. Interspersed among the forests are old iron-mining towns, many of which are ghosts of their former selves. Those that have

Iron Mountain is proud of its best-known residents. Wikimedia Commons

The Sylvania Wilderness Area is one of the largest protected, untouched wilderness areas in the country. Peter Gorman

survived the departure of the iron industry are known not for attractive downtowns, of which there are few in these parts, but for shockingly good Italian restaurants run by the ancestors of Italian immigrants who moved here in the early 1900s to work the iron mines. Although the ski resorts surrounding nearby Ironwood are better known, a handful of popular family resorts are located here in the Menominee Range, and Piers Gorge, near Norway, offers some of the Midwest's most rough-and-tumble whitewater.

WATERSMEET

Located almost entirely within the confines of the Ottawa National Forest and known predominantly for fishing, the Watersmeet area is chock-full of lakes, the best of which are surrounded by old-growth forests in the Sylvania Wilderness Area. The Sylvania's forests are unique in the U.P. in that they were protected from the lumber industry early on, which allowed trees, wild mushrooms, and wildflowers—including some incredibly rare breeds—to flourish, and kept its 34 lakes clear of sediment and full of fish.

Though Watersmeet is an entirely unassuming little place, the town came to national attention a few years back when its high school basketball team, the Nimrods, was included in an ESPN commercial spotlighting the most unusually named U.S. high school teams and subsequently in a Sundance Channel documentary that focused on the Native American ancestry of half the team and the school. In recent years, Watersmeet, unlike most other U.P. towns, has actually grown in population, thanks to its large and popular casino (Dancing Eagles Lac Vieux Desert Resort & Casino, owned and operated by local Ojibwa) and the increasing popularity of its affordable lakefront property with retirees from southern Michigan and Chicago.

Just across the state border, a few miles away, the Wisconsin resort village of Land O'Lakes is beautiful and charming and full of the restaurants and shops that Watersmeet lacks. Plenty of visitors stay in Watersmeet for the good prices and the solitude and head over to Land O'Lakes when they feel like being more sociable.

ONTONAGON AND THE PORKIES

Possibly the most underappreciated region of the U.P., Ontonagon and Porcupine Mountains Wilderness State Park (the Porkies) are often passed over by visitors in favor of more popular sights such as Pictured Rocks, Tahquamenon Falls, and Mackinac Island. Locals, however, know better. The park is Michigan's largest, with 60,000-odd acres of forest, over half of it virgin. Some of the U.P.'s most beautiful views can be had here; the region's mountains contain dozens of fantastic hikes; the lakeshore is sandy, pleasant, and rarely crowded; and there is no better spot in the U.P. to see fall color. In the winter, cross-country skiers are delighted by woodland paths and panoramic lake views, while skiers and snowboarders get a kick

The Watersmeet area is dominated by stretches of untouched nature. Courtesy U.S. Forest Service

Ontonagon is a small but charming little town near Porcupine Mountain State Park. Tim Kiser

out of some of Michigan's highest mountains. The only real town in the area is sleepy, pleasant Ontonagon. If you're looking for a wide selection of restaurants, hotels, and entertainment options, this probably isn't the spot for you. If, however, you're looking to head off the beaten path a bit, hike, backpack, and immerse yourself in nature, look no further.

Pick Your Spot

Best places to stay in south-western U.P., and nearby . . .

Although there are a number of lodging options in this area, it's not particularly overrun with hotels, and you won't find many over-the-top bed & breakfasts or five-star resorts here. Which is probably a good thing—who needs a resort when you can stay in a cottage on the lake or camp in a forest that's thousands of years old? That said, the ski condos and lodges around Iron Mountain can book up quickly during winter holidays, so if you're planning a trip during late December or early January, be sure to reserve lodging early.

A number of chain hotels have properties in this area, some of which offer decent rooms for good prices. I have not included reviews of specific chain properties but generally recommend the following chains in the area: AmericInn, Best Western, and Holiday Inn Express.

IRONWOOD AND THE GOGEBIC RANGE

The Black River Crossing B&B (906-932-2604; www.blackrivercrossing.com; open year-round; $$$), in Bessemer (just east of Ironwood) is about as swanky as log cabins get. Three rooms, each with a private bath, occupy this large and beautiful log home just a short walk away from the Black River. Rooms are lovely, with log walls, big comfy custom wood beds decorated with the dark greens and cranberries typical of the North Woods. High-quality handmade wooden furnishings add to the coziness. Bathrooms are all done in marble, and two of the three rooms (Black River Waterfalls Room and Black River Pines Room) have whirlpool tubs. The same two rooms also feature private fireplaces, and two more fireplaces are located in the house's shared areas. All the rooms also have wireless Internet access and TVs with cable and DVD—a nod to the high-tech side of the computer consultant owners. In addition to sitting rooms with fireplaces, the B&B has a game room with foosball and board games, a wood-fired Finnish sauna, a landscaped garden with a waterfall pond, and bikes, snowshoes, and cross-country skis for rent. Breakfast is a warm and hearty, home-cooked affair, and

the innkeepers also invite their guests for evening drinks every night. In addition to its proximity to its namesake Black River, where trout fishing and kayaking are great, the B&B is in a great bird-watching zone and within short driving distance to the popular Big Powderhorn ski resort, as well as nearby waterfalls and the many attractions of the Ottawa National Forest.

The ski resorts themselves are a good bet for lodging in this part of the peninsula, although they get booked quickly during winter weekends. Indianhead Mountain Resort (1-800-346-3426; www.indianheadmtn.com; open year-round; $$) is a large, modern full-service ski resort with a wide variety of lodging options. In addition to the 22 runs and nine lifts on the mountain, Indianhead has a 46-room main lodge with fairly large rooms decorated in the usual North Country colors (dark green and cranberry) with a number of Native American design accents. The resort also has several freestanding chalets available for rent that sleep anywhere from 4 to 12 people and a complex of fairly new, modern condos in one-, two-, three-, and four-bedroom layouts. For the best blend of value and comfort, we suggest the Trailside Condos for their spacious layout, updated décor, saunas, and hot tubs. Neither the condos nor the chalets get maid service, but guests at both have access to all of the lodge amenities, including an indoor pool, fitness club, sauna, and game room. The Lodge Restaurant, popular with locals and guests alike, serves dinner nightly in a large, renovated swayback barn, while Dudley's Saloon serves as an après-ski or sun hot spot. In addition to the ski slopes, Indianhead provides a number of activities for guests, especially for families with children. In the summer the resort maintains numerous bike trails, a nine-hole golf course, and outdoor tennis courts.

ONTONAGON AND THE PORKIES

Lodging options around the Porcupine Mountains are either in chain hotels or in completely unusual (in a good way) situations. Kaug Wudjoo Lodge (906-885-5275; www.michigan.gov/dnr; open year-round; $$$) is an option of the latter variety. Constructed in 1945 as the park manager's residence, the lodge is now available to park guests for weekly rentals, providing an ideal spot from which to explore Porcupine Mountains Wilderness State Park, the state's largest park. A charming dark brown lodge with a stone foundation and wood trim, Kaug Wudjoo (Ojibwa for "place of the crouching porcupine") has hardwood maple floors, a large stone fireplace, and a giant picture window overlooking Lake Superior. It sleeps up to 12 and is furnished with locally made cedar log beds. A fully equipped kitchen makes it easy for families

to move right in for a week of incredible experiences.

IRON MOUNTAIN AND IRON RIVER

On the banks of the Michigamme River just outside charming Crystal Falls, Edgar's Riverview Bed & Breakfast (906-875-6213; open year-round; $$) offers three rooms with private baths and river views. The most expensive room also includes a private Jacuzzi. Room décor is not amazing—think 1970s shag carpet and wood paneling—but the house is cozy and the river views are lovely. The property is nestled in the woods, and its nearest neighbor is a distance away, which makes for maximum quiet and privacy and excellent wildlife spotting opportunities, including deer and eagles. Guests can fish in the river or borrow canoes in the summer and have direct access to snowmobile trails in the winter. Edgar's also offers cross-country skis and snowshoes for guest use during winter. A central sitting room has a large stone fireplace, cathedral ceiling, and comfy couches. All guests are treated to a hot and hearty North Woods breakfast every morning, no matter what time of year it is. The only potential problem with Edgar's is that it's not walking distance to much, but it is located just off the highway, making it easy to get from the B&B to various local attractions.

Over in Iron River, Lac O'Seasons Resort (906-265-4881;

www.lacoseasons.com; open year-round; $$) offers larger, more modern cabins, ideal for families. Fourteen two-, three-, and four-bedroom cottages are available for rent, about half of which are located on the shores of Stanley Lake. The resort sits on nearly 40 wooded acres, and each cabin has a decent amount of space around it so visitors don't feel piled on top of each other. Popular Furnishings are basic, but comfortable; five of the cottages are traditional log cabins, and several also have fireplaces. A communal recreation building provides an indoor pool, sauna, and whirlpool hot tub. In the summer, visitors fish or swim in placid Stanley Lake, lie on the lake's sandy beach, or meander along numerous wooded paths, when not making short car trips to the area's other attractions. In the winter the resort is bordered by two snowmobile trails and is within a five-minute drive of the Ski Brule lifts.

Ski Brule (1-800-362-7853; www.skibrule.com; open year-round; $$$) also offers its own lodging on-site. A large winter (and summer, despite the name) family resort Ski Brule has 16 chalets that sleep anywhere from 4 to 12 people, plus a lodge with 15 separate condos. In the summer the resort offers boating, tubing, rafting, fishing, and guided horseback rides, and in the winter seven lifts carry skiers and snowboarders all over the mountain. Each of the chalets has a completely different look, but all are very well kept, if simple.

Some of the larger chalets have indoor saunas and hot tubs, and the Pioneer Lodge condos have access to two large outdoor hot tubs, but there is no pool on resort grounds (lake swimming is just a short drive away). Some of our favorite chalets include Anderson Lake Lodge, which is completely private, right down to its own private lake; Beaver Lodge Bottom for its sauna, updated kitchen, and beautiful stone fireplace; Wildwood for its almost ridiculously large stone fireplace and beautiful hardwood floors; and Heaven's Window for its groovy loft, stained-glass window, outdoor covered hot tub, and wood-burning stove.

Pine Mountain Golf & Ski Resort (906-774-2747; www.pine mountainresort.com; open year-round; $$), in Iron Mountain, also offers lodging on-site, walking distance to the lifts. Developed in the 1930s by Milwaukee brewer Fred Pabst, the resort features the newly renovated 34-room Pine Mountain Lodge, two dozen condos at the base of the mountain, and the five-star TimberStone Golf Course. Rooms and condos have all been recently spruced up with new carpet, paint, and linens, and the lodge includes an indoor pool, hot tub, and sauna. Two-room family suites are a great deal for families traveling with children. In addition to skiing in the winter and golf in the summer, the resort is just 2 miles from Piers Gorge, which offers some of the Midwest's best white-water rafting in summer. The resort's Famers restaurant serves decent if not exceptional classics like pizza, fish-and-chips, and ribs.

WATERSMEET

In a lovely, natural area like Watersmeet, staying at a casino may seem like an odd choice, but Lac Vieux Desert Vieux Dancing Eagles Hotel (1-800-895-2505; www.lvd-casino.com; open year-round; $$) is a decent option, especially in winter, when the heated pool is a nice perk. The 132-room hotel connects to the large and popular casino next door. Standard rooms are simple and basic; if you splurge a bit, the suites are fitted out with hot tubs and fireplaces. Lac Vieux is also close driving distance to the Sylvania Wilderness Area and has an adjacent golf course.

Vacationland Resort (906-358-4380; www.vacationlandresort.com; open year-round; $$$) is more along the lines of what one would expect a Watersmeet resort to be. A picturesque spot with several independent cabins on Thousand Island Lake, along the Cisco Chain of Fifteen Lakes, Vacationland looks like a perfect photograph taken out of someone's family vacation photo album. Each of the lovely pine cabins has a huge picture window looking out on the lake, a full kitchen, and a 14-foot fishing boat. Some cabins also have fireplaces, and tree-shaded RV spaces are available as well. In addition to a sandy beach, grills, and picnic tables for each cabin, the resort provides docks, boat rentals, and a great floating swimming platform out in the lake. Fishermen will love the access to 15 great fishing lakes, kids will love the lakes' 270 miles of shoreline, and everyone will love the idyllic permanent vacation feel of the appropriately named Vacationland.

Local Flavors

Taste of the town—restaurants, cafés, bars, bistros, etc.

As with the rest of the U.P., you cannot go wrong with whitefish in this area, but the dozens of inland lakes provide numerous other fresh seafood options as well, including walleye, trout, and perch. The shores of Lake Michigan have also benefited gastronomically from the influence of numerous immigrants. From handmade pastas to house-cured meats, some of the best Italian food in the state is available in Iron Country (Iron Mountain, Iron River, and the Menominee Range).

IRON COUNTRY

Ironwood, like nearby Iron Mountain, is known for its great Italian food, the welcome result of the large number of Italians who once worked the area's iron mines and whose children still live here. Italians also introduced the area to delicious *porchetta* (also spelled *porketta*)—a spicy, slow-roasted pork roast—and *cudighi*, a spicy sausage patty sandwich.

Manny's (906-932-0999; 316 E. Houk St.; Ironwood; $) is somewhat of an institution in Ironwood; hidden away in a residential neighborhood (near the World's Tallest Indian statue), it feels like a secret find. Truth be told, not all the food is amazing. But the homemade ravioli is worth a trip, and some would argue that the noodle omelet is as well, if only to say that you once had a noodle omelet for breakfast.

In downtown Ironwood, Tacconelli's Downtown Towne House (906-932-2101; www .tacconellis.com; 215 S. Suffolk St., Ironwood; $) is a very popular spot, especially during its famous Sunday lunch buffet. The restaurant's ribs, gnocchi, homemade soup, and lasagna are all great, and Tacconelli's To-Go will even deliver food—handy if you're camping in the area and don't feel like cooking out of a can.

Equally popular Don & GG's Food and Spirits (906-932-2312; 1300 E. Cloverland Dr., Ironwood; $) gives Tacconelli's a run for its money with classic North Woods fare with just enough twists to make the menu feel unique. It's also one of the few restaurants in the area that really makes an effort to offer an assortment of vegetarian dishes. Fresh whitefish and trout are always on offer, homemade soups are outstanding, the nachos are delicious, and they serve sandwiches and inventive entrée-size salads all day along, with a dinner menu of pastas, fish, chicken, steaks, and a rotating assortment of specials. The outdoor deck is a huge bonus during the summer.

Iron River's strongest contender in the area's "best Italian food" contest is Alice's (906-265-4764; 402 W. Adams, Iron River; closed Mondays; $), where the menu revolves around home-cooked Italian specialties passed down from generation to generation in the owner's Italian family. Everything is handmade, from the pasta and gnocchi to the delicious *cappelletti* soup. Though the restaurant touts chicken Valdostanna as its specialty, it's actually an Americanized version of an Italian dish. Stick instead with the traditional dishes—meat or cheese ravioli with meat sauce or handmade gnocchi served with portobello mushrooms (delicious!) and a grilled pork chop or steak on the side for the very hungry. The wine list includes a number of great and affordable choices from the old country, and Alice's lounge is a pleasant place to relax and try a few. Save room for the chef's infamous three-chocolate mousse—it's well worth it.

With three really solid Italian kitchens going strong, Iron Mountain may just hold the crown. At

Damian's Pasta Works (906-774-3058; 909 S. Stephenson, Iron Mountain; closed weekends, take-out only; $), hungry customers wait in their cars or in the tiny front room and salivate over fresh-baked breads and sweets while hints of their meal waft through from the back of this terrific hole-in-the-wall take-out favorite. Locals know this place is amazing, and visitors are consistently blown away by just how good it is. Located in an old house east of downtown Iron Mountain, Damian's is strictly take-out, and the owner-chefs make everything—pasta, 10 different sauces, lasagna, bread, roasted and cured meats for sandwiches—from scratch. Though it's all delicious here, there are a few standouts: gnocchi, ravioli, lasagna, and the porchetta (spicy, slow-roasted pork) sandwiches are all favorites. Fresh pastas are ready from three in the afternoon onward, and the lunch menu includes an assortment of salads. Portions are enormous, and prices are so low they're actually hard to believe.

At the opposite end of the spectrum, **Fontana Supper Club** (906-774-0044; closed Sundays; $$) is where I imagine couples went for a "fancy" dinner back in the 1970s; it's the sort of spot that makes you want to dress up, just for fun. Fontana's also serves good, straightforward Italian fare similar to what you'd find in the south of Italy served up in a blast-from-the-past supper club, complete with dim lighting, cavernous booths, and big leather menus. Fontana's is a long-time local favorite, particularly for family meals out. Homemade pasta dishes and steaks are the specialties of the *casa*, and one order of pasta, which comes with soup and salad, is more than enough for two, particularly if you order the Italian Holiday (gnocchi, cheese ravioli, and spaghetti with meatballs), which we did one night and lived to regret once the heavy food coma set in. Our favorite is the cheese ravioli with a meatball on the side for good measure. Service can be a little slow here, but it sort of adds to the charm. The bar, with its sports memorabilia and beer signs, is a fun place to hang out at night, with regular drink and appetizer specials.

Another classic Iron Mountain Italian family restaurant, **Romagnoli's** (906-774-7300; 1603 N. Stephenson Ave.; closed Sundays; $$) has been around for more than 20 years. House specials include homemade pasta (made fresh daily), ribs with a secret family sauce, roasted chicken, local fresh seafood specials, and steaks. The meat, chicken, and seafood entrées are all served with a salad, a warm loaf of homemade crusty bread, and your choice of spaghetti, gnocchi, or french fries. It's a lot of food. The lounge offers a full bar and appetizer menu, and the dining room is pleasantly nondescript. The restaurant's slogan is "Come as you are!" and they mean it. This is a casual dinner spot with friendly, excellent service.

Picnic Provisions

Angeli's Central Market

(906-265-7103; www.angeli foods.com; 426 W. Genesee St., Iron River) is an extraordinary market with great fresh produce, homemade local foods, bread baked fresh daily, lots of organic options, high-quality meats, imported cheeses, a fantastic wine selection, and various tasty treats from the infamous Zingerman's Deli down south. It seems entirely out of place in tiny Iron River, but the locals aren't complaining, and neither are savvy visitors. This is the best place for miles around to stock up on picnic provisions.

ONTONAGON AND THE PORKIES

Known for its one-third-pound burgers and its thin-crust pizza, Antonio's (906-885-5223; $) is a western U.P. institution. The original Antonio's was opened in Iron River by the Italian father of the owner of this Antonio's. The son also owns another outpost in nearby Bergland. Both locations are local hangouts with a 1950s diner feel, and both serve up a fairly tasty Italian menu in addition to the pizza and burger standbys for unbelievably low prices. Pasties are also made fresh daily.

Despite its name, Henry's Never Inn (906-886-9910; $) is open every day, a fact that makes fans of their homemade soups and chili very happy. An old miner's bar turned restaurant, Henry's also serves up a mean burger and a great Reuben. Nightly dinners feature weekly, rotating specials, including build-your-own-pizza night on Wednesday, smorgasbords on weekends, Italian night on Saturday, and, of course, the Friday fish fry.

WATERSMEET

A quaint log cabin with red trim and knotty pine interior, the Bear Trap Inn (715-547-3422; closed Mondays, only open Thursday through Saturday in winter; $$) has been serving hearty North Woods meals to happy customers for several decades. Walleye is delicious here, and the Friday fish fry is a terrific deal. Other favorites include pork chops, duck, and garlic-stuffed tenderloin, and the Bear Trap offers a long and decent wine list as well. From some tables diners can watch deer feeding outside or check out the fish in the restaurant's back pond.

Just over the Wisconsin border, in Land O'Lakes, Bent's Camp (715-547-3487; www.bents-camp .com; $$$, closed Tuesdays in winter) offers a similar sort of experience. A former logging camp turned into a popular fishing resort, Bent's also features an outstanding

Latest and Greatest U.P. Sights

Mining and lumber may have come and gone, but you can't keep a Yooper down. From small local foods businesses to burgeoning beer, maple syrup, and clean energy industries, the U.P. is experiencing a wave of innovation at the moment, economic downturn be damned. Chronicling that wave is Sam Eggleston, Marquette-based journalist and managing editor of weekly news site U.P.'s *Second Wave* (www.up.secondwavemedia.com). Always up on what's new and notable in the peninsula, Eggleston offers this list of six new and/or improved attractions not to be missed:

Marquette County. The **Republic Wetlands Preserve and Iron Ore Heritage Trail** (www.republicmi.com/IronOreTrail.php) are a prime examples of how an area can turn an industrial history into something beautiful. The town of Republic, in western Marquette County, joined forces with Cliffs Natural Resources and federal and state agencies to create wetlands out of a former mining site. There, over 2,000 acres of land are now home to birds, coyotes, wolves, moose, deer, and bear. A two-mile nonmotorized trail opened in 2008, and maps and information are available at the Republic Township Hall. In addition to being a lovely hike in itself, the Republic Preserve is also the trailhead to the Iron Ore Heritage Trail, which, when completed, will span 48 miles from Republic to Chocolay Township. Parts of the trail are motorized while others, like the 3-mile stretch between Ishpeming and Negaunee, are nonmotorized.

Sault Ste. Marie. The **Soo Theatre** (www.sootheatre.org), which had its heyday back in the 1930s before closing in 1998, has been the focus of restoration efforts by the city of Sault Ste. Marie and some dedicated people. The results have been amazing, and the theater is now back on its feet and offering a slew of entertainment options. It's providing a welcome economic boost and attraction to the city, which is the oldest settlement in Michigan. If you're looking for a chance to catch some live shows in a wonderfully restored historic setting, then the Soo Theatre should find its way onto your list of places to see.

Harris (near Escanaba). The **Sweetgrass Golf Club** (www.sweetgrass golfclub.com), at Island Resort & Casino in Harris, is just a baby compared to many attractions in the U.P. Built in 2008, it didn't take the course long to start earning much-deserved recognition. In 2009, the course was named Best New Course by both *Golfweek* and *Golf Digest* before earning Best Casino Course in 2010 by *Golfweek*. That same year, the course also earned the honor of being listed 13th on *Golf Magazine*'s Best Courses You Can Play list as well as *Golfweek*'s Best Courses You Can Play. If that isn't enticement enough for a links fanatic, then the fact that the Ladies' Pro Golf Association chose the course as a stop on its Futures Tour for 2011 should be.

Marquette. The **Marquette County History Museum** (906-226-3571; www.marquettehistory.org), which reopened in spring 2011 after moving to a new location in downtown Marquette, is worth seeing in rain, sleet, snow, or the nicest of sunshine. The museum is part of the oldest historical society in the U.P. and includes collections of artifacts from the prehistoric copper culture all the way through the modern face of the county. And don't worry about seeing the same old stuff each time you visit—out of the three large exhibit galleries, one houses the permanent local history exhibit. The other two galleries are changed regularly, because only about 20 percent of the museum's artifacts can be shown at once.

In February 2011, President Obama visited Donckers on a trip to the U.P. Matt Girvan

While many people will be jamming into the pasty shops across the U.P., fans of history and politics should make their way to **Donckers** (www.donckersfudge.com) in downtown Marquette. The store, which started as an open-air stand in 1896, has seen a transformation over the past few years. Below, in the original candy store, Donckers handmade fudge and candies are still available, but with the addition of a soda fountain and newly restored wooden booths. Upstairs is the real treat, however, where lunch and dinner feature U.P.-raised grass-fed beef, from-scratch soups, and even some classic menu items from days past, like olive and nut sandwiches. The food is so tasty, in fact, that President Barack Obama stopped in during his 2011 visit to Marquette.

Iron Mountain. It's hard to believe the **Pine Mountain Music Festival** (906-482-1542 or 1-888-309-7861; www.pmmf.org), founded in 1991 in Iron Mountain, has grown to be such an integral part of the U.P.'s music scene. The festival, which was started by cellist Laura Deming as a weeklong chamber music series, has grown from a handful of events to more than 40 performances, classes, and workshops around Houghton, Marquette, and Iron Mountain and spans a five-week period from June through July. The Pine Mountain Music Festival—which has won awards like the Governor's Award for Arts and Culture and the Great Lakes Community Arts Award and earned the first-ever National Endowment for the Arts grant in the U.P.—was once called "a miracle of ambition, idiosyncrasy and geography" by the *Detroit Free Press*.

restaurant, famous for its Friday fish fry, Saturday prime rib, juicy roast duck, and homemade pizzas. Located in the main lodge of the resort, Bent's Camp restaurant features wood tables in a large wooden, open-beam interior decorated with Native American trinkets and local hunting trophies. The restaurant has its own dock for those boating in for a meal. The Friday fish fry is renowned throughout the region, so plan on getting there early or waiting awhile if you want to find out what the big fuss is about—it's worth it. If you don't feel like braving the crowds, order up one of their famous deep-dish pizzas for take-out. For lunch, the burgers are great, but they also offer an assortment of large fresh salads if the Midwest meat diet is getting to you. And save room for dessert—homemade pies baked fresh daily are delicious. The adjoining bar is always a good time, though it can get very smoky; it's almost always packed in summer, and some sort of event or live music is often scheduled.

Extend Your Stay

If you have more time, try these great places to see and things to do . . .

If the U.P. in general is heavy on outdoor pursuits and a little light on entertainment of the indoor variety, in this part of the peninsula that is especially true. Unlike the east, which has Mackinac Island as a draw and the industrial economy of Sault Ste. Marie, or Marquette or the Keweenaw Peninsula, where long periods of prosperity brought with them lavish homes and elaborate public buildings, in this part of the U.P. for the most part either areas were left undeveloped, or economic development happened in such rapid boom-and-bust cycles that towns couldn't quite keep up. In particular, towns around Ironwood and the Gogebic Range never seemed to hold on to the iron money long enough to invest much in the area's buildings, and after the mines closed, the area languished for years in economic depression that some would argue is still going on today. Nonetheless, there are still bits of human history to be explored here.

HISTORIC BUILDINGS AND SITES

The Ironwood Memorial Building (906-932-5050; 213 S. Marquette St.), for example, was built in the 1920s to commemorate local men who died in World War I. The ornate Ironwood Memorial Building now plays triple duty as a city hall with civic offices and a community center. Its auditorium is used for various community gatherings. The memorial is still intact, with

various statues and plaques commemorating the nearly 1,600 Gogebic-area soldiers killed in the war. Built in the beaux-arts style, the building's central rotunda, inset with stained-glass windows, is not to be missed. The main lobby boasts the strangest stained glass we've ever
seen, depicting the Battle of the Argonne, complete with flying shrapnel. The memorial building also includes various displays of Ironwood's history, and it still houses the Women's Club, which helped raise money for the building.

Also built in Ironwood in the 1920s was the Ironwood Theatre (906-932-0618; www.ironwoodtheatre.net), which opened as a vaudeville and silent movie palace in 1928. In addition to its organ—the original, installed to provide a soundtrack to silent movies, and still playable—the theater's domed ceiling features an elaborate proscenium mural that was discovered in the process of restoring the theater in the mid-1990s. It had been covered by a coat of dark blue paint in the 1970s, but a local artist helped the theater to bring back what could be salvaged—the outline of the mural— and restore it to its original glory. Though it no longer screens films, the theater is now used for Ironwood's musical concerts, for community theater productions, and for various community programs.

Another Ironwood landmark, the World's Tallest Indian (Burma St.) is nowhere near as elegant. The 53-foot-tall fiberglass Indian on the outskirts of town is clearly not an Ojibwa artwork or a tribute to the local tribes. It

Crystal Falls is a charming town with several historical buildings. Andrew Jameson

was part of a push by local business bureaus to promote tourism as the iron mines were closing. Not that the huge kitschy statue could be mistaken for authentic Native American art, with its red skin and giant headdress. Still, the idea wasn't wholly off the mark. Hundreds of U.P. visitors have had their picture taken with the fiberglass statue since it was raised, despite the fact that it's in a residential Gogebic Range location that's not near much except a shut-down mine and Manny's, a local favorite Italian restaurant (see "Local Flavors").

MUSEUMS AND GALLERIES

The Northwoods Niche (906-932-3316; www.northwoodsniche.com; 210 S. Suffolk St.), in Ironwood, is part coffee shop, part gift store, and part gallery, but its primary goal is to provide a marketplace for local artists. Currently the shop sells the work of 70 local artists, including everything from hand-carved wood bowls to photography. The artists also help to staff the store, which sometimes creates the rare situation of a customer buying directly from the artist. The store also saves a room in the back for Northwoods Treasures, a collection of local antiques and collectibles, also for sale.

Housed in a former grocery store, the Ontonagon County Historical Society Museum (906-884-6165; www.ontonagonmuseum.org; 422 River St.; closed Sundays; $3) is so endearing you'll wish you could take it home in your pocket. The museum's treasures are collected in one large room. And there's a whole lot of artifacts packed in there, from the various phases of Ontonagon's history—as a harbor town, a mining town, and a Scandinavian village. Trinkets from early settlers, before and after pictures of an 1899 fire, and an exhibit of minerals and rocks pulled from the mines all combine to make this a charming and interesting small-town museum, well worth a stop if you're in Ontonagon. You can't miss the museum if you're driving through town—its building is painted baby blue with royal blue trim, and it's got the brightest pink door you've ever seen.

Despite its name, the Menominee Range Historical Museum (906-774-4276; www.menomineemuseum.com; 300 E. Ludington St.) is not in Menominee, but Iron Mountain. A stately Carnegie library built in 1901 is now home to over 100 exhibits showcasing life in Iron Country during the 1800s and 1900s, including an exact replica of an 1800s classroom, a full livery stable complete with horse carriages, and a hands-on general store stocked with typical goods from a bygone era. In addition to its permanent exhibits, the museum hosts a series of rotating exhibits. The building itself is large and beautiful, with imposing white columns and a balcony overlooking the front lawn. Next door, its sister Cornish Pump Museum contains the largest steam-driven pumping engine built in the United States.

Crystal Falls is home to two very interesting bits of Native American heritage. Open only in the summer, the Harbour House Museum (906-875-4341; 17 North Fourth St.) is a painstakingly restored Victorian house that's great fun to explore. Surprisingly, although it does hold a few steamer trunks filled with Great Gatsby–style garments of the area's ladies, the most complete collection in the house is in the Ojibwa room, where the traditional handicrafts and clothing of a local Ojibwa family are on display.

Pentoga Park (www.pentogapark.net; 1630 CR 424), a pretty park on the south shore of Chicaugon Lake, is also a preserved Ojibwa burial ground, complete with traditional wooden burial structures known as spirit houses. Dedicated in 1922 in honor of the Ojibwa tribe, the park is named, sort of, after the wife of the local tribal chief at the time, Chief Edward (his real name was Mush-Quo-No-Ns-Bi). His wife's name was Biindigeyaasi-nokwe, shortened to Biindige and mispronounced by the newcomers as Pentoga, meaning "bullhead."

SHOPPING

Antiques and Books

Don't let the name scare you off, some real antique treasures are to be found at Bargain Barn Antiques in Crystal Falls (906-875-3381; 60 Superior Ave.), a huge shop occupying an old hotel in the charming downtown area. You could easily spend all day here: Bargain Barn sells both the store's own collection and has stalls filled with collectibles from outside dealers as well. The name is no mistake; they actually do have a number of bargains here.

Gift and Specialty Shops

Iron Mountain isn't exactly the first town to come to mind when you think "shopping," but the fabulous Vintage Sundries (906-774-1324; 101 W. A St.) is a great spot to find all sorts of interesting gifts. Electric blue with orange trim, the shop sells retro-styled gifts and, well, sundries.

The Great Outdoors

Outdoor adventures and activities in southwestern U.P.

The U.P. is as much a nature lover's dream as it is an outdoorsman's paradise, equal parts wildlife refuge and hunter's haven. This particular region is especially popular with sportsmen for its dozens of inland lakes, which are incredible for fishing in the summer, and its large deer population, which makes for excellent hunting in the fall. Meanwhile, birdwatchers love the Sylvania Wilderness, home to numerous species, many of them rare.

In the fall, visitors flock to view the beautiful colors as the leaves turn and to hunt various deer and fowl; and in the winter, the well-groomed cross-country ski trails, mile after mile of snowmobile trails, and family-friendly ski resorts bring almost as many visitors in December as the summer sun brings in July.

BEACHES

Just west of Crystal Falls, Bewabic State Park comprises several lakes, footbridges, walkways, sandy beaches, and tennis courts. Fishing is great in several of the lakes, and canoes and kayaks are available for rent.

In the case of Clark Lake, in the Sylvania Wilderness Area near Watersmeet, one lake is plenty. With its sandy beach and jewel-toned, crystal-clear water, this is a perfect spot to spend a day (or more.)

Henes Park, off MI 35 in north Menominee, is a 50-acre city park with a playground, lily pond, and pleasant sandy beach.

BICYCLING

Over 200 miles of trails run through Iron County and down into Wisconsin to make up the Pines and Mines Trails. The Pomeroy/Henry Lake Mountain Bike Complex (1-800-659-3232) is part of that system, featuring a family-friendly 100-mile complex of loops provides a number of options, from shorter 7-mile rides to challenging longer rides. Trails lead through Ottawa National Forest and pass by various lakes, streams, and wetlands.

In nearby Ironwood, close to Big Powderhorn ski resort, a popular cross-country ski complex becomes Wolverine Mountain Bike Trail (906-932-5858)—a network of mountain biking trails—in the summer.

The lush, beautiful George Young Recreational Complex, a 3,000-plus-acre recreational complex between Iron River and Crystal Falls, features not only a golf course and a pool, but also 7.5 miles of mountain-bike trails that wind through woods, up and down hills, and beside the lake that adjoins the recreation area.

Porcupine Mountains Wilderness State Park (906-885-5275; www .michigan.gov/dnr) offers dozens of trails, many of which provide access to parts of the park that are otherwise tough to get to. Park officials have prepared a detailed and comprehensive mountain biking map that guests can pick up at the park's visitors center or download and print from the Michigan Department of Natural Resources (DNR) Web site.

Watersmeet is full of great trails as well, starting with the Agonikak

Clark Lake, in the Sylvania Wilderness Area of the Ottawa National Forest, provides excellent paddling. Aaron Landry

Trail, from Watersmeet to Land O'Lakes. An easy-to-moderate 12-mile ride that begins in the Ottawa National Forest near Watersmeet and meanders through dense forest and past inland lakes to Land O'Lakes. Head out in the late morning, stop in Land O'Lakes for lunch, and then take it easy on the flat return route to Watersmeet. For a longer but flatter version of this ride, stick to the Watersmeet Rails-to-Trails, an old railroad line converted to a biking, hiking, and ATV path, which begins at the U.S. Forest Service Visitor Center in Watersmeet and ends at the public library in Land O'Lakes.

BIRD-WATCHING

The Sylvania Wilderness Area rivals the Seney Wildlife Refuge as a great bird-watching spot, and with several parks in the area, including the Ottawa National Forest and Porcupine Mountains Wilderness State Park, it's not even the only spot around.

The DNR has developed two interpretive trails in the region. The Black River Songbird Trail (906-667-0261), just outside Bessemer, is a prime spot to view migrating waterbirds during spring and fall migrations. Merlins have also been known to nest in the bluffs around the harbor. Deer Marsh Interpretive Trail, south of Sidnaw, is an easy 3-mile hike that loops through wetlands and around Deer Marsh, which is positively brimming

Porcupine Mountains State Park features several lovely hiking trails.   Wikimedia Commons

with interesting wildlife. Ospreys, bald eagles, hooded mergansers, great blue herons, and American bitterns are all common here, and you may also spot black-backed woodpeckers, boreal chickadees, and the ever-elusive trumpeter swans.

Also in this area, near Crystal Falls, Bewabic State Park, with its chain of five Fortune Lakes surrounded by acres of mature birch-maple forest, is a great place to see a variety of U.P. birds, particularly during the spring migration. Warblers are often in full view, some of the lakes are quiet enough for loons, and eagles build their nests around two of the five lakes (First and Third).

And then of course there's the Sylvania Wilderness Area, less than 5 miles west of Watersmeet. If you needed any more reasons to visit the pristine lakes and stately hushed forests of the 21,000-acre Sylvania Wilderness Area, how about the fact that a pair of loons nests at nearly every lake, or that barred owls are out in abundance at night, only to be replaced by pileated woodpeckers, blackburnian warblers, black-throated green warblers, red-eyed vireos, and ovenbirds in the morning? The area is also home to bald eagles, broad-wing hawks, and ospreys, which stick around for the abundance of fish in the lakes.

CAMPING

Camping areas abound in the U.P., thanks in large part to the region's extraordinary number of protected nature areas, from state parks to wildlife refuges to enormous national forests. In this area, the Hiawatha National Forest, the Ottawa National Forest, and the Sylvania Wilderness Area provide a variety of options, as do numerous smaller parks. Whether you prefer to camp in untouched wilderness, in a shady campground with modern conveniences, or on the beach, you'll find plenty of options here.

What follows are our favorite campgrounds. For more detailed information about all the campgrounds in this region, visit the Web sites for Hiawatha National Forest (www.fs.fed.us/r9/forests/hiawatha) and Ottawa National Forest and Sylvania Wilderness Area (www.fs.fed.us/r9/ottawa).

Ironwood and the Gogebic Range

Located on the west shore of the largest inland lake in the U.P., Lake Gogebic State Park (1-800-447-2757; open mid-May through late September;

The Sylvania Wilderness Area features several pristine lakes, such as Katherine Lake.
Wikimedia Commons

Sylvania Wilderness Area is one of the largest untouched nature reserves in the country.
Aaron Landry

$10–16) is a large campground that includes a mile of shoreline. Almost a quarter of the sites are right on the lake—a pretty choice spot when you consider that the rest of the shoreline has been gobbled up by private cottages. Thanks to its shallow waters, Lake Gogebic is great for swimming, and the campground includes a large sandy beach, as well as a boat launch for fishermen eager to test the lake's famed waters. Taken purely on its own, the campground is not amazing—there are few trees, which means not a lot of privacy, and the proximity of the campground to the state highway isn't ideal—but the location and modern conveniences like showers and flushing toilets more than make up for what any of the individual sites lack.

A popular local campground situated on a bluff overlooking Lake Superior, near Ironwood, Little Girl's Point (906-932-1913; open May 15 through September 30; $12–14) has it all—sandy beach, boat launch, wildlife, large wooded campsites, electrical hookups, bike trails that connect with the Powers Trail System, and proximity to local sights. The only slight drawback is that the trees between sites aren't tall enough or thick enough to provide privacy.

Ontonagon and the Porkies

Renting a yurt or wilderness cabin in the Porcupine Mountains Wilderness State Park will put you in one of the coolest spots in the U.P. (www .michigan.gov/porkies; open May 15 through October 15; $60). Accessed only by trail, the yurts are sturdy dome-shaped tents built on top of wood platforms with built-in bunk beds. The fabric walls are so durable and pulled so snugly to the platform that the weatherproof yurts can accommodate campers in all seasons. The park's 19 rustic cabins are also accessed by trail—anywhere from 1- to 4-mile hikes—and have long been popular with visitors, especially the seven cabins that overlook Lake Superior. Even without the Lake Superior views, all of the cabins are located near the park's most scenic points. The cabins and yurts get booked up quickly, so it's best to reserve as far in advance as possible, especially if you're hoping to score one for a summer trip.

In general, the state park in the Porcupine Mountains (aka the Porkies) provides some of the best camping spots in the U.P. And Presque Isle River Campground (1-800-447-2757; www.michigan.gov/porkies; open May 15 through October 15; $14) is one of the best of the best. Located in one of the area's most picturesque (and popular) settings, just a quarter mile from the mouth of the Presque Isle River on a bluff overlooking Lake Superior, it's a fantastic site. Four nearby waterfalls are easily reached via a 2-mile trail loop. The sites themselves are large and well placed. Many have lake views, while others are tucked back into the forest.

Watersmeet

The Sylvania Wilderness Area (1-877-444-6777; www.reserveusa.com; open year-round; $10 May through September, free October through April) offers wilderness camping at its finest and purest. Sites are well placed around the 34 pristine lakes and acres of old-growth forest, which make Sylvania the treasure it is. Even on a crowded summer weekend, campers feel like they've got the forest to themselves. In addition to viewing various other wildlife and birds of all kinds, campers should remember that this is bear country: Black bears are a regular sight, and campers should prepare accordingly. If handled appropriately, of course, a bear sighting could be the highlight of your trip. Fishing in the lakes is spectacular, but highly regulated—be sure to visit the Ottawa National Forest's Web site for details. Canoeing, kayaking, and swimming are all absolutely amazing here; no mechanized items of any kind (which includes bicycles and sailboats) are allowed.

For those who want access to the Sylvania Wilderness without the wilderness camping, Clark Lake Campground (open May through September, first come, first served; $12) offers drive-up sites in the forest with all the amenities, including the rarest: hot showers. Close to a lovely swimming beach on Clark Lake and a pleasant stretch of the Clark Lake Trail surrounded by old-growth forest, the campground truly offers the best of all worlds.

CANOEING AND KAYAKING

With dozens of lakes and rivers in a half-dozen large state, national, and local parks, there's no end to the options for paddlers in this part of the peninsula.

The Ontonagon River (906-932-1330) has something for every level of paddler, from slow, scenic rides on the Middle Branch to a mix of easy paddles with decently challenging whitewater at the end of the South Branch to nonstop rapids on the East Branch.

Considered some of the Midwest's most challenging whitewater, the last few miles of Presque Isle River (906-885-5612) draw experienced paddlers from all over the state.

The Menominee Watershed creates a boundary between Michigan and Wisconsin; part of the Menominee also includes Piers Gorge, a whitewater for experienced paddlers only. The National Park Service (www.nps.gov) produces canoe trail maps for the region. A variety of trips are possible here, ranging from easy to advanced.

Sylvania Wilderness Area includes 34 named lakes, plus 25 miles of portages, all waiting to be explored. The canoe launch at Clark Lake is simple and straightforward; get a map from the Ottawa National Forest Service for details on other lakes and portages. Due to the area's vast size and the remote location of some lakes, we highly recommend a guided trip with Sylvania Outfitters (the only Special Use Permit holder for canoe trips into the Sylvania Wilderness and Recreation Area), or at least stopping in to talk to those guys before heading out on your own.

Rentals

Porcupine Mountain State Park Concessionaire. 906-885-5612; near Silver City

Northwoods Wilderness Outfitters. 1-800-530-8859; www.northwoodsoutfitters.com; Iron Mountain

Sylvania Outfitters. 906-358-4766; www.sylvaniaoutfitters.com; Watermeet

CROSS-COUNTRY SKIING

In addition to being home to most of the state's downhill ski resorts, this part of the peninsula has several great cross-country ski trails.

Fumee Lake Natural Area (1-800-236-2447; www.fumeelakes.org; west of Norway along the US 2) offers a few quiet, well-groomed trails across an 1,800-acre "no motors allowed" park surrounded by trees and hills. Groomed trail loops wrap around Fumee Lake, Little Fumee Lake, and Indiana Mine Pond, as well as up the hill and through the forest to the north of Fumee Lake on the Fumee Mountain Trail. In addition to the groomed trails, several single-track trails run through the park. Be careful away from the lakes, as trails in these areas are near the designated hunting area and a handful of snowmobile trails.

Nearby in Iron River, the Iron River Nordic Cross Country Ski Center (906-265-3401; www.georgeyoung.com), located in the George Young Recreational Complex, includes 6 kilometers of groomed cross-country ski trails that head to nearby Wagner Lake or through the hills and woods of the recreational complex. After skiing, relax your muscles and warm up at the complex's indoor pool, spa, and sauna complex.

There are two great cross-country ski complexes in Ironwood. ABR Trails (906-932-3502; www.abrski.com) is a huge 600-acre cross-country ski resort with 42 kilometers of spectacular trails, groomed daily. Wolverine Ski Club Nordic Trails (906-932-5858) has five different loops through rolling hills and woods that provide 18 kilometers of skiing for both striders and skaters of all levels, though the emphasis is on more experienced skiers. Wolverine also allows snowshoes on its tracks and provides a warming lodge for all. Some of the loops cross over onto Big Powderhorn ski resort and can also be accessed from the resort side.

DOWNHILL SKIING AND SNOWBOARDING

This is one of the few spots in Michigan that offers downhill skiing. Despite all the snow the state gets, its relatively flat landscape doesn't make it a downhill destination. The mountains here don't exactly compete with the Alps, but there are still a few decently challenging runs, and it's a great spot to teach kids to ski.

Norway Mountain (1-800-272-5445; www.norwaymountain.com) has a 500-foot vertical drop, 16 runs, three lifts, terrain park, ski and board rentals, a ski school, restaurant, bar, and lodging. Pine Mountain Golf & Ski Resort (906-774-2747; www.pinemountainresort.com), in Iron Mountain, is nearly twice as large; with the same 500-foot vertical drop, the resort boasts 26 runs, four lifts, two terrain parks, ski and board rentals, and a ski school. Pine Mountain also has lodging on-site, as well as a restaurant and bar. Size-wise, Ski Brule (1-800-362-7853; www.skibrule.com), in Iron River, is in between the two, but despite having only 18 runs, the resort boasts five lifts, as well as a half-pipe and a terrain park. Ski Brule also has lodging and dining on-site, and it opens early in the season (by early November) and stays open late (May).

In Bessemer, Big Powderhorn Mountain Resort (1-800-501-7669; www.bigpowderhorn.net) is one of the larger resorts in the area. It has a steeper drop (600 feet), as well as nine chairlifts, 29 runs, and three terrain parks, plus on-site lodging and dining. Bessemer's other ski resort, Blackjack Resort (906-229-5115; www.skiblackjack.com) is smaller, with a 466-foot drop, six chairlifts, and 20 runs. It does, however, have two terrain parks and two half-pipes, making it popular with local snowboarders. Nearby, in Wakefield, Indianhead Mountain Resort (1-800-346-3426; www.indianheadmtn.com) is the largest resort in the Big Snow Country part of the region, with a 638-foot drop, nine lifts, 28 runs, and two terrain parks. Indianhead is also the nicest all-around resort in Big Snow Country, with the most options for everyone in the family and the best-kept lodging and restaurants.

One of the few state parks in the country to offer prime downhill skiing, Porcupine Mountains Wilderness State Park (231-420-5405; www.skithe porkies.com), with its 787-foot vertical drop, makes for better skiing than the Big Snow Country resorts, especially with its 16 newly double-black-diamond Everest runs. There are just a few caveats: First, although there are plenty of options nearby, there is no lodging available on-site. Then, there are sometimes lines; although the park has 42 runs, there are only two chairlifts. You'll also need to bring your own mountain snacks, as there is no restaurant on-site.

FISHING

The best fishing spot in this part of the peninsula is the Sylvania Wilderness Area. Comprising 34 lakes, all great for fishing, Sylvania is well known for its catch-and-release bass program. All the lakes in the tract except for Crooked Lake abide by a set of regulations specific to Sylvania, which can be picked up at the park's entrance. Motors are allowed only on Crooked Lake, where the regular state of Michigan fishing regulations apply and not the Sylvania regulations. Sylvania Outfitters (906-358-4766; www .sylvaniaoutfitters.com), in Watersmeet, is the only outfitter with a permit to conduct tours in Sylvania, and they offer a couple of great fishing trips.

GOLF

The golf trend that hit Escanaba spread west to Iron Country, where summertime golf seemed like a good match for winter ski resorts. Gogebic Country Club (906-932-2515), in Ironwood, is one of the older courses in the area, opened in the early 1920s. Despite its country club name, the course is public. With its hills, tree-lined fairways, and a very pleasant clubhouse (with a restaurant and bar), it's a great place to spend a morning.

Surrounded by the large oak trees that give it its name, Oak Crest Golf Course (906-563-589; www.oakcrestgolf.com) in Norway is a moderate course, made more difficult by the rolling hills on which it is built.

Iron Mountain boasts two of the best courses in the area, TimberStone Golf Club and Pine Grove Country Club. TimberStone Golf Club at Pine Mountain Golf & Ski Resort (906-774-2747; www.pinemountainresort .com) is rated a five-star course by *Golf Digest*. It's a championship course designed by Jerry Matthews and draws as many visitors to Pine Mountain in the summer as the ski runs do in winter. Offering the sort of manicured beauty you'd expect golf magazines to rave about, TimberStone is surrounded by birch and maple trees and takes advantage of its panoramic Pine Mountain views. Though the course has a 300-foot vertical drop, golfers only have to contend with two uphill holes.

Pine Grove Country Club (906-774-3493; www.pinegrovecc.org), a semiprivate club founded in 1902, is surrounded by dense virgin stands of white and red pine, maple, and oak and features a challenging hilly terrain with an 84-foot elevation change. Another course that began life as a 9-holer, Pine Grove was expanded and redesigned by Roger Packard in the 1960s. A bit swankier than some of the other clubs because of its semiprivate status, Pine Grove is nonetheless incredibly affordable and friendly when compared to private or semiprivate clubs elsewhere in the country.

Just as George Young Recreational Complex (906-265-3401; www .georgeyoung.com) has some of the best fishing, bicycling, and cross-country skiing in the area, it also features a fantastic 18-hole course in the middle of its 3,000-plus acres. Donated to the public by a Chicago millionaire in the early 1990s, the complex is the jewel of Iron River. Young built the course himself, one hole at a time, modeling each after a personal favorite hole of his at various courses throughout the country. It's no wonder that the resulting course is the longest in the U.P.! With its narrow fairways and large greens, hills and panoramic views, the course was awarded four stars by *Golf Digest*, which called it "a gem off the beaten track." In addition to the design of the course itself, its surroundings make George Young very pleasant to play, with acre after acre of undeveloped forest, woodland wildlife, and a neighboring lake. The colors in the fall are vivid and beautiful. The main lodge is well designed, with plenty of windows and open beams that create a perfect blend of North Country rustic style and modern architectural design.

HIKING

Porcupine Mountains Wilderness State Park has some of the best hiking trails in the state. One of the best of the best is Escarpment Trail (906-885-5275). Starting at the Government Peak trailhead, this popular loop trail follows a high ridge over the Big Carp River Basin, offering dramatic views

Family Fun

DeYoung Family Zoo (906-788-4093; www.thedeyoungfamilyzoo.com; US 41 in Wallace, north of Marinette; $12 adults, $8 children) Recently featured on the National Geographic Channel reality show *My Life Is a Zoo*, the DeYoung Family Zoo is owned and operated by Bud DeYoung and is home to over 400 animals, including tigers (40 big cats and growing), brown and black bears, monkeys, wolves, foxes, hyenas, hippos, and an assortment of local critters, such as raccoons and porcupines. In addition to the regular zoo, there's also a small petting zoo, where kids can feed and pet an assortment of animals.

Iron Mountain Iron Mine (906-563-8077; www.ironmountainironmine .com; US 2 in Vulcan, 9 miles east of Iron Mountain) Though it might not have been much fun to work in the mines, it sure is cool to tour them now. Armed with raincoats and hard hats—and who doesn't get a kick out of a hard hat?—families can tour the 2,600-foot East Vulcan Mine, marveling at the life the miners must have had. An underground train takes visitors into the mine in much the same way the miners would have ridden to work back in the late 1800s and early 1900s. Experienced guides point out various rocks, recount the history of the mine, and guide visitors to large man-made mine chambers called stopes. The mine feels a bit like a Disneyland attraction now, with a huge "Big John—the world's largest miner" statue and sign out front, a gift shop selling toy pickaxes, and folksy blues mining songs playing on a loop, but it's a blast for kids, and it's interesting to learn a bit about the mining history of the area.

Pine Mountain Ski Jump (906-774-2747; www.pinemountainresort.com; N3332 Pine Mountain Rd., Iron Mountain) The best time of year to visit the ski jump is in February, during the Pine Mountain Ski Jumping tournament, when jumpers fly down the mountain and fling themselves off it, but in summer it's still fun to climb up to the top of the jump and check out the view. Just keep an eye on the little ones around the vertical drop!

Humongous Fungus (US 2, about 7 miles south of Crystal Falls) This bizarrely large honey mushroom was labeled the world's largest and possibly oldest living organism when it was discovered back in the early 1990s. Although Crystal Falls's fungus was soon surpassed by other, larger fungi, it's still an impressive sight. The mushroom extends over 30 acres south of Horserace Rapids, just south of Crystal Falls, and is celebrated every year at the Humongous Fungus Fest. Some people are just grossed out by a 'shroom this size, but kids usually get a real kick out of it.

Copper Peak International Ski Flying Hill (906-932-3500; www.copper peak.org; Ironwood) The tallest man-made ski jump in the world, Copper Peak is open to visitors during the summer, when you can crawl up its 18 stories and marvel at both the view and how terrifying it would be to go hurtling down this monster on skis. Just to put the hill into perspective, in the Olympics, ski jumpers compete on two different-size hills, small (90 meters) and large (120 meters). Copper Peak is a 170-meter hill. There are five ski-flying hills in Europe, but Copper Peak is the only ski-flying facility in the Western Hemisphere. Copper Peak is in the process of finishing various improvements required by the FIS (Fédération Internationale de Ski) in order to host ski-flying competitions. When the hill hosts another competition, it will be an event not to be missed!

Paulding Mystery Light (from US 2 at Watersmeet, take MI 45 north toward Paulding; in about 5 miles the road will begin a slow bend to the right; watch for Robbins Pond Rd.—old MI 45—on the left; turn down Robbins Pond Rd. and follow it about .375 mile to a dead end) A mysterious light is seen in the woods here, which some believe to be

continued next page

People huddle together and watch intently for the Paulding Mystery Light. Aaron Landry

supernatural, while others insist it's just headlights from a nearby road. Everyone has a different explanation for the light. Even the local chamber of commerce and the National Park Service have gotten in on this piece of folklore. The National Park Service posts a sign every summer that reads, "This is the location from which the famous Paulding Light can be observed. Legend explains its presence as a rail-road brakeman's ghost, destined to remain forever at the sight of his untimely death. He continually waves his signal lantern as a warning to all who come to visit." Whether you believe in ghost stories or not, it's great fun to take the kids out to the forest for a glimpse of the friendly ghost and his mysterious light. Face north and look for the light in the distance along the power line rights-of-way.

Presque Isle River Waterfalls (see "Waterfalls" for complete description) Kids absolutely love the suspension bridge here, and the wooden boardwalk provides an easy, safe way for small children to do a water-fall hike.

Summit Peak Observation Tower (Porcupine Mountains Wilderness State Park, middle of S. Boundary Rd.) A wooden boardwalk leads through hemlock and maple groves to this 40-foot tower at the park's highest point. The climb up is fun, and it feels like you can view the whole county and then some from up here, with views of Wisconsin's Apostle Islands in the distance. In the fall, the tower looks out over a sea of brilliant colors.

Summit Peak Overlook in Porcupine Mountains State Park. Matt Girvan

View from Lake of the Clouds Scenic Overlook. Bill Grove

of the valley and spectacular fall color. The slightly shorter Overlook Trail starts in the same place and provides similar views, and for those short on time, the Lake of the Clouds Scenic Overlook provides the terrific view without the hike.

The Porkies aren't the only great hiking spot in the region, of course. A section of the North Country Trail runs through the Trap Hills (906-932-1330), part of the Ottawa National Forest in Ironwood. Though it's a bit remote, the views from these hills are spectacular, incorporating Lake Superior, the Porcupine Mountains, and Lake Gogebic in one panoramic sweep.

Closer to the Wisconsin border, Piers Gorge is worth a visit, even if you haven't got the experience or courage to brave its whitewater rapids. You can enjoy the Gorge from a safe distance on a wonderful trail that goes from cedar forest to a ridge 70 feet above the river, with a view of Misicot Falls. The gorge's namesakes are actually outcroppings of rock that look a bit like piers and create small waterfalls as the water rushes over them. Adventurous hikers can make their way down closer to the river and sit on the rocks near the third pier to catch the spray off the whitewater, or even dip into some of the river's quieter sections. In addition to the river and the whitewater, the wildflowers are especially beautiful here in the late spring and early summer.

North of Piers Gorge, the Sylvania Wilderness Area offers some nice hiking spots as well, despite the fact that most people believe that the Sylvania is best experienced by canoe. Clark Lake Loop is one of the better hikes in the park; there is something absolutely magical about walking through the immense peace and silence of trees that are hundreds of years old. That section of the trail alone would be enough to make it memorable, but add to it the delight of happening upon rare wildlife or flowers and possibly a swim in the crystal blue quiet of Clark Lake, and you've got yourself a day you'll never forget.

HUNTING

Nearly all of the Porkies' 60,000 acres are open to hunters during the season. Deer and black bear are plentiful here, and the park's cabins and yurts are well placed in the wilderness for hunters. The stretch of Ottawa National Forest in Ironwood is also open to hunters during most of the year. Greenwoods Outfitting (906-863-5033; www.greenwoodsoutfitting.com) in Menominee and Northwoods Wilderness Outfitters (1-800-530-8859; www.northwoodsoutfitters.com) in Iron Mountain offer equipment, advice, and guides. For information about state hunting regulations and hunting seasons for various game, see chapter 7.

SNOWMOBILING

The state maintains over 6,000 miles of groomed snowmobile trails, and maps of the state-maintained trails are available online from the Michigan DNR (www.michigan.gov/dnr). Of particular interest in this part of the peninsula are Alligator Eye (MI 64, 2 miles south of Gogebic), a short and steep trail that leads to the top of a bluff with a panoramic view, and Greenland-Bruce Crossing Trail (also known as Trail 3), which runs through the Ottawa National Forest near Ontonagon to connect to Bruce Crossing. From there, it connects with dozens of other trails in the forest. Riders can stay on Trail 3 to Watersmeet, head west to Bergland (near Lake Gogebic) or ride east to Agate Falls. State Trails 2 and 3 intersect at Watersmeet, making it possible to go any direction you like from the town. The surrounding Ottawa National Forest is full of trails, but the forest's Sylvania Wilderness Area does not allow snowmobiles.

Snowmobiles can be rented from Timberline Sports (906-575-3397; www.timberlinesport.com) near Bergland.

Agate Falls are among the U.P.'s most popular waterfalls. James Phelps

WATERFALLS

Some of the prettiest falls in the peninsula are in this southwest corner, starting with **Agate Falls**, a large, tiered, multilevel waterfall created by the Ontonagon River. Nearby, in Porcupine Mountains State Park, Presque Isle River Waterfalls are reached via a pleasant woodland boardwalk that follows the river, revealing various falls along the way. On one end of the trail, a suspension bridge over the river provides a fantastic view of the falls and a great photo op; at the other end the boardwalk stops, but the trail continues a quarter mile to a final set of falls.

Five different waterfalls—Great Conglomerate, Potawatomi, Gorge, Sandstone, and Rainbow—are viewable along the **Black River** via either Black River Road by car or the North Country Scenic Trail on foot. At the end of the river, **Black River Harbor** (906-667-0261) provides a pleasant beach and picnic area known for bird-watching. West of Ironwood, near Hurley, Wisconsin, the dramatic **Superior Falls** are created as the Montreal River flows through a steep and narrow gorge on its way to Lake Superior near the Wisconsin-Michigan border. The Wisconsin Electric Power Station harnesses the power of the water to generate electricity and has built a viewing platform for the falls. The river first thunders 40 feet over a sheer cliff, pools, then flows on through the tree-lined walls of the gorge.

5

Northwest

HOUGHTON, KEWEENAW, AND ISLE ROYALE

THOSE EARLY COPPER MILLIONAIRES sure did know how to put a town together. From Houghton and Hancock at the base of the peninsula, to Calumet and Laurium in the middle, to Copper Harbor at the northern-most point, the Keweenaw is chock-full of darling towns, beautifully designed buildings, and great views.

At one point the Keweenaw was the world's largest supplier of copper, a fact that drew to its mines thousands of immigrants, primarily of Finnish, Italian, and Eastern European descent. As with the Upper Peninsula's vari-ous other former mining regions, the descendants of those immigrants still call the Keweenaw home and have woven their food, music, and culture into the fabric of the remaining towns.

Houghton—which is so close to nearby Hancock that most people just run the names together and think of them as one town—is the U.P.'s other university town. Though Northern Michigan University in Marquette is better known, Michigan Technological University in Houghton is well respected for producing world-class engineers. It was established to train mining engineers but quickly broadened its scope and has grown into a highly regarded university. And Houghton is the better for it. The students have given the town a young, but smart, vibe that's enjoyable and has a way of making the small town seem much more urban than it is.

Isle Royale, on the other hand, is truly untouched wilderness. The park holds the dubious honor of being the least visited park in the National Park System. That's not a huge surprise, given that it's a six-hour, 73-mile journey

LEFT: Isle Royale's Rock Harbor Lighthouse.   Matt Girvan

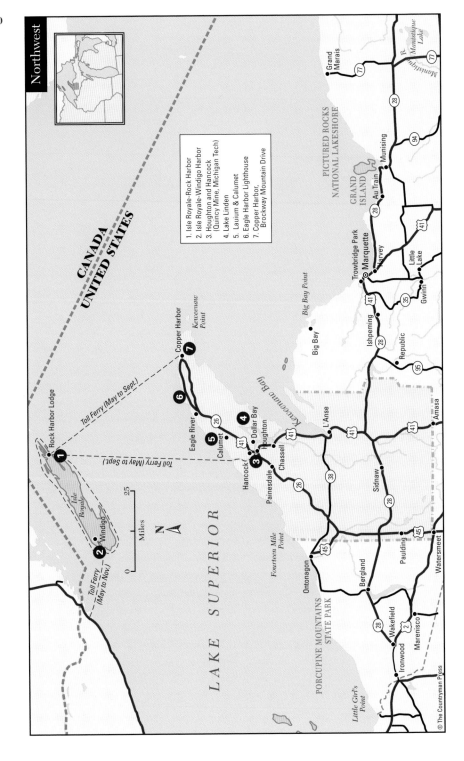

CANADA
UNITED STATES

1. Isle Royale–Rock Harbor
2. Isle Royale–Windigo Harbor
3. Houghton and Hancock
   (Quincy Mine, Michigan Tech)
4. Lake Linden
5. Lauium & Calumet
6. Eagle Harbor Lighthouse
7. Copper Harbor,
   Brockway Mountain Drive

LAKE SUPERIOR

Isle Royale

Windigo

Toll Ferry
(May to Nov.)

Rock Harbor Lodge

Toll Ferry (May to Sept.)

Toll Ferry (May to Sept.)

Keweenaw Point

Copper Harbor

Eagle River

Calumet

Hancock

Painesdale

Houghton

Dollar Bay

Chassell

Keweenaw Bay

Big Bay Point

Big Bay

L'Anse

Ishpeming

Republic

Trowbridge Park

Marquette

Harvey

Little Lake

Gwinn

Fourteen Mile Point

Ontonagon

Bergland

Sidnaw

Paulding

Watersmeet

Amasa

PORCUPINE MOUNTAINS STATE PARK

Wakefield

Marenisco

Ironwood

Little Girl's Point

PICTURED ROCKS NATIONAL LAKESHORE

GRAND ISLAND

Au Train

Munising

Grand Marais

Manistique Lake

Manistique R.

N

Miles

0   25

26

41

41

38

28

26

45

45

28

22

28

41

95

28

35

41

41

94

28

77

77

© The Countryman Press

Downtown in the mining-turned-college town of Houghton. Matt Girvan

from Houghton Harbor at the base of the Keweenaw Peninsula, and a three-hour, 56-mile voyage from Copper Harbor, at the northernmost tip. Once you dock, however, this 45-mile-long, 10-mile-wide island is essentially all yours. Visitors are welcome to explore as much or as little of the island as they like. Hard-core backpackers head for the farthest corners of the island, exploring its shores, caves, falls, streams, forest, and wildlife. Tent campers set up camp at one of the campgrounds near Rock Harbor, or hike farther into the woods for more privacy. And, for those who require a real bed and a hot shower, the Rock Harbor Lodge offers 60 guest rooms, each with two beds, a private bath, and a choice view of Lake Superior. Boaters and paddlers love Isle Royale almost as much as hikers and backpackers do: The island's many inland lakes, bays, and streams provide countless miles of paddling, and kayakers can just bring their camps along with them, making their way around and through the park easily.

Because of its remote location and near-total lack of development, Isle Royale is an ideal place to study nature and wildlife. The longest-running large mammal predator study on earth is the ongoing study of the gray wolves on Isle Royale. You may come across one of the subjects of this study if you're very quiet and catch it off guard. Equally elusive moose

Isle Royale's wilderness was once home to copper mines, first excavated by so-called Old Copper Indians. Matt Girvan

abound on Isle Royale to such an extent that they have become a sort of mascot for the island. Head to one of the bays in the early morning for the best chance of spotting one. Keep in mind that it gets cold here even in the summer months, especially the closer you get to Lake Superior. It is not uncommon to need long pants and a fleece on Isle Royale in July.

Pick Your Spot

Best places to stay in north-western U.P., and nearby . . .

There are plenty of great lodging options up and down the Keweenaw Peninsula, where the mansions of some of the region's old mining titans have been turned into charming B&Bs. Camping is great both on Isle Royale and in Baraga County, where beaches and forests around both Lake Superior and several inland lakes make for great spots to wake up in the morning.

On Isle Royale, Rock Harbor Lodge (1-888-644-2003; www.rock harborlodge.com; open May 25 through September 7; $$$$) is the only lodging facility on IsleRoyale, (campgrounds are listed under "Camping"), which goes a long way toward explaining why its room rates are some of the highest in the

U.P. Fortunately, it's also a very pleasant, well-kept lodge, the best aspect of which is the Lake Superior views from every one of its 60 rooms. All-inclusive packages that include room, three meals a day, and half-day use of a canoe are available. In addition to the views, each lodge room has two beds and a private bath. Twenty duplex housekeeping cottages are also available. Each cottage sleeps up to six people and comes equipped with a kitchenette, dishwasher, utensils, electric heat, double bed and bunk bed, linens and towels, and private bath.

A ferry ride away, on the northernmost tip of the peninsula in Copper Harbor, the **Bella Vista Motel and Cottages** (1-877-888-8439; www.bellavistamotel.com; open mid-May through mid-October; $) is a quaint red motel with white trim that fits exactly with Copper Harbor's whole vibe and provides basic rooms in one of the loveliest settings on the Keweenaw Peninsula. Most of the motel rooms offer a view of a lovely rock garden dotted with bright wildflowers in the spring and summer that stand out nicely against the deep blue of the lake just beyond. Even those without a view of the garden have a harbor view, and all have windows and sliding doors leading out to decks—sometimes shared, sometimes private. All guests also have access to free wireless Internet service. The cottages are darling vintage numbers,

some of which have been renovated recently, others of which could probably use an overhaul. Only some of the cottages face the water; others are closer to the road and have no real view, so be sure to ask for a lakefront cottage if you opt for the privacy of the cottages over the motel. The Bella Vista is within walking distance of the Isle Royale Ferry dock and various Copper Harbor restaurants. A picnic area on the lake side of the motel is probably the most picturesque picnic spot in Copper Harbor.

A mile outside town, the **Keweenaw Mountain Lodge** (1-888-685-6343; www.atthelodge.com; $$) was built in the 1930s as part of the government's public works program. It gave dozens of out-of-work miners a purpose for a few months—hand-building several lovely log cabins, a log lodge, and a rolling golf course in the woods on a hillside a mile south of Copper Harbor. Since then the lodge has added an eight-unit motel. Though the motel offers large, newer rooms, nothing beats the vintage architecture of the cabins, most of which also include hand-built stone fireplaces. The main lodge itself is equally special, with its Alpine-inspired dark logs and rows of white-trimmed windows. The lodge's dining room turns out consistently good meals and has become somewhat of a "special occasion" restaurant locally.

A half hour down the peninsula,

the Dapple-Gray Bed & Breakfast (906-289-4200; www.dapple-gray .com; open year-round; $$$) in Eagle Harbor is a large, beautiful log B&B, with the owners' fantastic antiques shop occupying one of the ground-floor rooms. The inn and shop's namesake, a dapple-gray steeplechase horse, greets visitors to both. Four suites are each decorated according to a theme that infuses everything from the style of furniture to the pattern on the comforters—Americana, North Woods, Seashore, and Lincoln (as in Abe). Each suite has its own bathroom and its own private lakeview deck. Antiques displays are dotted through the house, but guests also have access to modern amenities like satellite TV and highspeed Internet. Common rooms include a sitting room with cathedral ceiling and a 28-foot fireplace and well-stocked library, laundry room, kitchen, and a freestanding wood sauna. Breakfast is warm and usually a notch above, with eggs Benedict, Michigan blueberry pancakes, and Midwest corn fritters all making an appearance. The Van Goors also rent a private twobedroom summer cabin in the woods on 27 acres of forest with 600 feet of private rocky shoreline.

In the middle of the peninsula, Laurium and Calumet are two of the prettier towns in Copper Country, filled with lovely buildings that hearken back to a time when captains of industry liked to see their names on opera houses. The Lau-

rium Manor Inn and its sister property the Victorian Hall fit right in.

Built in 1908 as the opulent, 45-room mansion of a Keweenaw copper baron, the Laurium Manor Inn (906-337-2549; www.laurium manorinn.com; $$$) now delights guests with its grand columns, ornate moldings, clawfoot tubs, and tales of Theodore Roosevelt having slept in one of the inn's beds. The folks at the Laurium have become preservation experts in the course of restoring the inn to its former glory, so much so that they went ahead and bought the Victorian across the street too and have also turned it into a B&B (see Victorian Hall listing below). Ten guest rooms with private baths offer guests 10 totally different experiences. Room 1, where Teddy Roosevelt is said to have stayed, boasts a stately private balcony, a huge fireplace, and is large enough to accommodate up to five guests. Each room has been restored to a version of its former self, and the Sprengers provide a description of what each room was and whom it once housed. Still, though all have been fitted out with the antique furnishings (sometimes original items from the manor) befitting their former lives, they also include modern luxuries such as LCD TVs with cable and free wireless Internet access, and some of the rooms have whirlpool tubs and DVD players. The Keweenaw Suite, housed in the manor's carriage house, is one of the loveliest structures we've

Laurium Manor Inn is a restored 45-room mansion that has been beautifully converted into a popular B&B. Laurium Manor Inn

ever seen. It's architectural perfection wrapped in a neat package of classic French doors and beautiful hardwood floors offset by sage green walls with crisp white trim and furniture of rich, dark brown leather. The suites are over-the-top beautiful, but even the former maids' quarters here are something special, and the common areas are jaw-droppingly beautiful, partly because of the quality of the materials that have gone into this house—stained glass, marble, beautiful woods, gilded and embossed elephant leather wall covering— and partly for the sheer larger-than-life scale of everything, from the 100-foot wraparound tile balcony to the grand triple staircase flanked by

a 9-by-14-foot stained-glass window. A full buffet breakfast is served in the formal dining room every morning for all guests, but the Laurium Manor Inn is also within walking distance of a handful of local eateries.

Also built as a mansion for a wealthy copper baron, and just as well preserved as its sister property across the street (the Laurium Manor Inn), the Victoria Hall (906-337-2549; www.lauriummanorinn .com; $$) is all dark wood and candlelight, where the Laurium is vaulted ceilings and windows. It just depends on whether you're in more of an Edgar Allen Poe sort of mood or a Walt Whitman flight of fancy. Either way, you can't help but be delighted by these grand old houses. Four of the eight guest rooms at Victoria Hall are blessed with ornately carved fireplaces, and elaborate molding and stained glass abound. As with Laurium Manor, Victoria Hall's crown jewel is its former carriage house, which has been transformed into a darling private cottage complete with wood-burning fireplace, hardwood floors, clawfoot tub, four-poster bed, and private porch. Victoria Hall guests are also treated to a full buffet breakfast every morning, served in the dining room of Laurium Manor across the street. Something to keep in mind: There are no phones at Victoria Hall, although most people get decent cell phone service.

In nearby Calumet, Michigan House (906-337-1910; www.michiganhousecafe.com; $) is not quite so grand as the mansions of Laurium, but it's still delightfully vintage. A former 26-room hotel constructed by the Bosch Brewing Company in 1905, the Michigan House now houses two delightful apartments, both decorated with vintage furniture and retro kitchens that will make visitors feel like they've traveled back in time 40 or 50 years. Located in historic downtown Calumet, the hotel is in walking distance to a few great eateries and shops and is conveniently close to the highway, making it easy to head north to Copper Harbor or south to Houghton and Hancock. The smaller of the two suites,

called the Corner Walk-Up, accommodates up to two people comfortably with a bedroom and sitting area, a kitchen with a half-size Wedgewood stove, and a bathroom with a clawfoot tub. The larger Angler Suite is decorated in vintage fishing décor and includes a separate living room and bedroom, a full kitchen, and a private bath with a shower. Both suites have free wireless Internet access. The popular brewpub on the first floor serves lunch and dinner every day but Wednesday, when the cooks are busy brewing their Red Jacket Oatmeal Espress microbrew.

Also in this area, Sand Hills Lighthouse Inn (906-337-1744; www.sandhillslighthouseinn.com; $$$)—largest and last manned lighthouse on the Great Lakes—is now a fantastic bed & breakfast with eight lovely rooms and stunning Lake Superior views. Listed on the National Historic Register, the lighthouse was built in 1913 to house the keeper and his family and was painstakingly restored in the mid-1990s by its warm and very proud owner. Decorated in a Victorian style that fits with the original details and moldings, all of the rooms are lovely, but the two standouts feature private balconies with sweeping Lake Superior views, king beds, and whirlpool tubs. It really doesn't get much more romantic than escaping to an old lighthouse, lighting a fire in the fireplace, and watching the moon twinkle on Lake Superior.

The influence of early Finnish and other Scandinavian settlers on this part of the peninsula is evident in everything from architecture to accents, but it's perhaps most evident in the local cuisine.

The terrific food at Copper Harbor's Harbor Haus (906-289-4502; www.harborhaus.com; $$$), for example, is varied, interesting, and delicious, with an assortment of German, Austrian, and Swedish imports, mixed with local specialties. Though the menu changes daily, certain items are almost always in rotation, including a fantastic duck pâté with crostini and lingonberries appetizer and of course fresh Lake Superior whitefish and trout. The fish is cooked absolutely perfectly, and German specialties like sauerbraten (vinegar-marinated slow-roasted beef), served with the traditional braised red cabbage and *spaetzle* (potato dumplings) are delicious. Steaks are cooked exactly to order: It's no easy task to cook a rare steak so that it's good and bloody but not cold in the center. A dinner companion who always orders steak rare and almost never gets the steak he's after was stunned to silence by the perfection attained here. Homemade desserts also change regularly, but the special raspberry cobbler is always on the menu and well worth ordering when you order your meal, as the kitchen bakes each order fresh. Finally, of course a restaurant called the Harbor Haus has to have good beer on draft, and here they continue to impress with imported German Hefeweizen (wheat beer) and pilsner.

As with Iron Country, Copper Country attracted several Italian workers as well, and their descendants are still a vibrant part of the community. The Gemignanis have been making spaghetti for hungry Copper Country diners for 75 years and counting. Gino, the grandfather of the current owner, Tony, started back in the late 1920s and early 1930s with a restaurant in Hancock called Gino's. Gino's meat sauce became so famous the family began canning it and selling it in grocery stores in the 1960s and 1970s. In 1982, Gino's son Rudy opened Gemignani's (906-482-2902; closed Sundays; $$) in Hancock in the same bright red and green building it occupies now. By 1994 Rudy was ready to retire and sell the place, but his son Tony decided to buy it from him instead and keep it in the family. Now, Tony is selling the Gemignani sauce, too, but not in cans—just spice packs so that people can make the famous sauce at home. In addition to the sauce, Tony and his wife, Rose, hand make most of the pastas, including delicious ravioli and cannelloni. The restaurant also serves a variety of traditional meat dishes, including chicken marsala and veal piccata, and an assortment of vegetarian options. At lunchtime, big sandwiches on crusty bread are a local favorite.

The other culinary influence on peninsula is not from the old country, but from the young students who flood into Houghton each year. Every college town needs its pizza joint, and the **Ambassador Restaurant** (906-482-5054; open lunch and dinner; $) is Houghton's. Except, this being the U.P., it's not just any old pizza place. This one is housed in a historic barroom with century-old booths and stained glass, offset by German-inspired murals of drinking and carousing gnomes thought to have been painted during Prohibition. In the summertime, an outdoor beer garden is a great place to sit and watch the boats go by on the Portage Canal. And the pizza is good too—thin crust with a variety of toppings, including all the usual suspects plus a very tasty assortment of specialty pies, among them the popular Garlic Chicken, Tostada Pizza, Chicken Broccoli, and Super Vegetarian.

Tucked away in a lovely old redbrick building on a Houghton side street, with a fantastic waterfront view, the **Library Restaurant and Brew Pub** (906-487-5882; $$), with its varied menu, French waitress, and large dining room, feels like it's in a much bigger town. The food is still mostly locally inspired, however, with fresh whitefish daily,

as well as an assortment of other fish, including salmon, sea bass, and a Hawaiian fish special that changes daily. We're not quite sure why they feel the need to fly fish in from Hawaii when they're surrounded by fish-filled waters, but I suppose one does get tired of whitefish after a while. In addition to the seafood, the restaurant offers a dizzying assortment of pastas, sandwiches, burgers, steaks, chicken, salads, appetizers, and even sushi and Mexican food. Usually when you get that kind of variety, none of it's all that good. Here, though, they somehow manage to handle it all well. The Library also brews its own beer, which goes nicely with almost everything on the menu— particularly the light and refreshing Keweenaw Golden Ale. The restaurant also offers a beer sampler for those who want to try a few of the creations.

The Library's not the only brewpub in the peninsula. The **Michigan House Café & Brew Pub** (906-337-1910; www.michiganhousecafe.com; closed Wednesdays; $) in Calumet is a real gem in every way, from the early-1900s mining vibe to the outstanding food, which includes pub classics like a Black Angus burger, with modern additions like a Kahlua pig sandwich and a black bean quinoa patty substitute for the burgers. The Michigan House's on-site brewery (the Red Jacket Brewing Company, in honor of Calumet's first name) completes the establishment's trip

The Gay Bar in Gay, Michigan

The only bar in this tiny town has taken advantage of the town's name and created a booming T-shirt business. Dozens of shirts in various designs sporting slogans like "I Went Straight to the Gay Bar" draw tourists well off the beaten path to Gay. Once they're here, they take a photo next to the Gay Bar sign and head inside to grab lunch and another giggle: The Gay Bar's specialty is footlong hot dogs and brats.

Tourists travel several miles out of their way for a photo and a T-shirt from The Gay Bar in Gay, Michigan.   Matt Girvan

down memory lane. It occupies the site of a former hotel/saloon/restaurant/brewery, and with two vintage apartments for rent upstairs and a bar and restaurant downstairs, the brewery was all that was missing. The brewery is focusing on reviving the past as well, working with a recipe that's reminiscent of pre-Prohibition ales. The resulting Oatmeal Espress Stout has a higher alcohol content than most beers and uses oatmeal and espresso to give it its flavor and some of its oomph. The beer is brewed one barrel at a time on Wednesday when the restaurant is closed. When it's not being used for beer, the espresso here is delicious on its own—fresh-ground beans brewed in a vintage hand extraction process, of course. In addition to burgers, salads, and sandwiches, the restaurant serves an assortment of pastas, steaks, pork chops, shepherd's pie, and locally caught fish

Tasty Treats

Berry Patch (906-289-4602; 920 Gratiot Ave., Copper Harbor) Delicious fresh wild berry jams and sauces, as well as assorted gift items. Open in summer only.

Four Seasons Tea Room (906-482-3233; www.fourseasonstearoom .com; 606 Shelden Ave., Houghton) A 1940s-inspired tearoom with a variety of tea services, sandwiches, and

cakes, Four Seasons is a fantastic place to while away an afternoon. All the teas and some of the cakes are also sold in the shop, along with teapots, teacups, and various other tea accessories.

Jampot (www.societystjohn.com; 6500 MI 26, 3 miles east of Eagle River and 5 miles west of Eagle Harbor, right next to Jacob's Creek Falls) The jam, fruit butters, and baked goods here are delicious, but people are equally motivated to visit this tiny store on the road between Eagle River and Eagle Harbor just for the story behind it. Started by three monks from the Society of St. John, the store is still run by the order, who have since grown in number and built an ornate church just up the road. The monks felt the area lent itself well to a monastic life, and they now also lead monastic retreats here for others. Although they are always very friendly and pleasant, don't expect the monks to be too chatty; they prefer to spend most of their time in quiet reflection. When they're not tending to their booming online jam business, that is.

Sheldon's Pasties & Bakery (906-487-6166; www.sheldonsbakery .com; 901 W. Sharon Ave., Houghton) Sheldon's was the winner of the 2007 Pasty Fest Copper County award in the commercial division and the nontraditional division. Its traditional pasty won't pass muster with pasty purists for its blend of ground pork and beef and the addition of carrots, but for those without any hard-and-fast pasty rules, they are delicious. The breakfast pasty, which is what won the nontraditional award, is filled with pork sausage, potatoes, cheese, eggs, and seasoning. In addition to pasties, which Sheldon's ships anywhere in the country, the bakery also sells pies, muffins, pastries, and doughnuts.

Toni's Country Kitchen and Bakery (906-337-0611; 79 Third St., Laurium) Toni's wins many "best pasty" honors for its famous 1-pound pasty, made with ground chuck, potatoes, onion, and rutabagas.

Michigan House serves up its own microbrews and delicious grub. Matt Girvan

prepared a variety of ways, including fish-and-chips. Desserts such as cheesecake and beer-battered chocolate are homemade.

A steak lover's steakhouse, the Pilgrim River Steakhouse (906-482-8595; open lunch and dinner; $$$) in Houghton does just about everything right, from the huge assortment of cuts to the homemade bread served with every meal to the fact that they serve prime rib every day and not just on Sunday. And, as with any great steakhouse, the sides are just as good as the meat, whether you choose homemade soup, its famous spinach salad with hot bacon dressing, or the homemade steak fries. Despite the word *steakhouse* in its name, the Pilgrim River does seafood exceedingly well, especially white-fish and trout and the Friday special seafood platter. Homemade desserts are worth saving room for, and this is a great lunch spot as well, with big juicy burgers and tasty entrée-size salads.

Extend Your Stay

If you have more time, try these great places to see and things to do . . .

Skilled miners and unskilled laborers from England, Finland, Germany, the Balkans, and Italy flocked here to take the numerous mining jobs available. Their influence is still felt throughout the region today. Hancock, for example, is considered "the most Finnish town in America." Just under half of Hancock's population is of Finnish descent, a fact that is evident in many of the town's business names and annual events, like Heikinpaiva, the annual midwinter celebration (the word means "when the bear rolls over"), during which various town residents take a frigid plunge in Lake Superior.

The Keweenaw did eventually suffer the same fate as the other mining boom areas, resulting in the abandonment of several beautiful buildings throughout the peninsula and particularly in Calumet. The upside of that downturn is the recent reimagining of those old schools, libraries, and factories into restaurants, B&Bs, and galleries. In some cases, the old theaters and opera houses have been restored to their original glory and purpose as well. Either way, Copper Country is an architecture buff's dream.

HISTORIC BUILDINGS AND SITES

Calumet

Calumet was more directly created with money from the mines than most towns. Initially called Red Jacket, the town was taken over, planned, and paid for by the Calumet & Hecla mining company. The town has since been designated a historic preservation area by the National Park System, through legislation describing Calumet as an unprecedented example of American corporate paternalism. Its Main Street and North End (intersection of Fifth and Sixth with Pine) were built out to include the mansions of

Downtown Calumet is filled with historical buildings.   Andrew Jameson

wealthy copper barons, ornate office buildings for successful businessmen, an opera house, a theater, and fanciful stores and saloons. Although it suffered a period of depression after the mines closed that is still evident in an assortment of derelict houses around town, recently Calumet has been on an upswing. In addition to the National Park Service's commitment to preserving several historic landmarks downtown, in 2003 Calumet began receiving grant money from the National Trust for Historic Preservation to aid in the restoration of its downtown. Far from a depressed mining town, Calumet has become somewhat of a magnet for artistic types, many of whom are working hard to restore its historical buildings. Their work has been rewarded with an increase in both visitor interest and transplants moving to Calumet, mostly from elsewhere in Michigan or the U.P.

Calumet Preservation

The legislation designating Calumet as a historic preservation site provides a good summary of the history lesson this town continues to tell: "The corporate-sponsored community planning in Calumet, Michigan, as evidenced in the architecture, municipal design, surnames, foods, and traditions, and the large scale corporate paternalism was unprecedented in American industry and continues to express the heritage of the district. The . . . picture of copper mining on Michigan's Keweenaw Peninsula is best represented by . . . the Village of Calumet, [and] the former Calumet & Hecla Mining Company properties."

A large, freestanding, sandstone and brick archway on Seventh Street leads to Italian Memorial Park, a small park on the site of the former Italian Hall, commemorating a bleak point in Calumet history. The story goes that five months into a bitter copper mine strike, at a Christmas Party at Calumet's Italian Hall, someone yelled "fire!" though there was, in fact, no fire, and the resulting stampede of people rushing out of the building killed 73 people, mostly children, who were trapped in a stairwell with doors that opened inward and were said to have been locked shut. Some speculated that the mine bosses staged the whole thing, which is entirely possible, but no evidence was ever found to prove it. Lack of evidence didn't keep Woody Guthrie from composing a song about it, "1913 Massacre," that blamed the bosses, and it hasn't kept people from blaming them ever since.

The fantastic Gothic-style St. Anne's Church (25880 Red Jacket Rd.) sits at the head of downtown Calumet, reclaiming its place as a central structure in the town. As with many of the buildings in the area, St. Anne's is made of red sandstone from the Jacobsville quarry, cut into large rectangles like bricks. The facade's three entries feature ornate door-ways typical of late French Gothic buildings, and the interior features the vaulted ceilings and ornate moldings and eves also typical within the aes-thetic. Historians believe the church was built with various French design touches to please what was at the time predominantly French Canadian parishioners. Deconsecrated by the Catholic Church in the late 1960s, the building hosted a flea market for a time in the 1980s before lying vacant and neglected for decades. Now a designated Keweenaw Heritage Site, the church serves as the heritage center for the town and has been almost com-pletely restored to its former glory.

Also downtown, on Sixth Street, **Michigan House Café & BrewPub** (906-337-1910; www.michiganhousecafe.com) is on the site of an 1896 rail-road hotel, restaurant, and saloon by the same name that was torn down and rebuilt in 1905 by the Bosch Brewing Company. Michigan House still boasts its early 20th-century interiors, including ornately tiled floors and murals of jolly Germans drinking Bosch beer. The mammoth bar and fire-place complete the historical feel of the place, and the new owners have really brought the building back to its roots, starting a restaurant, a brewery, and a couple of hotel suites upstairs. The Milwaukee artists group that painted the mural here may well be the folks behind the mural at the Ambassador Restaurant in Houghton (see "Local Flavors"), but the link has never been proven.

Down the street former Red Jacket fire station is now the **Firefighters' Memorial Museum** (906-337-4579), a very handsome building made of Jacobsville sand-stone that seems to be of a brighter red than average, highlighted by bright red painted doors over the old fire truck garages. The arched windows, bell tower, and elaborate eaves make it an interesting build-ing to check out, even if the museum it encloses isn't all that fascinating.

Sixth Street is also home to the historic Vertin Building. Vertin Brothers & Co. built a two-story sandstone building, originally a department store, with lots of win-dows in 1885 and in 1900 added

The former Red Jacket fire station is now a museum in Calumet   Andrew Jameson

A department store in the early 1900s, Vertin Gallery is now a popular art gallery filled with wonderful pieces from dozens of local artists. Matt Girvan

the two floors and atrium that make the building seem so gigantic today. Vertin Brothers sold not only groceries and appliances but the latest fashions, products, and home furnishings to supply the local copper millionaires. The building sat empty for a number of years, until 2004 when artists began renting studio spaces on the second floor. Soon thereafter, they formed a cooperative and turned the first floor into a gallery for local artists. In honor of its historic home, the gallery is called **Vertin Gallery** (906-337-2200; www.vertingallery.com).

A short stroll down the street will bring you to **The Calumet Theatre** (906-337-2610; www.calumet theatre.com), the jewel of Copper Country and maybe even the entire U.P. Originally known as the Red Jacket Opera House, the renamed Calumet Theatre is one of the oldest municipally built theaters in the country, predating those built in Detroit, as locals are fond of pointing out. The 1,200-seat theater is a Keweenaw Heritage Site, protected by the National Park

The jewel of Copper Country, The Calumet Theatre. Dan Johnson

System, and it still hosts plays, concerts, and a monthly film series. Built with a mix of light sand-colored brick and deep red Jacobsville sandstone, alternating in patterns around the windows and the theater's main clock tower, the theater is clearly a landmark, but it's the interior that really shines, with richly colored murals, arches flecked with gold, carved wood balconies, and antique chandeliers. Tours are conducted regularly, but the best way to really appreciate the theater is to see a production there.

In nearby Laurium, the Laurium Manor (906-337-2549; www.laurium manorinn.com) is a huge, opulent, 45-room mansion built in 1908 by a copper baron. No expense was spared in the building or furnishing of this house, and current owners Dave and Julie Sprenger have put their all into researching its past and restoring it faithfully. The imposing, white-columned manor is now a bed & breakfast (see "Pick Your Spot"), but history buffs not staying there are welcome to pop in for a self-guided tour between 11 AM and 5 PM (call if you want to stop by in the off-season).

Hancock

Like Calumet, Hancock was also founded by a mining company. Built in 1859 by the Quincy Mining Company, the bulk of downtown Hancock, including the main drag—Quincy Street, of course—was made of wood buildings, most of which burned in an 1869 fire. The mining company rebuilt the town, primarily using Jacobsville sandstone, and Downtown Quincy Street is now listed on the National Register of Historic Places.

The row of storefronts in the 100 Block of Quincy Street was built from 1870 to 1900 and contained the bulk of the town's commerce. That is still the case today, and though some of the front windows have been modernized, the buildings have remained essentially the same.

In the 200 block, the First National Bank Building is a giant neoclassical beauty, built in 1905 and updated in 1913, with limestone balustrade and imposing columns, that looks grandly over Quincy Street. It's easy to imagine the early copper millionaires swaggering into the bank in the glory days of mining.

Hancock City Hall, also on Quincy Street, just one block up, was designed by Charlton, Gilbert, and Demar, the same firm responsible for St. Anne's (now the Keweenaw Heritage Center) in Calumet. The building is reminiscent of the firm's other designs, with a large clock tower, gable-framed large arching windows, and a sprinkling of Gothic details. When it was built, in 1898–1899, the original clock tower was 90 feet tall. The building was used for a while as a jail but has reverted to its original use as a combination city hall, police, and fire station.

Two Finnish American landmarks round out the sights on Quincy Street. In 1990, a rundown former Catholic church was renovated with an

Historic Quincy Street in downtown Hancock.   Andrew Jameson

eye toward Finnish design and became the Finnish American Heritage Center (906-487-7302; www.finlandia.edu; 601 Quincy St.). With its clipped gable blue roof and white walls with white-trimmed windows, the building sticks out in the mostly red sandstone downtown as being different and decidedly Finnish. The center also regularly hosts interesting Finnish art and history exhibits that tend to be very well curated and displayed.

Up the street, a Finnish high school was opened in 1896 by the Finnish Lutheran Church of the Suomi Synod (*suomi* means homeland in Finnish; *synod* refers to a religious council). This academy eventually became Suomi College in 1924 and later changed its name to Finlandia University. The Jacobsville sandstone edifice is built in a Richardsonian Romanesque style, with an arched entryway and large, somewhat intimidating tower. The complex holds various classrooms, a chapel, offices, and dorm rooms and is listed on the National Register of Historic Places.

The Quincy Dredge, near Calumet.   Matt Girvan

For a less touristy, prettified view of the area's mining days, local photographers frequent the Quincy Mill and Quincy Dredge right outside town. Set along the Hancock waterfront, directly across from each other, the mill (a copper stamp mill) was built in the late

1800s, with the dredge coming shortly thereafter in the early 1900s. Both are now empty shells of their former selves, but still provide a fascinating look at the remains of an industry and make for some eerily beautiful shots of Hancock.

Houghton

If Calumet and Hancock are reminders of the well-to-do mining giants, Houghton gives visitors a peek into how life might have been for the miners during those days. The **Adventure Copper Mine** (906-883-3371) leads a well-respected, authentic copper mine tour that gives visitors a firsthand look at what life was like in the mines. A few copper deposits were actually left behind in this mine, which makes for great viewing now. Guests are provided with hard hats and headlamps, but sturdy shoes and lightweight jackets are recommended. Certain areas of the mine are popular bat hibernation spots as well: The tour operators keep those sections closed off to protect the bats, but are happy to get into some bat talk if you're interested. For adventurous families with older kids, a rappelling and spelunking prospectors tour is also available.

In downtown Houghton, the **Douglass House Saloon** (906-482-2003; 517 Shelden Ave.) hosted early visitors to Houghton in 1902 and is now a popular local watering hole. With all its original fixtures, from the large wooden bar to the Tiffany lamps hanging from the ceiling, the bar really feels like an old-time saloon. The building itself remains a Houghton landmark, with its large redbrick facade and ornate white turret watching over downtown. Douglass House was originally conceived by local businessmen who thought Houghton needed a first-class hotel; they would be rolling over in their graves to hear that despite all its finery, Douglass House is generally considered a fun and funky dive bar, whose name is shortened by the local college kids to Doghouse.

The popular Douglass House Saloon in Houghton. Bobak Ha'Eri

LIGHTHOUSES

As with the other U.P. regions along Lake Superior, the northwest boasts a number of postcard-worthy lighthouses. There are three that are particularly worth a visit: Copper Harbor Lighthouse, Eagle Harbor Lighthouse, and Rock Harbor Lighthouse.

The tower at Eagle Harbor Lighthouse. Matt Girvan

Copper Harbor Lighthouse is a small white brick lighthouse with a red roof, located at the point of the peninsula that forms Copper Harbor. The site includes an interpretive trail in the woods, with information about the discovery of copper here and the various ships that have wrecked on the rocky peninsula, as well as a handful of exhibits in the lighthouse and the small adjacent keeper's quarters. Visitors are taken by boat over to the lighthouse for tours. The lighthouse can also be reached by kayak or private boat.

The picturesque Eagle Harbor Lighthouse and Museums (906-289-4990)—a redbrick lighthouse with bright white turret—is now joined by a maritime museum, commercial fishing museum, mining museum, and automotive museum, as well as the preserved keeper's quarters in the lighthouse, where visitors can marvel at the 14-inch-thick brick walls, built to keep keepers safe during harsh Lake Superior winters. The museums are delightful and well worth the $4 donation entry fee. Showcasing everything from examples of copper jewelry made by very early Native American miners to a handful of early automobiles that were rescued from a shipwreck on Lake Superior and providing an in-depth look at how and why the lake has claimed so many ships (and lives), this spot gives a pretty comprehensive overview of the history of the Keweenaw.

Set on its own little island near Isle Royale's shore, the Rock Harbor Lighthouse (www.nps.gov/isro) elicits squeals from visitors passing it on their way to Isle Royale. It's the first indication that they will soon reach their destination. Small and white and nestled between interesting rock formations, the lighthouse is a favorite photo subject. Tours to the lighthouse are available from the island during the summer and include a look at the connected commercial fishery—once truly commercial and now focused on providing the island's diners and scientists with fish.

MUSEUMS AND GALLERIES

This part of the peninsula has a good number of both galleries and interesting museums devoted to its mining past.

Calumet, with its lovely old buildings and interesting past, is a natural draw for local artists, who keep the town's two great galleries—the Vertin and the Omphale—stocked with unique paintings, sculptures, and glass art. Vertin Gallery (906-337-2200; www.vertingallery.com; 220 Sixth St.) is housed in a huge historic building that has been carefully and faithfully restored. The gallery itself, on the first floor of what was once a department store, is large and beautiful, with big display windows that let in plenty of natural light, hardwood floors, and freestanding white walls thrown up here and there for hanging artwork and dividing up the space. The layout pulls you in right off the bat, and then you slowly notice that absolutely every piece in this gallery is of very high quality. People from cities tend to assume that only city people can be artists. Not so, and the Vertin proves it emphatically. Displaying the work of the 50-odd artists who work in the studios above the gallery, the store sells beautiful handcrafted pottery, sculptural wood bowls, stunning jewelry, gasp-worthy paintings, photographs, and sculptures. It would be easy to spend a few hours in this place, carefully examining each beautiful thing. And the prices make it easy to actually purchase some of this original work.

A block away, Omphale Gallery & Café (906-337-2036; 431 Fifth St.) is charged with so much creative energy and artistic experimentation, it feels more like Brooklyn than Calumet. The gallery is a co-op of artists, each of whom acts as curator for various shows throughout the year. Supported by donations and commissions from art sales, Omphale also functions as a group work studio, with various local artists meeting here occasionally to work together. Focused on contemporary art, the gallery showcases the work of local artists, as well as that of some out-of-towners and even out-of-staters. In 2011, the gallery shut down for a time as Julie Depaul Johnson & Katie Jo Wright set about researching kitchen equipment and turning part of the Omphale into a café, much to locals' delight. Reopened in June 2011, the Omphale is once again a buzzing community center in addition to a great local gallery.

Down at the base of the Keweenaw Peninsula, in Hancock, the Copper Country Community Arts Center (CCCAC) (906-482-2333; www.copper

countryarts.com) is an active and popular arts center and gallery housed in a large historic art deco brick building on Quincy Street. The CCCAC is one of Hancock's gems. In addition to its exhibition gallery and education programs, the art center's Artists' Market sells the work of over 200 local artists and craftspeople. If it feels like a curated collection, that's because it essentially is. Each artist's work is evaluated by a panel of artists before it is allowed to be sold in the store. The center also hosts a couple of large fundraiser sales every year, including the Poor Artists' Sale, a popular holiday shopping event.

Nearby Houghton may not have a groovy gallery, but it makes up for it with the **A.E. Seaman Mineral Museum** (906-487-2572; www.museum.mtu .edu; open July through September, closed Saturdays and Sundays), a hidden gem on the fifth floor of the Electrical Resources Center at Michigan Technological University (MTU). Displaying around 8,000 specimens from its 30,000-piece collection of rare rocks and minerals from the Lake Superior region and the rest of the world, the museum is well worth a visit, even if you're not a hard-core geologist. Despite the small, obscure space, the museum is very well laid out; the MTU campus is also very pretty, and the walk from downtown is pleasant. In late 2011, the museum will move to its new digs, currently under construction at 1404 Sharon Avenue, next to MTU's Advanced Technology Development Complex.

Those interested in the area's minerals and mining past should also check out the **Quincy Mine Tour**, (906-482-3101; www.quincymine.com; tours available April through late October), a fantastic underground mine tour in the landmark Quincy copper mine, overlooking Hancock. There are three tour options: I recommend going for the full tour, which includes a cog-rail tram car ride down the hill to the mine entrance and a tractor-pulled wagon ride into the mine, seven levels underground. The underground tour includes a look at a large stope—a hole through which copper was excavated. All tours also include a video tour of one of the mine shafts, a guided tour through the mine's museum, and a tour of the 1918 Nordberg Steam Hoist, the world's largest steam-powered hoist engine. It's a lot of fun, and a great history and science lesson at the same time.

NIGHTLIFE

A handful of bars on Shelden Avenue cater to the Michigan Tech students and provide most of Houghton's nightlife. The **Douglass House Saloon** (906-482-2003; 517 Shelden Ave.), known locally as the Doghouse, is an old-time saloon with a pool table, a great long wooden bar, and a quieter, older feel than the other spots. Added bonus: free popcorn from a vintage popcorn maker.

Many of the historic buildings along Shelden Avenue in downtown Houghton are now home to popular bars. Andrew Jameson

A block away, the **Keweenaw Brewing Company** (906-482-5596; www .keweenawbrewing.com; 408 Shelden Ave.) is Copper Country's entry in the U.P. microbrew scene. A classic taproom, this spot serves beer only (no snacks), but with eight great local brews, that's not a bad thing.

Nicknamed the DT, the **Downtowner Lounge** (906-482-5054; 126 Shelden Ave.), down the street, is popular for its large outdoor patio. A few doors down, the **Ambassador Restaurant** (906-482-5054; www.the ambassadorhoughton.com; 126 Shelden Ave.) is another favorite watering hole, as beloved for its pizza as it is for its famous fishbowls—giant cocktails served in bowls—and bizarre murals of mischievous elves.

For entertainment of a different variety, MTU's **Rozsa Center for the Performing Arts** (906-487-3200; www.rozsa.mtu.edu) has a fantastic sched-ule of lectures and concerts, including performances from local bands and orchestras, as well as visiting performers. The current schedule of events includes a night with Maya Angelou, a production of Monty Python's *Spa-malot*, and several performances by the Superior Wind Symphony and the Keweenaw Symphony Orchestra.

SHOPPING

Given that this is Copper Country, various copper items are for sale throughout the Keweenaw Peninsula, from jewelry to cookware, but the peninsula's concentration of artists makes it a good place to find unique noncopper gifts as well.

The Last Place on Earth (906-337-1014), on US 41 just outside Kearsarge, is as well known as a landmark on the highway as it is for its selection. A bright redbrick building with a sign that announces in white block letters LAST PLACE ON EARTH, the popular store sells antiques and collectibles, landscape paintings by one of the owners, and the bird's-eye spoons the store is locally famous for. After all, as their sign clearly states, this is "the home of the spoon maker."

Farther south, housed in the historic First National Bank building in downtown Laurium, Keweenaw Keepsakes (906-337-4326, 305 Hecla St.) is worth a visit just to check out the original tin ceiling, tile floors, and display windows. The antiques collection is decent as well, with furniture, jewelry, and knickknacks culled from throughout the peninsula. The vintage clothes racks occasionally provide a good find, and the store also sells an assortment of new items, including toys and local crafts.

Over in Calumet, Artis Books & Antiques (906-337-1534; 425 Fifth St.) is one of those rare bookshops that makes readers want to move in. The store specializes in used and rare books, which makes it an excellent place to spend an afternoon ogling beautifully kept classics. The store also sells a small selection of antiques, all carefully selected by the owners. A fantastic old-book smell, combined with the antiques and the shop's historic building, create a lovely time-warp experience here.

Gift and Specialty Shops

Copper World's (906-337-4016; www.calumetcopper.com) name says it all: This is your one-stop Copper Country shop for all things copper. Housed in a darling historic building painted red with white trim in downtown Calumet, Copper World is a good place to stop if you need to bring gifts back home or if you want to be sure to pick up something copper while you're in the area.

Located in the Laurium Manor B&B, Julie's Ballroom Giftshop (906-337-2549) is a charming little shop run by Julie Sprenger, one part of the couple responsible for the amazing restoration of the manor. Julie's good taste is in evidence throughout the manor, but it really shines through in her store, where she has gathered an outstanding assortment of jewelry, apparel, gifts, and home furnishings. The added bonus, of course, is that the shop is located in the grand third-floor ballroom of the manor.

At the base of the Keweenaw peninsula, in Houghton, Keweenaw Gem & Gift (906-482-8447; www.copperconnection.com) is a large, red, wood-sided store owned by a gemologist and geologist couple who keep it stocked with gifts and jewelry all made from locally found rocks and gems. It's a great place to find something truly unique to the area.

The Great Outdoors

Outdoor adventures and
activities in northwestern U.P.

From the untouched wilderness of
Isle Royale to the off-piste downhill
runs at Mount Bohemia, Copper
Country has something for every
outdoor enthusiast.

BEACHES

Jutting out into Lake Superior, the Keweenaw Peninsula boasts an array of
picturesque beaches, all worth a visit even when the lake is at its choppiest
and the weather turns cold.

Agate Beach (take MI 26 to Toivola, about 15 miles southwest of Houghton,
then head west on Misery Bay Rd.) This sandy crescent beach, also known
as Santa Monica Beach, is good for swimming, and there are plenty of colorful rocks to be found, including agates from time to time. Picnic facilities
are available.

Baraga State Park (off US 41 in Baraga) This long sandy beach overlooking
Keweenaw Bay has sand tinged gray from iron ore. The park also allows
camping. Playground, picnic facilities, and flush toilets available.

Great Sand Bay (off MI 26 between Eagle River and Eagle Harbor) A perfect sandy crescent and a calm bay for swimming, ringed by woods and
backed by dunes.

Lake Manganese and Manganese Falls (Lake Manganese Rd., just south
of Copper Harbor off US 41) The crystal-clear, fairly shallow waters here

Great Sand Bay is an idyllic sandy beach and protected bay between Eagle River and Eagle
Harbor. Matt Girvan

Brockway Mountain Drive provides great views of Lake Superior and the Keweenaw Peninsula. Charles Dawley

warm up early in the summer. The sandy beach is bordered by hemlock groves, and a boat launch is provided for those who want to take advantage of the lake's good fishing. A short hike to nearby Manganese Falls reveals a lovely 45-foot waterfall tumbling through a deep gorge covered in bright green moss.

McLain State Park (18350 MI 203, Hancock) Wind surfing is popular on this 2-mile-long sand beach on Lake Superior, as is berry picking from nearby fields.

BICYCLING

As with most of the peninsula, bicycling is a great way to not only get around the various towns of the region but also to travel between them. The Jack Stevens Hancock–Calumet Rail Trail starts at the Portage Lake lift bridge that connects Hancock to Houghton and runs 14 miles along a former railroad grade from Hancock to Calumet. The trail is rough, with ATVs on it regularly in summer and snowmobiles in winter, so is suitable only for mountain bikes, but the MI 203 has a paved bike lane for road cyclists from Hancock to Calumet as well.

BIRD-WATCHING

According to the National Park Service, there are more species of birds on Isle Royale than any other living thing. Interestingly, you won't always see the same birds here that you would on the mainland. Bring binoculars, as numerous trails provide great opportunities to spot birds.

Back on the main peninsula, Brockway Mountain Drive is known for its spectacular views of Copper Harbor and the Keweenaw Peninsula, but is also a great place to spot hawks.

CAMPING

As with the rest of the U.P., the Keweenaw boasts some truly breathtaking wilderness camp spots. There's really no better way to experience the beauty of the region than waking up in the woods alongside one of its many bodies of water. Isle Royale (www.nps.gov/isro/) is, essentially, one giant floating wilderness campground. With the exception of the Rock Harbor Lodge, at the Isle Royale harbor, there's no way to avoid camping out on the island. That said, there is a range of options, from easy, level sites in the woods near shore for camping newbies to rugged hike-in spots on the banks of the interior lakes. All campers need backcountry permits, but the permits are free and are handed out aboard the ferry on the way to the island. Be sure to book ferry reservations in advance. Isle Royale may be the least-visited national park in the country, but given that camping is only an option four months out of the year, spots on the ferry are in high demand.

Back on the main peninsula, Fort Wilkins State Park (www.michigand nr.com/parksandtrails) offers visitors a dose of history along with their immersion in nature. Over 100 campsites (all with modern hookups) are scattered around Lake Fanny Hooe, an inland lake just a mile or so from Lake Superior. In addition to easy access to both lakes, as well as nearby hiking trails, campers are just a short walk from a restored historic military fort. Built in 1844, Fort Wilkins is now staffed by costumed guides who explain the site's history and perform various reenactments. At the other end of the park, the Copper Harbor Lighthouse (one of the first lighthouses built on Lake Superior) can also be toured.

Between Houghton and Laurium, on the eastern shore of Lake Superior, McLain State Park (www.michigandnr.com/parksandtrails) is one of the most popular campgrounds in the Keweenaw, thanks not only to its central location (it's easy to get to all the peninsula's attractions from here) but also to its 2-mile sandy beach. Modern campsites (97 of them) are scattered throughout the woods; there are also six minicabins and one larger cabin available for use. Beyond the campground, McLain boasts over 400 acres of wooded trails, fishing rivers, and prime summertime berry picking.

CANOEING AND KAYAKING

One of the best ways to explore Isle Royale (www.nps.gov/isro) is by kayak. The park's newsletter *The Greenstone* includes a detailed map highlighting

Isle Royale's crystal-clear waters are popular with kayakers.   Matt Girvan

trails. Kayakers are encouraged to use the inland lakes as much as possible as opposed to unreliable Lake Superior. Park rangers also ask that kayakers wash off kayaks that have been in Lake Superior before entering one of the inland lakes on Isle Royale to avoid the transfer of invasive species from one to the other. Very experienced and fit paddlers can make a 14-mile circle tour through the island. Those who attempt it will be rewarded with solitude and breathtaking natural beauty.

CROSS-COUNTRY SKIING

The popular Swedetown Trails (906-337-1170; www.swedetowntrails.org; Agent St.) in Calumet feature more than 30 kilometers of groomed cross-country ski and snowshoe trails, including several loops with varying difficulty levels, from beginner loops with few if any hills to advanced, hilly loops. Swedetown also keeps 4.5 kilometers of trails lit until 10 PM during the winter, and the attached chalet includes a snack bar and a groomed sledding hill.

DOWNHILL SKIING AND SNOWBOARDING

An X Games–style extreme winter sports haven, Mount Bohemia (902-360-7240; www.mtbohemia.com), about 35 miles north of Houghton, near Lac Labelle, was hotly contested by locals when it was first built. People are never thrilled about development in these parts, and Mount Bohemia's

Superior Sunsets

There are numerous spots around Lake Superior known for incredible sunsets. Two of the best are in Copper Country.

Brockway Mountain Drive, Copper Harbor. With panoramic views as far away as Isle Royale, sunsets here are breathtaking, particularly during the fall color season.

Chicken Bone Lake, Isle Royale. This interior lake on Isle Royale is one of the best spots in the park to see moose, and they like sunset almost as much as they like sunrise. If you're quiet and still, you'll spot them cruising around the lake just about the time it starts to get that pretty evening glow.

developers weren't just talking about a ski resort but numerous lodges built out around the resort and Lac La Belle. Though it's still a sore point, the ski resort has gained fans fairly quickly for its steep and challenging runs and its hard-core backcountry. The mountain gets 270-plus inches of snow each season, and the average run is pitched at 31 degrees. The Extreme Backcountry runs include 40-foot cliff drops.

FISHING

Craig Lake State Park (906-339-4461), east of Houghton in Baraga County, is a gigantic 6,000-plus-acre state park with several lakes, the largest of which is Craig Lake. All the lakes in the park are known for good fishing, but Craig is particularly good for muskellunge, bass, walleye, and northern pike, while Teddy Lake has perch and panfish. Motorized boats are not allowed except on Keewaydin Lake. Fishing is allowed by artificial lure only, and a catch-and-release policy is in place for northern pike, muskellunge, and bass.

Farther west, up the Keweenaw Peninsula, the upper portion of the Gratiot River, including No Name Pond, is good for brook trout, while the last mile downstream from Lower Falls hosts spring runs of steelhead. From Upper Falls to the river's mouth, the Gratio is home to rainbow trout, along with the occasional Coho salmon.

GOLF

There's not much of a golf scene in Copper Country, but those looking to get a game will enjoy the pleasant 9-hole, 36-par course at the Keweenaw

Mountain Lodge (906-289-4403; www.atthelodge.com; $13). Built in the wooded hills overlooking the lodge, the course dates back to the government's public works program in the 1930s, when building both the lodge and the course helped put Depression-era Americans back to work.

HIKING

There might be no better place to hike in the world than Isle Royale, which offers a seemingly endless array of trails. Even during the most popular summer weeks, it's easy to take a hike on Isle Royale and not bump into another human. In addition to the numerous backcountry hikes on the island, the Scoville Point Loop, a marked 4-mile loop near Rock Harbor, is a great way for newcomers to acclimate themselves to the island and take in some fantastic views. The trail winds up and along the bluffs from Rock Harbor, through the trees, past old copper mines to lovely and isolated Scoville Point and loops back past an inland lake to Rock Harbor.

SNOWMOBILING

You could feasibly snowmobile from Houghton to Ontonagon via the Bill Nicholls Trail. The very popular trail follows an old railroad from Adventure Mountain in Ontonagon to Houghton. Once there, the Jack Stevens Hancock-Calumet Rail Trail will take you from nearby Hancock up to Calumet. Farther north, the Brockway Mountain Trail follows popular Brockway Mountain Road along a scenic route to the top of Brockway Mountain for a 360-degree view of the Keweenaw. Snowmobiles can be rented from Copper Country Rentals in Calumet (906-337-9905; www.coppercountryrental.com).

6

Information

THIS CHAPTER IS A QUICK AND HANDY GUIDE to the essential details. Compiled with both the local and the visitor in mind, information is presented on the following subjects:

AMBULANCE/FIRE/POLICE

Always dial 911 in an emergency situation—to report a fire or request an ambulance or immediate police response. For police assistance that doesn't require an emergency response, contact the number listed below for the city closest to your location.

AREA CODES

The entire Upper Peninsula uses the 906 area code. Mackinaw City, in Cheboygan County on the Lower Peninsula, uses 231.

LEFT: Grand Island.   Matt Girvan

INFORMATION

Town Police

Ahmeek	.337-2211
Allouez	.337-2211
Alpha	.875-3465
Amasa	.875-3012
Arnold	.346-9224
Atlantic Mine	.482-3102
Au Train	.387-2275
Aura	.524-6161
Baraga	.353-7181
Bark River	.466-7441
Bay Mills	.248-3244
Bergland	.787-2300
Bessemer	.667-0203
Big Bay	.485-1888
Brampton	.428-3131
Brevort	.643-8383
Brimley	.248-3251
Bruce Crossing	.884-4901
Calumet	.337-2345
Carney	.497-5511
Caspian	.265-3223
Cedarville	.495-5889
Champion	.485-1888
Channing	.875-3012
Chassell	.482-4411
Chatham	.387-2275
Christmas	.387-2275
Cooks	.341-2133
Copper City	.337-0528
Copper Harbor	.337-0528
Cornell	.428-4411
Covington	.524-6950
Crystal Falls	.875-3012
Curtis	.293-5151
Dafter	.495-5889
Daggett	.753-2275
Deer Park	.293-5236
Deerton	.249-4040
DeTour Village	.495-5889
Dodgeville	.482-4411
Dollar Bay	.482-2121
Drummond Island	.495-5889
Eagle Harbor	.337-0528
Eagle River	.337-2345
Eben Junction	.387-2275
Eckerman	.293-5151
Engadine	.293-5151
Ensign	.428-3131
Epoufette	.293-5151
Escanaba	.786-5911
Ewen	.787-2300
Faithorn	.774-2121
Fayette	.428-4411
Felch	.563-5801
Ford River	.497-5511
Foster City	.774-2121
Gaastra	.265-3223
Garden	.341-2133
Garden Corners	.341-2133
Germfask	.293-5151
Gladstone	.428-3131
Goetzville	.632-2216
Gould City	.293-5151
Grand Island	.387-2275
Grand Marais	.293-5236
Greenland	.884-4901
Gulliver	.341-2133
Gwinn	.346-9224
Hancock	.482-3102
Harris	.466-2911
Helmer	.293-5236
Hendricks	.293-5151
Herman	.524-6161
Hermansville	.497-5511
Hessel	.643-8877
Houghton	.482-2121
Hubbell	.296-9911
Hulbert	.293-5236
Ingalls	.753-2275
Ingallston	.863-4441
Iron Mountain	.774-1234
Iron River	.265-4321
Ironwood	.932-1234

Ishpeming	486-4416	Perkins	428-4411
Jacobsville	337-2345	Pickford	495-5889
Kearsarge	337-2345	Powers	497-5511
Kingsford	774-2525	Quinnesec	774-2121
Kinross	495-5889	Raco	248-3251
L'Anse	524-6050	Ralph	346-9224
Lac La Belle	482-3102	Ramsay	667-0313
Lake Gogebic Area	787-2300	Rapid River	428-4411
Lake Linden	296-9911	Republic	376-8800
Laurium	337-4000	Rock	428-4411
Limestone	387-2275	Rockland	884-4901
Loretto	563-5801	Rudyard	495-5889
Mackinac Island	847-3300	Sagola	875-3012
Mackinaw City	231-436-7861	Sand River	249-4040
Manistique	341-2133	Sault Ste. Marie	632-3344
Marenisco	787-2300	Seney	293-5151
Marquette	228-0400		
Mass City	884-4901		
Matchwood	787-2300		
McMillan	293-5151		
Melstrand	387-4540		
Menominee	863-5568		
Michigamme	485-1888		
Mineral Hills	265-4321		
Mohawk	337-0528		
Moran	643-8877		
Munising	387-2275		
Nadeau	497-5511		
Nahma	428-4411		
Nahma Junction	428-4411		
Naubinway	643-8877		
Negaunee	475-4154		
Newberry	293-5236		
Nisula	524-6161		
Norway	563-5801		
Ontonagon	884-4901		
Osceola	482-3102		
Painesdale	482-3102		
Palmer	475-4154		
Paradise	248-3244		
Pelkie	524-6161		
Pequaming	524-6161		

Big Shoal Beach is just one of several
secluded beaches on Drummond Island.
Matt Girvan

Branches for major banks are located in Escanaba, Hancock, Houghton, Iron Mountain, Ironwood, Mackinaw City, Marquette, Menominee, Munising, Newberry, Sault Ste. Marie, and St. Ignace. All banks have ATMs. In smaller towns without a major bank, ATMs are usually available on the street or in grocery and convenience stores.

CLIMATE, WEATHER, WHAT TO WEAR

There's a popular saying in Michigan that if you don't like the weather, just wait five minutes. Nowhere in the state is this more the case than in the U.P., where a warm summer day can turn into a thunderstorm and back again in minutes. Obviously, in winter it's winter, and that's not going to change until April, but even in the snow season, the wind can whip up and die down at a moment's notice, drastically increasing and decreasing the amount of bundling needed throughout the day. That said, in broad strokes, the weather is very seasonal: It's hot in the summer, cold in the winter, rainy in the fall, and sunny but cool in the spring. June brings blackfly season, so be prepared with bug spray, long sleeves, and pants. By August, the lakes are warm enough to swim in; more shallow, inland lakes warm up a bit earlier.

On Isle Royale, in the middle of Lake Superior, it can be cold even in August, so be sure to pack warm clothes if you're making the trip to the island. It does warm up there during the day, especially in August, but even on the warmest of days, it cools down at night and in the morning.

In the winter, you absolutely must have a warm winter jacket, gloves, a hat, and boots at a minimum. Certain areas get more snow than others, but in general, you're looking at around 150 to 200 inches of snow a season. If you're driving in the U.P., it's best to have a four-wheel-drive vehicle. Snow chains aren't allowed in Michigan.

In the fall, the colors here are absolutely spectacular, especially in the Porcupine Mountains. The leaves generally start to turn at the end of September and early October, when the U.P. gets its last surge of visitors before the winter sets in.

FISHING AND HUNTING REGULATIONS

A fishing or hunting license is required for all fishing and hunting in Michigan, and they are available from the state's Department of Natural Resources (DNR) (906-228-6561; www.michigan.gov/dnr). Different regulations apply to different species in different areas, so be sure to check the DNR's Web site before planning your trip. Every year, the DNR picks a weekend in June to be Michigan's Free Fishing Weekend; no fees are required on these days, but licenses are. To find out about the next free weekend, check the DNR's Web site. Applications may also be filed online for permits, and reservations can be made for most state park campgrounds through the site as well.

Persons with mental disabilities may fish or hunt in Michigan without a license, provided they are accompanied by an adult with a valid license. Senior citizens are offered a discounted rate on licenses, and legally blind persons are also eligible for the discount.

Game/Season

American woodcock. September 22 to November 5

Black bear. September 10 to October 26

Canada goose. September 18 to November 1

Duck and merganser. September 29 to November 27

Elk. August 25 to 29; September 15 to 18; December 11 to 18

Pheasant (males only). October 10 to November 14

Ruffed grouse. September 15 to November 14; December 1 to January 1

Russian boar. Year-round (hunters can hunt boar with any valid hunting license)

White-tailed deer. Bow: October 1 to November 14 and December 1 to January 2; regular firearm: November 15 to 30; muzzle loader: December 2 to 18

Wild turkey. October 8 to November 14

HANDICAPPED SERVICES

A surprising number of hotels and restaurants in the U.P. are handicapped accessible, and the DNR has a great program to provide information and assistance to disabled fishermen, hunters, and campers. Still, many of the buildings up here were built long before ADA regulations became law, and the historic buildings are not required to upgrade, so there are still some buildings with very narrow doorways and large staircases that are not easily accessed by the disabled.

The state and national parks and forests all have information regarding campsites for the disabled (most campgrounds have at least one accessible campsite) and handicapped access to parks and facilities, as well as TDD phone numbers to call for the hearing impaired. For an accessibility guide to Fort Mackinac and other Mackinac State Historic Parks properties, call 231-436-4100 or fax 231-436-4210.

All the hospitals listed here have 24-hour emergency care. The level of care tends to be better at the larger hospitals, purely because they have more money for equipment and staff. The good news is that once you're in the U.P., it doesn't take all that long to get from one place to the next, so no matter where you are, you're generally close to a good emergency facility. Because this is a wilderness area, there are trained search and rescue teams throughout the peninsula.

Baraga County Memorial Hospital. 906-524-3300; 770 Main Street, L'Anse

Bell Hospital. 906-486-4431; 101 S. Fourth Street, Ishpeming

Dickinson County Healthcare System. 906-774-1313; 1721 S. Stephenson Avenue, Iron Mountain

Grand View Health System. 906-932-2525; 10561 N. Grand View Lane, Ironwood

Helen Newberry Joy Hospital. 906-293-9200 or 1-800-743-3093; 502 W. Harrie Street, Newberry

Iron County Community Hospital. 906-265-6121; 1400 W. Ice Lake Road, Iron River

Keweenaw Memorial Hospital. 906-337-6500; 205 Osceola Street, Laurium

Mackinac Straits Hospital. 906-643-8585; 200 Burdette Street, St. Ignace

Marquette General Health System. 906-228-9440; 580 W. College Avenue, Marquette

Munising Memorial Hospital System. 906-387-4110; 1500 Sand Point Road, Munising

Ontonagon Memorial Hospital. 906-884-4134; 601 S. Seventh Street, Suite 1, Ontonagon

OSF St. Francis Hospital. 906-786-5707; 3401 Ludington Street, Escanaba

Portage Health System. 906-483-1000 or 1-800-573-5001; 500 Campus Drive, Hancock

Schoolcraft Memorial Hospital. 906-341-3200; 500 Main Street, Manistique

War Memorial Hospital. 906-635-4460; 500 Osborn Boulevard, Sault Ste. Marie

Fiercely independent and proud of their home and cultural heritage, U.P. residents boast a lively and entertaining publishing and radio scene. On the music front, the radio stations skew heavily toward country and oldies, and every once in a while you'll hear some classic Yooper folk songs as well. Following are some of the best local papers and stations—one of the best ways for visitors to truly immerse themselves in U.P. culture.

Newspapers and Magazines

The Daily Mining Gazette (906-482-1500; www.mininggazette.com; offices in Houghton and Calumet) Serving Houghton, Keweenaw, Baraga, and Ontonagon Counties since 1858, the paper obviously started in the mining days and has continued to cover what's near and dear to the locals ever since. This is a great place to find out about what's going on in local politics, both in this region and U.P.-wide.

The Finnish American Reporter (906-487-7549; www.finnishamerican reporter.com; Hancock) This is a great only-in-the-U.P. paper out of Finnish-centric Hancock. It's printed in English but covers Finnish and Finnish American news, as well as human-interest stories that are of interest to Finnish Americans.

Lake Superior Magazine (1-888-244-5253; www.lakesuperior.com) Although based in Minnesota, this magazine about all things Superior often covers news and events in the stretch of the northern U.P. that runs along the shores of the great lake.

Marquette Monthly (906-226-6500; www.mmnow.com; Marquette) Just the sort of magazine you'd expect to find in a college town like Marquette, jam-packed with cultural news, events, and commentary as well as local entertainment listings. This is a good place to find out about local art exhibits and upcoming concerts in the Marquette area.

Soo Evening News (906-632-2235; www.sooeveningnews.com; Sault Ste. Marie) Not an amazing paper for news coverage, but the *Soo Evening News* is a great slice-of-life read and offers excellent local sports coverage.

Upper Peninsula Magazine (906-789-7710; www.upperpeninsula.biz; 1007 Ludington St., Escanaba) The magazine mostly covers its advertisers, but its advertisers are mostly all businesses that visitors will be interested in, so it's not so bad. Its event listings are always very good.

Blogs and Web Sites

Eagle Herald (http://ehextra.com) A great little online paper serving Menominee and Marinette (interesting, given that the towns are in two different states!), the *Eagle Herald* focuses on local news and runs national and world news from the Associated Press.

EUP News (www.eupnews.com) A daily news blog covering the eastern U.P.

Ironwood Info (www.ironwoodinfo.com) A daily news site covering the city of Ironwood, and surrounding counties Baraga, Houghton, Gogebic and Ontonagon, as well as Iron County in Wisconsin.

Keweenaw Now (http://keweenawnow.blogspot.com) This local blog started out covering environmental issues in the Keweenaw, but now covers a variety of local happenings.

Marquette Social (www.marquettesocial.com) A new social media site that connects Yoopers, Marquette Social is a great way to both get a flavor for the local scene and find out about events, openings and closings.

Upper Peninsula News (www.upperpeninsulanews.com) This news aggregator pulls in stories from various outlets that cover the U.P.

Upper Peninsula's Second Wave (http://up.secondwavemedia.com) A great little blog, updated daily, UP's Second Wave runs positive local business and lifestyle stories, with an aim to highlighting the region's "second wave," the economic development happening postmining and -lumber. It's a great spot to find out about new restaurants, bars and events.

Radio

AM

590 WJMS. Ironwood; country
600 WCHT. Escanaba; news
680 WDBC. Escanaba; adult contemporary
920 WMPL. Hancock; talk
940 WIDG. St. Ignace; sports
970 WZAM. Ishpeming; news
1230 WIKB. Iron River; oldies
1230 WSOO. Sault Ste. Marie; adult contemporary
1240 WIAN. Ishpeming; talk
1320 WDMJ. Marquette; news/talk
1400 WKNW. Sault Ste. Marie; talk
1400 WQXO. Munising; nostalgia
1400 WCCY. Houghton; nostalgia
1450 WMIQ. Iron Mountain; talk
1490 WTIQ. Manistique; oldies

FM

88.5 WOAS. Ontonagon; variety
90.1 WNMU. Marquette; public radio/classical
90.1 WLSO. Sault Ste. Marie; variety
91.1 WGGL. Houghton; classical/news/talk
91.5 WUPX. Marquette; alternative
91.5 WVCM. Iron Mountain; religious
91.9 WMTU. Houghton; college
92.3 WJPD. Ishpeming; country
93.1 WIMK. Iron Mountain; classic rock
93.5 WKMJ. Hancock; adult contemporary
94.1 WUPK. Marquette; classic rock

94.3 WZNL. Norway; adult contemporary

95.7 WHWL. Marquette; religious

97.1 WGLQ. Escanaba; Top 40

99.1 WIKB. Iron River; oldies

99.7 WIMI. Ironwood; adult contemporary

97.7 WOLV. Houghton; classic rock

97.9 WIHC. Newberry; classic rock

98.3 WHCH. Munising oldies

98.3 WCNF. Sault Ste. Marie; public radio

99.5 WYSS. Sault Ste. Marie; Top 40

99.5 WNGE. Negaunee; oldies

100.7 WOBE. Crystal Falls; oldies

101.1 WUPY. Ontonagon; country

101.3 WSUE. Sault Ste. Marie; rock

101.5 WJNR. Iron Mountain; country

101.9 WKQS. Negaunee; adult contemporary

102.3 WHKB. Houghton; country

102.5 WCMM. Gulliver; country

102.9 WMKC. St. Ignace; country

103.3 WFXD. Marquette; country

103.7 WHYB. Menominee; country

104.3 WVCN. Baraga; religious

104.7 WYKX. Escanaba; country

105.7 WCUP. L'Anse; country

106.9 WUPM. Ironwood; Top 40

107.7 WMQT. Ishpeming; adult contemporary

TOURIST INFORMATION

Lake Michigan and Environs

Delta County Chamber of Commerce (Escanaba, Manistique, Bays de Noc) 906-786-2192; www.deltami.org; 230 Ludington Street, Escanaba

Delta County Tourism Bureau (Escanaba, Gladstone, Rapid River, Fayette) 906-789-7710 or 1-800-533-4FUN; www.deltafun.com; 230 Ludington Street, Escanaba

Escanaba and Bays de Noc Tourism Bureau. 906-789-7862; www.travel baysdenoc.com; 230 Ludington Street, Escanaba

Hiawatha National Forest Office. 906-341-5666; 449 E. Lakeshore Drive/US 2, Manistique

Iron County Chamber of Commerce. 906-265-3822; www.iron.org; east of downtown Iron River on US 2

Manistique Area Tourist Council. 1-800-342-4282; www.onlynorth.com

River Cities Chamber of Commerce. 906-863-2679; www.rivercities.net /tourism; Menominee and Marinette

Lake Superior and Environs

Alger County Chamber of Commerce. 906-387-2138; www.algercounty .org; 129 E. Munising Avenue, Munising

Baraga County Convention & Visitors Bureau. 906-524-7444 or 1-800-743-4908; www.baragacountytourism.org; 755 E. Broad Street, L'Anse

Ironwood Chamber of Commerce. 906-932-1122; 116 N. Lowell Street, Ironwood

Keweenaw Convention & Visitors Bureau. 906-337-4579 or 1-800-338-7982; www.keweenaw.info; 56638 Calumet Avenue, Calumet

Lake Gogebic Chamber of Commerce. 906-842-3611 or 1-888-464-3242; www.lakegogebicarea.com

Marquette Country Convention & Visitors Bureau. 1-800-544-4321; www.michigan.org/Property/Detail.aspx?p=G4597; 337 W. Washington Street, Marquette

Ontonagon Chamber of Commerce. 906-884-4735 or 906-458-4354; www.ontonagonmi.org

Pictured Rocks/Hiawatha National Forest Visitor Center. 906-387-3700; www.nps.gov/piro; H58 just east of MI 28, where the main highway turns west to follow the lakeshore in Munising

Western U.P. Tourism and Convention Bureau. 1-800-522-5657; www.westernup.com

Eastern Lake Superior and Whitefish Bay

Drummond Island Tourism Bureau. 906-493-5245; www.drummondislandchamber.com

Grand Marais Visitors Bureau. 906-494-2447; www.grandmaraismichigan.com

Les Cheneaux Tourism Bureau. 1-888-364-7526; www.lescheneaux.org; Cedarville

Mackinac Island Visitors Bureau. 1-800-454-5227; www.mackinacisland.org

Mackinaw City Chamber of Commerce. 231-436-5574; www.mackinawcity.com; 214 E. Central Street, Mackinaw City

Michigan Welcome Center. 906-863-6496; Mackinac Bridge exit, St. Ignace

Newberry Chamber of Commerce. 906-293-5562; www.newberrychamber.net

Sault Ste. Marie Convention & Visitors Bureau. 906-632-3301; www.saultstemarie.com

Tahquamenon Falls State Park. 906-492-3415; www.michigan.gov/dnr

Straits of Mackinac and Environs

St. Ignace Chamber of Commerce. 906-643-8717 or 1-800-970-8717; www.stignace.com; 560 N. State Street, St. Ignace

Bibliography

THE U.P. HAS INSPIRED MANY A POET, naturalist, and historian. A growing number of fictional works have also been based in the U.P., a handful of which—like *Anatomy of a Murder*, which was made into a film in 1959—have gained national fame. There are thankfully several independent bookstores throughout the U.P. that carry regional books, covering both the U.P. in its entirety and specific regions. These bookshops are worth a visit while you're in town. In the meantime, following is a reading list to get you started.

Biography and Reminiscence

Crowe, William S. *Lumberjack: Inside an Era in the Upper Peninsula of Michigan.* Skandia, MI: North Country Publishing, 2002. 144 pp., photos. A 1950s classic that has recently been reprinted, *Lumberjack* is a firsthand account of the logging industry in the U.P., particularly around the Manistique area, when the industry was booming.

Emerick, Lon L. *Going Back to Central: On the Road in Search of the Past in Michigan's Upper Peninsula.* Skandia, MI: North Country Publishing, 2003. 160 pp., photos. Very well researched and written travelogue through the U.P., full of rich characters, local folklore, and beautiful landscapes.

———. *The Superior Peninsula: Seasons in the Upper Peninsula of Michigan.* Skandia, MI: North Country Publishing, 1996. 216 pp. Emerick, a retired professor, pens a moving love letter to the U.P., organized by seasons. If anything could make you fall in love with six-month winters, it's this book.

Harju, Jerry. *Northern Reflections: A Lighthearted Account of "Growing Up North."* Marquette, MI: North Harbor Publishing, 1999. 123 pp. A fun and funny collection of stories about growing up in the U.P. in the 1940s, during a time when iron and lumber, though on a major decline, were still big business in the U.P., and the Mackinac Bridge hadn't yet been built.

Zechlin, Carol Brisson. *Growing Up Yooper: Childhood Memories of Michigan's Upper Peninsula*. St. Germain, WI: The Guest Cottage, Inc., 2004. 91 pp. A collection of charming short stories about being a kid in the U.P. in the 1950s.

Fiction

Anderson, Lauri. *Misery Bay and Other Stories from Michigan's Upper Peninsula*. St. Cloud, MN: North Star Press, 2002. 160 pp. A collection of short stories that celebrate the Finnish heritage of the U.P., especially in the Copper Country era. Lots of local customs and legends are introduced here.

Traver, Robert. *Anatomy of a Murder*. New York: St. Martin's Press, 1958. 448 pp. A novel based on a real murder and court case in Big Bay, Michigan, *Anatomy of a Murder* was highly praised for its character development and skillful description of courtroom drama. A film was made out of the book in 1959, bringing a bit of notoriety to the U.P.

History and Cultural Studies

Bohnak, Karl. *So Cold a Sky: Upper Michigan Weather Stories*. Negaunee, MI: Cold Sky Publishing, 2006. 350 pp., illus. A series of true tales chronicling Yooper weather battles from the pioneers to the present day.

Dodge, Roy L. *Michigan Ghost Towns: The Upper Peninsula*. San Diego, CA: Thunder Bay Press, 1994. 300 pp., photos. A detailed account of the many ghost towns in the U.P. The background of each town is given, how it was built, what it was like, what happened to it, and what's left of it today. A must for anyone interested in exploring the U.P.'s many ghost towns.

Graham, Loren R. *A Face in the Rock: The Tale of a Grand Island Chippewa*. Berkeley: University of California Press, 1998. 172 pp. Winner of the Follo Award of the Michigan Historical Society for its contribution to Michigan history, Graham's book details the plight of the Chippewa on Grand Island, from battles with other tribes to white encroachment and a loss of culture, language, and land. Graham finishes on a positive note, looking at the preservation of Grand Island and recent efforts to honor the Chippewa culture.

Lankton, Larry. *Cradle to Grave: Life, Work, and Death at the Lake Superior Copper Mines*. New York: Oxford University Press, 1993. 352 pp., illus., photos. An academic work, written by a Michigan Tech history professor, focused on both the technical side of the mining world (how technological advancements in mining affected the mining business) and what was happening socially and culturally both above and below ground during the Keweenaw's copper boom. It's a great precursor to a Copper Country visit.

Osborn, Chase S. *The Iron Hunter*. Detroit: Wayne State University Press, 2002. 248 pp., photos. A reprint of the fascinating autobiography of Chase Salmon Osborn, the eccentric publisher-turned-governor, who remains the only Michigan state governor to hail from the U.P. There are several monuments to Osborn in his hometown of Sault Ste. Marie.

Piljac, Thomas. *Mackinac Island: Historic Frontier, Vacation Resort, Timeless Wonderland*. Chicago: Chicago Review Press, 1996. 320 pp., photos. A very informative and comprehensive look at Mackinac's long and varied history.

Nature Guides

Dufresne, Jim. *Isle Royale Foot Trails and Water Routes*. Seattle, WA: Mountaineers Books, 2002. 144 pp., photos, illus. An indispensable guide to what can be a very confusing island to navigate. Dufresne does an excellent job of unlocking the mystery of Isle Royale for visitors.

Glime, Janice. *The Elfin World of Mosses and Liverworts of Michigan's Upper Peninsula and Isle Royale*. Houghton, MI: Isle Royale Natural History Association, 1993. 154 pp., photo, illus. A field guide to mosses and liverworts, written for the layperson.

Hansen, Eric. *Hiking Michigan's Upper Peninsula*. Guilford, CT: Falcon, 2005. Hands-down the best hiking guide to the area. Hansen gives vivid descriptions and very detailed directions to hikes ranging from easy to challenging, popular to hidden.

Huggler, Tom. *Fish Michigan: 100 Upper Peninsula Lakes*. Davison, MI: Friede Publications, 1994. 112 pp., photos. A detailed guide to the best fishing lakes in the U.P., with information on when and where to find the fish you're looking for.

Photographic Studies

Phipps, Terry. *Seasons of Mackinac*. Ann Arbor: University of Michigan Press, 2004. 128 pp., photos. A lovely introduction to Mackinac in all four seasons, this is a great book for visitors to check out to see that there's more to the island than just summertime.

Index

DATE DUE